States and Citizens
History, Theory, Prospects

The imminent demise of the nation-state in the face of global capitalism and supra-national agencies has often been predicted, yet in practice the death of the state seems scarcely imaginable: indeed terrorist activity and corporate collapse have made states, if anything, more assertive in recent years, and the condition of 'statelessness' is regarded as grave in the extreme. This volume offers a coherent survey of perceptions of the state, its history, its theoretical underpinnings, and its prospects in the contemporary world. The coverage of the Western European experience is thorough and wide-ranging, with the greatest post-colonial democratic state, India, as a comparative example. The provocative and accessible contributions of a very distinguished and genuinely pan-European team of contributors ensure that *States and Citizens* provides a unique and valuable resource, of interest to students and teachers of the history of ideas, political theory, and European studies.

QUENTIN SKINNER is Regius Professor of Modern History at the University of Cambridge.

BO STRÅTH is Professor of Contemporary History at the European University Institute, Florence.

States and Citizens

History, Theory, Prospects

edited by

Quentin Skinner

and

Bo Stråth

CAMBRIDGE
UNIVERSITY PRESS

PUBLISHED BY THE PRESS SYNDICATE OF THE UNIVERSITY OF CAMBRIDGE
The Pitt Building, Trumpington Street, Cambridge, United Kingdom

CAMBRIDGE UNIVERSITY PRESS
The Edinburgh Building, Cambridge, CB2 2RU, UK
40 West 20th Street, New York, NY 10011–4211, USA
477 Williamstown Road, Port Melbourne, VIC 3207, Australia
Ruiz de Alarcón 13, 28014 Madrid, Spain
Dock House, The Waterfront, Cape Town 8001, South Africa

http://www.cambridge.org

First published 2003

Printed in the United Kingdom at the University Press, Cambridge

Typeface Times 10/12 pt.   *System* LATEX 2$_\varepsilon$ [TB]

A catalogue record for this book is available from the British Library

Library of Congress cataloguing in publication data
States and citizens: history, theory, prospects / edited by Quentin Skinner, Bo Stråth.
    p.   cm.
Includes bibliographical references and index.
ISBN 0 521 83156 3 (hardback) – ISBN 0 521 53926 9 (paperback)
1. State, The – History – Congresses.   2. Citizenship – History – Congresses.
I. Skinner, Quentin.   II. Stråth, Bo, 1943–
JC11.S775   2003   320.1 – dc21   2003046039

ISBN 0 521 83156 3 hardback
ISBN 0 521 53926 9 paperback

Contents

List of contributors   *page* vii
Acknowledgements   viii

Introduction   1
BO STRÅTH AND QUENTIN SKINNER

PART ONE: States and citizens: setting the scene

1 States and the freedom of citizens   11
   QUENTIN SKINNER

2 The concept of the state: the sovereignty of a fiction   28
   DAVID RUNCIMAN

3 Citizens and the state: retrospect and prospect   39
   GIANFRANCO POGGI

PART TWO: The medieval background

4 Freedom, law, and the medieval state   51
   MAGNUS RYAN

5 States, cities, and citizens in the later Middle Ages   63
   ALMUT HÖFERT

PART THREE: Early-modern developments

6 The state and its rivals in early-modern Europe   79
   MARTIN VAN GELDEREN

7 The development of the idea of citizens' rights   97
   ANNABEL S. BRETT

PART FOUR: **Citizens, states, and modernity**

8   Enlightenment's differences, today's identities   115
    JUDITH A. VEGA

9   Citizen and state under the French Revolution   131
    LUCIEN JAUME

10 A state of contradictions: the post-colonial state in India   145
    SUDIPTA KAVIRAJ

PART FIVE: **After the modern state**

11 The state and its critics: is there a post-modern challenge?   167
    BO STRÅTH

12 Citizenship and equality of the sexes: the French model in
    question   191
    MICHÈLE RIOT SARCEY

13 States, citizens, and the environment   208
    ANDREW DOBSON

    Index   226

Contributors

ANNABEL S. BRETT is Lecturer in History at the University of Cambridge and a Fellow of Gonville and Caius College, Cambridge, UK.

ANDREW DOBSON is Professor of Politics, Department of Government and Politics, The Open University, UK.

MARTIN VAN GELDEREN is Professor of European Intellectual History at the European University Institute, Florence.

ALMUT HÖFERT is Assistant in Early Modern History in the Department of History at the University of Basel, Switzerland.

LUCIEN JAUME is Directeur de recherche at the CNRS and Professor at Sciences Po., Paris.

SUDIPTA KAVIRAJ is Senior Lecturer in Politics at the School of Oriental and African Studies, University of London.

GIANFRANCO POGGI is Professor of Political Theory at the European University Institute, Florence, Italy.

MICHÈLE RIOT-SARCEY is Professor of Contemporary History at the University of Paris 8.

DAVID RUNCIMAN is Lecturer in Political Theory in the Faculty of Social and Political Sciences, University of Cambridge, UK.

MAGNUS RYAN is Lecturer in Late Medieval Studies at The Warburg Institute, University of London, and a Fellow of All Souls College, Oxford, UK.

QUENTIN SKINNER is Regius Professor of Modern History in the University of Cambridge and a Fellow of Christ's College, Cambridge, UK.

BO STRÅTH is Professor of Contemporary History at the European University Institute, Florence, Italy.

JUDITH A. VEGA is Lecturer in Social and Political Philosophy in the Faculty of Philosophy of the University of Groningen, The Netherlands.

Acknowledgements

This book originated in a conference held at the European University Institute in October 2000. For advice at the planning stage we are particularly grateful to Annabel Brett and David Runciman. To the Institute we are deeply indebted for its warm hospitality and the use of its magnificent conference facilities. Special thanks to Sylvie Pascucci for helping to organise our meetings, and for tireless secretarial assistance. We are also much indebted to the audiences at our discussions, whose questions and interventions made us aware of several ways in which we needed to expand and reshape our coverage. Above all we are grateful to those who agreed to write the additional chapters we commissioned, and to those who delivered papers at the conference itself. We thank them in particular for being so willing to revise their contributions, sometimes extensively.

It is a pleasure to express our appreciation to the staff of the Cambridge University Press. Richard Fisher showed an early faith in our project, supported it with excellent advice at every stage, and edited the resulting book with superb professionalism. We are likewise grateful to the Press's three anonymous referees, each of whom provided valuable suggestions, all of which we have followed. Jean Field acted as our sub-editor and brought to bear on the task an exceptional level of commitment and meticulousness. We are also most grateful to Michael Leach for compiling the Index.

The division of editorial labour has been as follows. Bo Stråth was responsible for the organisation of the conference itself. He wishes to thank Liz Fordham, Thomas Jørgensen, and James Kaye for research and editorial assistance, and additionally to thank Liz Fordham for her outstanding translations of the papers originally delivered in French. Quentin Skinner revised the individual chapters and conducted negotiations with the Press. He wishes to thank the Leverhulme Trust for the award of a Major Research Fellowship, during the tenure of which this book was completed. He is also indebted to the staff of the Faculty of History at the University of Cambridge, especially Joanne Nichols, for much essential help. Most of all, we both wish to thank our contributors for meeting their deadlines so cheerfully, and more generally for showing so much forbearance and goodwill.

QUENTIN SKINNER
BO STRÅTH

Introduction

Bo Stråth and Quentin Skinner

The imminent demise of the nation-state is regularly reported.[1] It is certainly true that contemporary states attempt to do less than they used to do. They rarely claim the power or even the right to control economies, and increasingly they ask their citizens to take responsibility for their own welfare. It is also true that contemporary states have more rivals than they used to have. They live in a world of supra-national agencies – the IMF, the World Bank, the United Nations – which have partly usurped their traditional functions. Meanwhile, investment and employment have fallen so much into the hands of multinational corporations that these agencies, we are constantly told, have now become the true rulers of the world.[2]

It only needs a little reflection, however, to remind us that the death of the state can hardly be an imminent or even a readily imaginable event.[3] We can even point to a number of ways in which states are becoming increasingly assertive. Consider, for example, current reactions to the large-scale migration of those fleeing poverty or tyranny. This has turned increasing numbers of desperate people into candidates for citizenship in the rich states of the West. So far the response of these states has been to re-assert their powers of exclusion with a new ferocity, while the response of their citizens has often been even more stridently nationalistic in tone.

Furthermore, it is or ought to be obvious that corporations have not taken over from states and cannot be expected to do so. Everyone, especially in a world beset by terrorism, increasingly demands security. Who but the state and its agencies can provide it? Do we seriously suppose that corporations stand ready to create their own armies, police forces, and intelligence services? Moreover, even the largest corporations remain vulnerable to collapse, as several spectacular instances have lately reminded us. If they expect to be provided

[1] For a recent historical survey which issues in the conclusion that the modern state is in rapid decline, with its functions increasingly being taken over by other organisations, see van Creveld 1999.
[2] For a strong statement of this claim, see Hertz 2001. For some valuably sceptical remarks, see the review by Corey Robin in *Times Literary Supplement*, 15 February 2002, p. 29.
[3] On the difficulties of thinking beyond the idea of the state see Bartelson 2001.

with a safety-net, to whom can they turn except the state? Besides which, corporations need contracts to be enforced, money to be printed, interest-rates to be set, while at the same time they themselves need to be regulated. They turn out, indeed, to need far more regulation to prevent them from lapsing into sheer criminality than it has lately been fashionable to suppose. Who other than states can hope to perform these tasks? States, in short, are here to stay, at least in the foreseeable future.[4] Not for nothing is the condition of statelessness regarded as an extremely grave predicament.

Taking the importance of the state for granted, the contributors to this book reflect on its history, its theoretical underpinnings, and its prospects in the contemporary world. This is a vast theme, and we make no pretence of offering anything like systematic coverage. One limitation we have imposed on ourselves has been a geographical one. We have concentrated on the Western European experience, to which we have added the case of the greatest of the post-colonial democracies, India. We have little to say about state-formation in China or Japan, or about the two federated states that confronted each other for much of the twentieth century, the USA and the USSR. There is no implication that the Western European case is of unique importance. But we certainly believe it to be of exceptional importance, historically as well as conceptually, and it remains a legacy worth examining in depth.

Within our chosen geographical area, we concentrate specifically on the relationship between states and citizens. We have little to say about the embodiment of Western polities before the advent of the state, and accordingly begin no earlier than the medieval period. Equally, we have little to say about the role of intermediate groups within states or about the relations between states and nationhood. We are not unaware that citizens have always possessed multiple identities, and that one of these has normally been a sense of national identity. But nationality and nationalism are two further topics which, while obviously cognate to our theme, would have expanded it beyond all bounds if we had tried to include them.[5]

What, then, are the issues we address as we focus on states and citizens? We begin with three scene-setting chapters, the first of which examines the idea of state power in relation to the freedom of citizens. While this has always been an inescapable confrontation, Quentin Skinner shows that it has been conceptualised in a number of divergent and even incommensurable ways. Concentrating on the Anglophone case, Skinner provides a review of leading traditions of thought about the concept of political liberty. During the early-modern period,

---

[4] For further sceptical reflections about the supposed 'crisis' of the nation-state see Dunn 1996, pp. 196–210.
[5] For a valuable attempt to provide a broader historical survey, see the research reported in Hindle 2002.

the liberty of citizens was generally treated as a status and equated with conditions of legal and social independence. During the eighteenth century, however, this understanding began to be replaced by the view that liberty simply consists in absence of interference. Despite the efforts of many nineteenth-century thinkers to expand the concept of freedom to take in the notion of real human interests, the idea of freedom as non-interference eventually attained a hegemony which it has never lost. This opening chapter ends by reflecting on the moral limitations inherent in the resulting vision of the relationship between the freedom of citizens and the power of the state.

We next turn to examine the character of the state. David Runciman's chapter highlights the extraordinary elusiveness of the concept, the difficulty of identifying the state with anyone or anything in particular. Runciman emphasises the classic importance of Thomas Hobbes's contribution to this view of the state in his *Leviathan* (1651). It is in Hobbes that we first encounter the paradoxical modern understanding of the state as at once the bearer of sovereign power and at the same time as little more than a fictional entity. Runciman concludes that, as in the case of the analogous institution of money, the fictional nature of the state does not undermine but rather helps to explain the power it continues to exercise over us.

The last of our scene-setting chapters looks at the other side of the coin, examining how the experience of citizenship has been conceptualised. After asserting that citizens should always be regarded in the first instance as subjects, Gianfranco Poggi reviews a number of ways in which individual subjects have represented themselves to the state. They have variously seen themselves as soldiers, as tax-payers, as bearers of rights, and sometimes as nothing but spectators of government. Against the background of this conceptual reconstruction, Poggi outlines the prospects for the state in the light of a number of contemporary developments, in particular the rise of globalisation and the formation of supra-national agencies.

After these conceptual clarifications, we shift our attention to the history of the changing relationship between citizens and states. Magnus Ryan traces the way in which the concept of civic liberty first emerged from the background of medieval law. When the concept of law first became a dominant preoccupation of medieval theorists, they did not think of it as a means to ensure the liberty of those living under it. Rather it was seen as a means to discipline the evil, to reward the good and thereby to keep the peace. However, one of the traditional means of rewarding the good was to grant them liberties, that is, special privileges, often in the form of limited rights of self-government. Such privileges frequently created communities by bringing entire populations under the rule of one lord. It thus became possible to regard privileges or liberties as expressive of the geographical area in which they applied, not simply of the power of the lord who applied them. In some cases this process went so far that the area itself was dubbed a liberty. Liberties had the potential, therefore, to become liberty, especially where traditional hegemonies were challenged and replaced by communal or corporate organisations. This raised questions about who should be regarded as the beneficiaries of such liberties. The way out of such problems was frequently to construct an abstract entity to act as the bearer of these rights. Ryan concludes that, while it would be impetuous to call these entities states, it would be a serious error to ignore the relevance of this development. As he ends by showing, there was a coherence in these discussions about law, liberty, and the abstract expression of collective organisation out of which the modern state partly emerged.

We next turn to the later Middle Ages, and specifically to the much-debated question of how far the civic traditions and experience of that period contributed to the crystallising of the modern state. Recent historiography has discredited the idealisation of the medieval city as an island of free burghers in a sea of feudal arrangements. But we are still left with the Weberian view that the urban legal systems of the later Middle Ages made an important contribution to the establishment of the impersonal legal rule of the modern state. As Almut Höfert shows, however, we need to abandon that conception too. Urban court decisions were not made in correspondence with town charters or other legal prescriptions. Rather they were based on an underlying social system of hierarchy and honour. During the fifteenth century, city councils managed to establish an almost complete sovereignty over citizens and so created in their place the concept of the subject. With Jean Bodin's concept of the *civis*, this authoritarian relationship was finally transferred from the city to the sovereignty of the state.

Because the state has become the master noun of our political discourse, it has become almost unavoidable for those reflecting on its history to write in teleological terms about its rise and triumph. The pull of this meta-narrative makes it all the more important to stress that, until a relatively late stage in Western European history, the state continued to face rivals to its absolutist and centralising tendencies. One of the main arguments of Martin van Gelderen's chapter is that too many historians of the nineteenth and twentieth centuries glorified the state as the hallmark of modernity. Even those who, like Friedrich Meinecke, had a more subtle and ambivalent view of modernity failed to give a genuinely historical account of the emergence and development of the modern state. They all failed, in particular, to appreciate the significance of a number of rival conceptions of political community that developed in the course of the seventeenth century. These included Grotius's republican model, Althusius's consociational theory and Arnisaeus's account of the sovereign *ordo civitatis*. Taking the work of Meinecke as its pivotal example, van Gelderen's chapter argues that historians and theorists of modernity have oversimplified a complex picture by failing to pay due attention to the conflict between the state and its rivals in the early-modern period.

Our other chapter on early-modern developments focuses on the emergence of the discourse of rights. The idea that we are citizens, not just subjects, and accordingly hold rights, not just in respect of each other but also in respect of the state, has become central to European political self-consciousness. As Annabel Brett shows, however, if we look at the historical development of both these notions – 'rights' and 'citizens' – we can see that there is something highly problematic about their association in the modern idea of 'citizens' rights'. The language of rights arose in the context of articulating the moral claims of human beings independently of the positive order of the *civitas*. These claims were developed by appealing to a normative, pre-civic notion of human nature and natural law, generating the idea of natural rights. During the wars of resistance at the end of the sixteenth century, the appeal to natural rights was used as a means of legitimating revolt against the *civitas*. In reaction, seventeenth-century theorists of natural rights sought to analyse them in such a way as to neutralise this revolutionary force and to see them as guaranteed by the state. By contrast, the classical figure of the citizen, revived in the course of the humanist Renaissance, implied that a human being achieved morality only within the *civitas*, thus removing any grounds for appeals to nature against it. Although citizenship implied a form of government which could be used as a critique of tyranny, by the mid-seventeenth century it too, like rights, had been refigured to neutralise its radical edge. During the seventeenth century, a new focus on the history of the *civitas* allowed theorists to draw together the notions of citizen and rights as a critical weapon against current regimes. However, this did not resolve the inherent conflict between rights and citizenship, a theoretical dilemma that has never finally been overcome.

The modern state has traditionally been seen as a product of the Enlightenment and the French Revolution, and we next consider the merits of this argument. Judith A. Vega focuses on Enlightenment conceptions of identity and citizenship, and specifically on the place of women's rights within these debates. She questions a received view of the struggle for women's rights as centring on the desire for equality. The demand for citizenship on behalf of women was frequently articulated in terms of the inadmissibility of slavery, while the vocabulary of slavery was challenged by the vocabulary of sociability. Both vocabularies made the idiom of rights incumbent on historical anthropology, but in different ways. As Vega shows, the struggle about rights gave rise to a language of gender difference, one distinguishable from claims to universal equality or group identity. A conception of justice alert to cultural and economic asymmetries originated in the space where the precise meaning of natural rights for civil existence was contested.

With Lucien Jaume's chapter we reach the French Revolution itself, and its influence on the history of citizenship in France. Jaume distinguishes three different views of the *citoyen* associated with the Revolution. One was that of the moderates in 1789, for whom citizenship was not an end in itself but a means of protecting private individuals and rights. A second view was associated in particular with Condorcet, for whom citizenship must aim (notably through the use of education) to create what he described as 'public reason'. Finally there was the perspective of the Jacobins, for whom citizens were seen as members of the people, parts of a whole and thereby subject to the common norms of civic virtue.

Jaume goes on to show that, in the two centuries following the Revolution, the French concept of citizenship came to be characterised by its universalist and abstract nature, irrespective of all horizontal ties, whether communitarian or associative. Recently, however, these elements have been profoundly questioned by the extension of pluralism, by the growing autonomy of civil society and by the forms of standardisation introduced by the European Community. Jaume concludes by suggesting that liberty and equality, the two leading principles of citizenship according to the Revolution, need careful rethinking if they are to accompany these new features of citizenship now coming to birth.

The eighteenth century not only witnessed the crystallisation of the modern concepts of state and citizen in Western Europe; it also saw the beginnings of the great phase of Western European imperialism. What types of state were set up as a result of these colonial adventures? We focus on the case of India, an example of exceptional importance not only by virtue of its scale, but also because it illustrates the successful implanting of the modern state and its conversion to popular government. Sudipta Kaviraj's chapter begins by considering the organisation of power in traditional Indian society. This operated through the structure of the caste system, which segmented society and subjected political power to an inflexible religious order, thereby denying sovereignty to the state. As Kaviraj demonstrates, colonial power in India did not enter through a conflict with the Mughal state but through a slow, insidious process of commercial, administrative, and cultural control. By the mid-nineteenth century it had established a state structure which claimed sovereignty over society. But the unwillingness of the colonial state to overextend itself gave increasing opportunities to Indian elites, who eventually shaped the nationalist ambition to seize control from the British. Kaviraj ends by suggesting that the most significant elements in the evolution of the Indian state since independence have been the immense expansion of its bureaucracy together with an irresistible impulse towards democracy. The democratic effects of lower-caste electoral mobilisation have undermined the caste-based society, a transformation of enormous and continuing significance.

We end with a group of chapters in which the history and prospects of the contemporary state are surveyed. Bo Stråth traces the ironic trajectory of the conflict between the state and its critics in the latter part of the twentieth century.

Beginning with the challenge posed by the social movements of the 1960s, Stråth emphasises their individualistic thrust: cries for freedom and equality were essentially cries for personal emancipation from the state or from parental authority. This individualism was in turn inspired by a Marxist critique in which the state was cast as an instrument of bourgeois repression. This critique developed within a framework of disintegration: the optimistic image of Western modernisation, industrialisation, and democratisation was seriously undermined by the dollar collapse, the oil-price shock, and the recurrence of mass unemployment in the first half of the 1970s. The outcome, however, was not the realisation of Marx's prophecy of a classless society. A new political language emerged in which the values of flexibility and responsibility were emphasised and a growing role was assigned to individual workers in friendly relationships with their employers. The ironic outcome was that the changes of the 1960s were followed not by the triumph of the working class but by its gradual dissolution as an historical category. What emerged was the surprisingly robust structure of the neo-liberal state.

We end by addressing two of the most pressing questions facing contemporary states. First, how can they accommodate the equality of their citizens, men and women alike? Michèle Riot Sarcey considers the issue in relation to the French experience. Although the French democratic system is nominally constructed on the basis of liberty and equality, the establishment of representative democracy in the nineteenth century went hand in hand with a social hierarchy grounded on inequalities of sex and class. Women were regarded as naturally inferior, and were limited to their reproductive role, thereby creating a social difference that became, over time, a difference in kind. Politics meanwhile developed as the prerogative of the free man, to whom the privilege of representation was alone accorded. Eventually a new word – parity – had to be invented to enable women to participate in the system of political representation. Parity, however, is very different from liberty and equality, and it is Riot Sarcey's conclusion that a genuinely democratic state, in which men and women are equally gathered together, has yet to be created.

We conclude by asking whether we can hope to create a more internationalist conception of citizenship. Andrew Dobson considers the question in relation to the environmental problems that every state is now obliged to face. Since many of these problems are global in character, states cannot be the only locus of environmental action. But states remain dominant in our political thinking, making it difficult to generate internationalist or inter-generational conceptions of citizenship. We need to recognise, Dobson argues, that it is a mistake to link citizenship too firmly to the state. He proposes a 'non-bounded' view that could underpin an environmentally oriented conception of citizenship, buttressing it by showing that the obligations of citizenship are not exhausted by the citizen–state relationship. We accordingly end by peering beyond the boundaries of this relationship, the millennial-long history of which we have principally been concerned to trace.

BIBLIOGRAPHY

Bartelson, Jens (2001). *The Critique of the State*, Cambridge: Cambridge University Press.
Creveld, Martin van (1999). *The Rise and Decline of the State*, Cambridge: Cambridge University Press.
Dunn, John (1996). *The History of Political Theory and Other Essays*, Cambridge: Cambridge University Press.
Hertz, Noreena (2001). *The Silent Takeover: Global Capitalism and the Death of Democracy*, London: Heinemann.
Hindle, Steve (ed.) (2002). 'Discussion Group on the State: "When and What Was the State?" St Peter's Oxford. 29–31 March, 2001', *The Journal of Historical Sociology* 15, pp. 59–165.

PART ONE

States and citizens: setting the scene

1   States and the freedom of citizens

Quentin Skinner

What is the extent of the lawful power of the state over its citizens? Or, to put the question the other way round, what is the extent of the freedom and rights of citizens within the state? The claim that these are among the central issues in political philosophy would nowadays be accepted by almost everyone. But this makes it all the more important to begin by stressing that these questions, in the form I have raised them, are distinctively modern ones. Among political theorists writing in the English language, the suggestion that the fundamental confrontation is between states and citizens arose only in the course of the constitutional upheavals of the seventeenth century. It was only once the opponents of the Stuart monarchy began seriously to question the powers of the crown in the 1640s that they started to describe themselves as freeborn citizens rather than as subjects of their king.[1] And as David Runciman indicates in chapter 2, it was only in the same period that they began to think of the holders of sovereign power not as persons acting in their own name but rather as representatives of the state.[2]

The same applies to the belief that, when we speak about the freedom of citizens, we are speaking about the extent of their individual rights. This assumption likewise came to the fore in Anglophone political theory only in the course of the seventeenth century. As late as the Jacobean period, conservative legal and political writers continued to construe civil liberties as nothing more than privileges allowed by the crown as a matter of grace. They were still living, in short, in the world described by Magnus Ryan in chapter 4. When they spoke about the liberty of the Church, they had in mind its special exemptions from the law; when they spoke about the liberty of subjects, they had in mind whatever immunities the crown had chosen to bestow on them.

---

[1] See, for example, Overton 1998, which is headed (p. 33) 'A remonstrance of many thousand citizens and other freeborn people of England'. Here the category of *subject* is silently but vehemently repudiated.

[2] Hobbes in *Leviathan* is perhaps the first Anglophone political theorist to insist in so many words that the figure of the sovereign merely 'carries the person' of the state – that is, serves as its representative. See Hobbes 1996, ch. 17, p. 121 and cf. David Runciman's discussion in chapter 2 of the present work.

If all this is so, it might seem that we ought to avoid discussing the Anglophone case. But there would be a similar story to be told about the concept of the state and the rights of citizens in all the leading polities of early-modern Europe. Furthermore, there are at least two good reasons for concentrating, as I propose to do, on the way in which these issues were debated in the history of Anglophone political thought. One is that, in a brief and impressionistic survey, it is necessary to follow one specific story if the materials are to be kept under any kind of control. But the more important reason is that the Anglophone story is, as it happens, of peculiar importance in the evolution of modern theories of state power and civic liberty. This in turn is due to the fact that so many commentators throughout the eighteenth and nineteenth centuries paid particular attention to the British experience, accepting at face-value the self-image of the British as a nation peculiarly blessed with a constitution guaranteeing freedom under the law.

I began by noting that, as late as the start of the seventeenth century, many defenders of the royal prerogative still insisted that the king's subjects held their property and personal liberty merely by grace of the crown. As John Cowell maintained in his law dictionary of 1607, the term *libertas* refers to 'a priviledge held by graunt or prescription, whereby men enjoy some benefit or favour beyond the ordinarie subject'.[3] It was precisely this understanding, however, that parliamentary critics of the prerogative began to dispute. They complained that, to the extent that they were obliged to rely for the preservation of their liberties on the goodwill of the crown, they were condemned to living in the condition not of free subjects but of slaves. The knowledge that they were living under an arbitrary power capable of interfering with the exercise of their liberties served in itself, they claimed, to undermine their freedom as subjects.[4]

The immediate inspiration for this way of thinking appears to have come from a number of medieval common-law texts, above all those of Bracton and Littleton. These were the authorities that Sir Edward Coke and his followers in the early Stuart Parliaments loved to invoke. Henry de Bracton in his *De Legibus et Consuetudinibus Angliae* of *c.* 1260 had distinguished in his opening chapter between free persons and slaves, and had defined as a slave anyone who 'lives in subjection to the dominion of someone else'.[5] Sir Thomas Littleton's fifteenth-century treatise, *Un lyver de exposicion de parcell de les tenures*,[6] had drawn

---

[3] Cowell 1607, sig. Ss1ʳ.

[4] Note the implicit definition of arbitrariness. A power is arbitrary if the person wielding it is capable of interfering with others solely on the basis of his or her *arbitrium* or will, and hence with no obligation to take into account the interests of those who are subject to the interference. For further discussion see Pettit 1997 and Skinner 1998.

[5] Bracton 1968–77, vol. II, p. 30: '*Quid est servitus*. Est quidem servitus . . . qua quis dominio alieno . . . subicitur.'

[6] This is the title found in the earliest extant manuscript. See Cambridge University Library MS Mm. v. 2, fo. 2ʳ.

a similar set of distinctions between freemen, villeins, and slaves, repeating that a slave is someone whose lack of liberty is such that his person – and not merely, as with a villein, his property – is *sub potestate*, within the power or at the mercy of someone else.

The striking feature of these definitions (although later common lawyers did their best to ignore the fact) is that they owe their phraseology entirely to the analysis of freedom and slavery at the start of the *Digest* of Roman law. There we are first informed that 'the fundamental division within the law of persons is that all men and women are either free or are slaves'.[7] Then we are given a formal definition of slavery. 'Slavery is an institution of the *ius gentium* by which someone is, contrary to nature, subjected to the dominion of someone else.'[8] This in turn is held to yield a definition of individual liberty. If everyone in a civil association is either bond or free, then a *civis* or free subject must be someone who is not under the dominion of anyone else, but is *sui iuris*, capable of acting in their own right.[9] It likewise follows that what it means for someone to lack the status of a free subject must be for that person not to be *sui iuris* but instead to be *sub potestate*, under the power or subject to the will of someone else.

It was this Roman vision of political liberty that a number of spokesmen in Parliament began to deploy in criticism of the crown in the early decades of the seventeenth century. One aspect of this campaign has been extensively discussed, and forms the cornerstone of the traditional 'whig' explanation for the outbreak of the English Civil War in 1642. The government was repeatedly accused, most notably in the Petition of Right of 1628, of forcibly interfering with fundamental liberties, especially by imprisoning subjects without due cause and imposing levies without parliamentary consent. As I have intimated, however, some of the crown's critics were also concerned with a different argument about the relations between the freedom of subjects and the royal prerogative. They argued that these acts of violence were merely the outward manifestations of a deeper affront to liberty. The underlying offence was held to be that of claiming that the king possesses the prerogative right to tax, imprison, and execute his subjects whenever he judges such actions to be in the public interest. To claim such discretionary powers, it was objected, is to leave everyone in dependence on the will of the king. But to live in such dependence is to live as a slave, and to live as a slave is to be bereft of liberty. Hence the claim that Charles I

---

[7] Mommsen and Krueger 1970, I. V. 3. 35: 'Summa itaque de iure personarum divisio haec est, quod omnes homines aut liberi sunt aut servi.' (Note that, in this and subsequent quotations from the *Digest*, I have made my own translations.)

[8] Mommsen and Krueger 1970, I. V. 4. 35: 'Servitus est constitutio iuris gentium, qua quis dominio alieno contra naturam subicitur.'

[9] Mommsen and Krueger 1970, I. VI. 1. 36: 'Some persons are in their own power, some are subject to the power of others, such as slaves, who are in the power of their masters.' ['quaedam personae sui iuris sunt, quaedam alieno iuri subiectae sunt . . . in potestate sunt servi dominorum'.]

was acting in such a way as to curtail not merely the specific liberties but the underlying freedom of his subjects.

We first encounter these arguments in the numerous debates about the alleged prerogative right to impose levies without consent of Parliament. Sir Thomas Hedley in his great speech to the Commons in 1610 maintained that such a prerogative places the property of free subjects 'in the absolute power and command of another'.[10] But if you 'take away the liberty of the subject in his profit or property' then 'you make a promiscuous confusion of a freeman and a bound slave'.[11] The same arguments were even more prominently invoked in later debates about the right to imprison without showing a cause. As the common lawyer Richard Cresheld argued at the time of the Petition of Right, if the crown is permitted such a right we 'become bondage'. To which he added, referring directly to the definition of slavery in the *Digest*, that this condition 'I am sure is contrary to and against the law of nature'.[12]

These were serious enough assaults on the royal prerogative, but the moment at which they provoked a fatal crisis came in the opening months of 1642. When the House of Commons brought forward a proposal early in February to take control of the Militia, Charles I made it clear that he would veto any such legislation by exercising his so-called prerogative of the Negative Voice. Parliament then took the revolutionary step of claiming that, at least in times of emergency, it must possess the right to legislate even in the absence of the royal assent. The reason why this must be so, a number of spokesmen now declared, is that the alternative is national servitude. Henry Parker in his *Observations* of July 1642 furnished the most influential statement of the parliamentary case. If the crown can block any legislation with the Negative Voice, this will reduce Parliament – which represents the entire kingdom – to a state of dependence on the will of the king. But if the kingdom is condemned to living under such a constitution, this will reduce the freeborn English to a nation of slaves. Once we permit the king 'to be the sole, supream competent Judge in this case, we resigne all into his hands, we give lifes, liberties, Laws, Parliaments, all to be held at meer discretion' and thereby consign ourselves to bondage.[13]

Parker was not the first to put forward this argument about the Negative Voice,[14] but the influence of his *Observations* helped to make it central to the rhetoric of the ensuing civil war. We encounter the same argument in Parliament's call to arms of August 1642, in which we are told that the king's advisers now aspire 'to destroy his Parliament and good people by a Civill War; and, by that meanes to bring ruine, confusion, and perpetuall slavery upon the

---

[10] Foster 1966, vol. II, p. 196. For an analysis of Hedley's speech see Peltonen 1995, pp. 220–8.
[11] Foster 1966, vol. II, p. 192.   [12] Johnson and Cole 1977, p. 149.
[13] [Parker] 1933, pp. 209–10.
[14] It is already adumbrated, for example, in the parliamentary Remonstrance of 26th May 1642. See Husbands *et al.*, 1643, pp. 263–4.

surviving part of a then wretched Kingdome'.[15] We encounter the argument once again at the conclusion of the war, when it was used to justify not merely the regicide but the abolition of the monarchy. The charge against Charles I at his trial was that he had sought 'to erect, and uphold in himself an unlimited and Tyrannical power to rule *according to his Will'*, a course of action designed not merely 'to overthrow the Rights and Liberties of the People' but 'to take away, and make void the foundations thereof'.[16] The Act of March 1649 abolishing the office of king duly confirmed that monarchy is 'dangerous to the liberty, safety, and public interest of the people', adding that in England the effect of the prerogative had been 'to oppress and impoverish and enslave the subject'.[17]

This neo-Roman analysis of what it means to possess our freedom carried with it a distinctive view of the relations between the liberty of citizens and the constitution of the state. The essence of the argument is that freedom is restricted by dependence. To be free as a citizen, therefore, requires that the actions of the state should reflect the will of all its citizens, for otherwise the excluded will remain dependent on those whose wills move the state to act. The outcome was the belief – crucial both to the republicanism of the Italian Renaissance and to that of the Dutch and English in the seventeenth century – that it is possible to enjoy individual liberty if and only if we live as citizens of self-governing republics. To live as subjects of a monarch is to live as slaves.

No sooner had the English proclaimed their 'free commonwealth' than the greatest of their political writers, Thomas Hobbes, picked up his pen to compose a furious reply to these anti-monarchical arguments. Hobbes's *Leviathan*, written in a white heat between 1649 and 1651, is among other things a violent attack on the theory of freedom propagated by the supporters of Parliament in the English Civil Wars. Hobbes writes as someone anxious above all to vindicate the necessity of absolute sovereignty. He accordingly needs to defend his Leviathan state against the charge that it is an arbitrary power incapable of respecting the liberty of its subjects. The defence he mounts is that, in claiming that absolutism automatically produces slavery, the parliamentarians completely misunderstand the concept of liberty.

As Hobbes defines it in *Leviathan*, liberty has nothing to do with conditions of dependence or independence. To be free is simply to be unhindered by external impediments from exercising one's powers. 'By LIBERTY, is understood, according to the proper signification of the word, the absence of external Impediments: which Impediments, may oft take away part of a man's power to do what hee would; but cannot hinder him from using the power left him, according as his judgement, and reason shall dictate to him.'[18] Freedom is taken away, in other words, only by identifiable acts of interference on the part of external

[15] Husbands *et al.* 1643, p. 509.   [16] *Charge of the Commons* 1649, pp. 3–4.
[17] Gardiner 1906, p. 385.   [18] Hobbes 1996, ch. 14, p. 91.

agents, acts of interference that have the effect of rendering actions within our powers impossible to perform. It is only when someone or something 'is so tyed, or environed, as it cannot move, but within a certain space, which space is determined by the opposition of some externall body, [that] we say it hath not Liberty to go further'.[19]

One startling implication of Hobbes's analysis is that coercion of the will does not infringe liberty. When the law coerces us by arousing our fears about the evil consequences of disobedience, we cannot be said to act unfreely in obeying it. Freedom is taken away only by external impediments, and fear is not an external impediment. What happens is that, by reflecting on the consequences of disobeying, we acquire the will to act as the laws prescribe. The predicament in which we find ourselves is exactly analogous to that of the man who 'throweth his goods into the Sea for *feare* the ship should sink'. Far from acting against his will, he performs the action 'very willingly, and may refuse to doe it if he will: It is therefore the action, of one that was *free*'. As Hobbes grimly summarises, 'Feare, and Liberty are consistent.'[20]

As Hobbes is at pains to point out, this analysis completely overturns the dangerously absurd belief that 'the Subjects in a Popular Common-wealth enjoy Liberty; but that in a Monarchy they are all Slaves'.[21] If we maintain that our freedom has been taken away, we must be able to point to some act of interference on the part of some external agency. It makes no sense to claim that we are less free simply because we live under absolute power than if we lived under conditions of republican self-government. The liberties of subjects basically depend on 'the Silence of the Law', so that the question is not who makes the laws but simply how many laws are made.[22] The fewer the laws, the greater the individual liberty.

Hobbes's counter-revolutionary analysis did not immediately commend itself to his fellow citizens. They were shocked in the first place by his contention that coercion leaves liberty unimpaired. John Locke in his *Two Treatises of Government* of 1690 was one of many who sought to reinstate the traditional point of view. He first does so in the course of dismissing the claim that conquest can give a valid title to rule. 'Should a Robber break into my House, and with a Dagger at my Throat, make me seal Deeds to convey my Estate to him, would this give him any title?'[23] Locke's rhetorical question answers itself: under such conditions of duress, no one can be said to act freely, so that no just title can arise from the perpetration of such an outrage. Later Locke makes the same point when reflecting on King James II's acts of arbitrary power, in particular his success in managing 'to corrupt the *Representatives*' of the people so that 'by

---

[19] Hobbes 1996, ch. 21, p. 145.   [20] All quotations from Hobbes 1996, ch. 21, p. 146.
[21] Hobbes 1996, ch. 29, p. 226.   [22] Hobbes 1996, ch. 21, p. 152.
[23] Locke 1988, para. 176, p. 385.

Sollicitations, Threats, Promises or otherwise' they were 'won to his designs'. This is to behave coercively, Locke responds, and again he takes it to be obvious that no one can 'freely act and advise' under such conditions of duress.[24]

A yet more thorough repudiation of Hobbes's analysis came from those who professed to see a resurgence of arbitrary government under the later Stuarts. Faced with an apparent drift towards absolutism, these critics revived and underlined the claim that an awareness of living in dependence on arbitrary power has the effect of limiting our freedom. This is the stance adopted by Locke in his attack in the *Two Treatises* on Sir Robert Filmer's *Patriarcha*, and this is the argument similarly pressed against Filmer by Algernon Sidney in his *Discourses of Government*, first published posthumously in 1694. At the outset of his analysis Sidney offers an emphatic restatement of the neo-Roman case. 'Liberty', as he defines it, 'solely consists in an independency upon the will of another, and by the name of a slave we understand a man, who can neither dispose of his person nor goods, but enjoys all at the will of his master'. We cannot accept that 'those men or nations are not slaves, who have no other title to what they enjoy, than the grace of the prince, which he may revoke whensoever he pleaseth'. For 'if it be liberty to live under such a government, I desire to know what is slavery'.[25]

The revival and restatement of these neo-Roman arguments proved a no less powerful weapon in the hands of the radical whigs in the generation following the constitutional settlement of 1688. Bolingbroke drew on these ideas in his attempt to prove that, under Sir Robert Walpole's oligarchy, the arbitrary power of the crown had been replaced by the no less arbitrary and hence enslaving power of a corrupt executive. When John Trenchard and Thomas Gordon published their *Cato's Letters* in the early 1720s, they too mounted a repeated contrast between the slavery produced by dependence on executive tyranny and the true freedom of a nation in which 'the people have no masters but the laws' and in which 'both laws and magistracies are formed by the people'.[26]

A generation later, Joseph Priestley, Richard Price, and their dissenting allies showed how the same neo-Roman arguments could be used to uphold the cause of the American colonists against the British crown. Perhaps the most powerful defence was that of Price in his *Two Tracts on Civil Liberty* of 1778. He begins by reiterating that a free person is someone not dependent on the will of another. So long as anyone is 'held under the power of masters', they 'cannot be denominated free however equitably and kindly they may be treated'. He then declares that 'this is strictly true of communities as well as individuals'. If the maintenance of free government depends on any human power 'which is considered as giving it, on which it depends, and which can invade or recall

---

[24] Locke 1988, para. 222, p. 413.   [25] Sidney 1990, p. 17.
[26] Trenchard and Gordon 1995, vol. I, p. 484.

it at pleasure, it changes its nature and becomes a species of slavery'.[27] With these considerations in mind, Price turns to the American colonists and their Declaration of Independence. Any country 'that is subject to the legislature of another country in which it has no voice, and over which it has no controul, cannot be said to be governed by its own will. Such a country, therefore, is in a state of slavery.'[28] But slavery is contrary to the law of nature, so that any such country must possess the natural right to liberate itself from its condition of servitude, just as the American colonists have done.

This use of neo-Roman arguments to call for parliamentary reform at home and the liberation of colonies abroad was too much for the more conservative political writers of the age. Rightly perceiving that these demands were grounded on the claim that dependence undermines freedom, they proceeded to revive the Hobbesian contention that there must be something amiss with this underlying definition of liberty. Hence we find David Hume mocking the absurdity of believing that the nominal dependence of the French upon the will of their king for the maintenance of their civil liberties has any deleterious effect on their lives.[29] Hence too we find Jeremy Bentham and John Lynd, in repudiating the American Declaration of Independence, reverting to a purely Hobbesian definition of liberty, although in Bentham's case with many protestations about his own originality.[30]

Of all these polemical responses, perhaps the most systematic came from William Paley in his *Principles of Moral and Political Philosophy* in 1785. Paley notes that 'the usage of common discourse, as well as the example of many respectable writers' have given rise to the view that liberty consists 'not merely in an actual exemption from the constraint of useless and noxious laws and acts of dominion, but in being free from the *danger* of having such hereafter imposed or exercised'.[31] But this commitment, Paley retorts, rests on confusing the concept of freedom with that of security, and describes 'not so much liberty itself, as the safeguards and preservatives of liberty'.[32] We may be less secure if we live in a state of dependence, but we cannot be less free, because our 'degree of actual liberty' always bears 'a reversed proportion to the number and severity of the *restrictions*' placed on our actions. Once we recognise that liberty is marked by the absence not of dependence but merely of interference, we shall be able to see that 'this liberty may be enjoyed under every form of government', and that 'those popular phrases which speak of a free people' and 'of a nation of slaves' are barely intelligible.[33]

The positive conclusion announced by these and other utilitarian writers is thus that the extent of our liberty as citizens must be measured by the extent to

[27] Price 1991, p. 77.   [28] Price 1991, p. 30.   [29] Hume 1994, pp. 51–7.
[30] For these protestations see Long 1977, pp. 54–5.   [31] Paley 1830, vol. III, p. 357.
[32] Paley 1830, vol. III, p. 359.   [33] Paley 1830, vol. III, p. 356.

which we remain free from interference by the coercive powers of the law.[34] As Bentham acknowledged, however, this commitment raised a new difficulty. What instances of bending the will are to count as coercive? Hobbes had never needed to confront the question, but it became unavoidable for anyone who rejected his claim that freedom of action and coercion of the will are compatible. Locke illustrates rather than addresses the difficulty when he speaks, as we have seen, of 'Sollicitations, Threats, Promises' and describes them all as exercises of coercive power. No doubt this is true of credible, serious, and immediate threats, but can we so readily say that offers and other such solicitations have a similarly coercive effect? Where and how is the line to be drawn?

Bentham is one of the first writers to face this question squarely and propose an answer to it. Suppose I affect your will by promising you a benefit or, in Bentham's phrase, 'by holding out the prospect of pleasure' if you comply with my demands. Then in Bentham's terms I am *alluring* you, for if you refuse my offer you are no worse off, whereas if you accept it you are better off. I may therefore be said to have presented you with a genuine choice, and your liberty remains intact. But suppose I act on your will 'by holding out the prospect of pain' for non-compliance with my demands. Then I am *coercing* rather than alluring you, for if you accept my offer you will be no better off, and if you refuse it you will definitely be worse off. I cannot be said to have presented you with a genuine choice, and have therefore undermined your liberty.[35]

So long as the power of the state appeared to pose the gravest threat to the freedom of citizens, the neo-Hobbesian analysis of liberty popularised by the classical utilitarians continued to hold the field. By the middle of the nineteenth century, however, the heirs of this school of thought – John Stuart Mill in particular – were becoming more concerned about the inhibiting effects on individual freedom of growing demands for social conformity. As Mill expresses the anxiety in his essay *On Liberty* of 1859, the yoke of law may in recent times have become lighter, but 'the yoke of opinion is perhaps heavier' in England than 'in most other countries of Europe'.[36]

Underlying Mill's argument is a challenge to one of the basic presuppositions of all the theories of freedom I have so far examined. Mill implicitly rejects the assumption that freedom is necessarily interpersonal in character, arguing instead that we ourselves may be among the agents capable of undermining our own liberty. As he repeatedly insists, the people of Victorian England find themselves condemned to living under 'the despotism of custom' in a society in which 'the traditions or customs of other people are the rule of conduct'.[37] They think of themselves as free, but the effect of this demand for conformity is

---

[34] Bentham 1970, p. 253: speaks of 'coercion, which it [sc. liberty] is the absence of . . .'
[35] All quotations from Bentham 1970, p. 259.   [36] Mill 1989, p. 12.
[37] See Mill 1989, p. 57, and on the despotism of custom see pp. 70–1.

to make them censor their desires in such a way as to prevent their choices from being authentically their own. They 'choose what is customary, in preference to what suits their own inclination' until 'it does not occur to them to have any inclination, except for what is customary' and 'the mind itself is bowed to the yoke'.[38] Genuine freedom of action is thereby forfeited, and they have only themselves to blame.

Mill is here reviving and restating the ancient belief that our passions can be one of the agents of our own enslavement.[39] The belief is as old as Plato's exploration of the geography of the soul in the *Timaeus*, in which he pictures the will as equally capable of aligning itself with reason or with passion. If we yield to passion, we enslave ourselves to our desires; only if we ensure that our will remains allied with reason can we hope to act freely. A number of early-modern writers – John Locke is prominent among them – emphasise a similar set of connections between freedom and reason, but John Stuart Mill's distinctive contribution is to place these considerations at the heart of his theory of social and political liberty.[40] His resulting analysis bears a striking resemblance to – and may partly have paved the way for – the Marxist contention that our freedom is capable of being undermined by our own false consciousness. If social being determines consciousness, and if our consciousness is determined by a bourgeois society in which our freedom is conceived in consumerist terms, we are liable to collude in our own servitude by endorsing a purely consumerist and hence a false account of what is in our own best interests. With these contentions, especially as refined and extended by Marx's modern disciples, the claim that the self is capable of undermining its own freedom became fully politicised.

Although Mill places a distinctive emphasis on custom as the enemy of freedom, he nevertheless agrees with earlier utilitarian theorists that potentially the most serious threat to individual liberty comes from the coercive powers of the state. No one had expressed this commitment more trenchantly than Jeremy Bentham. 'A law', Bentham had declared, 'whatever good it may do at the long run, is sure in the first instance to produce mischief'. He concedes that 'the good it does may compensate the mischief', but he insists that 'no law can ever be made but what trenches upon liberty', and that 'if it stops there, it is so much *pure* evil'.[41] This commitment had the effect of propelling the utilitarians inexorably in the direction of endorsing a minimal state. If liberty is the ideal to be cherished, and if law is the principal means by which it is undermined, then we have a powerful reason for controlling the state in the

---

[38] Mill 1989, p. 61.   [39] On this theme see James 1997, esp. pp. 11–14.

[40] Freud's achievement, in the next generation, could perhaps be analogously described as that of inventing a therapy capable of bringing to consciousness the repressed forces that inhibit us, thereby enabling us to attain a greater degree of liberty.

[41] Bentham 1970, p. 54.

name of maximising our freedom as citizens. The philosophy of liberalism accordingly came to centre on the defence of a *cordon sanitaire* of inviolable rights, a *cordon* beyond which the state must under no circumstances be allowed to trespass.

To many liberal theorists of the later nineteenth century, however, this came to seem a grossly uncaring creed, and one that underestimated the power of the state to improve people's lives, above all the lives of the less fortunate. Repudiating the idea of a *cordon sanitaire*, philosophers such as T. H. Green and Bernard Bosanquet went on to reconceptualise the notion of individual rights as contributions to the common good, declaring at the same time that the state must act to further the common good if it is to count as legitimate. The state on this analysis is no longer seen as an enemy of liberty, but is taken to have an obligation to hinder the hindrances (in Bosanquet's phrase) that we may encounter in fulfilling ourselves as citizens and thereby attaining our highest goals.

Green, Bosanquet, and their followers are notable for presenting this doctrine as a theory of freedom. The essence of their argument is that if and only if we succeed in acting in such a way as to fulfil our highest potentialities can we count as fully free. Genuflecting in the direction of Kant and Hegel, Green is perhaps the first Anglophone philosopher to articulate the argument in precisely these terms. The effect is to engineer a sharp break with earlier traditions of thinking about the idea of liberty. Although the utilitarian and neo-Roman writers had differed in many respects, they had agreed on one fundamental point: that the concept of liberty is essentially a negative one. They had agreed, that is, that the presence of liberty is invariably marked by an absence – absence of dependence according to the neo-Roman writers, absence of interference according to the utilitarians. By contrast, Green and his disciples accept the Hegelian contention that this is to speak only of the negative moment in the dialectic of liberty. If we are to attain true freedom, we must transcend this negativity by committing ourselves to following the specific way of life in which our liberty is most fully realised. 'Real freedom', as Green declares, 'consists in the whole man having found his object'.[42] To speak of the freedom of a man is thus to speak of 'the state in which he shall have realised his ideal of himself'.[43] Liberty is, in short, the name of an end-state; as Green concludes, it is 'in some sense the goal of moral endeavour'.[44]

With this image of freedom, the suspicion of the state so deeply embedded in earlier liberal traditions drains away. The state comes to be seen as the guarantor of freedom, not only because it is capable of enacting laws that create a *cordon sanitaire*, but also because it is capable of hindering the hindrances that prevent us from realising our highest potentialities. The outcome is a proposal for a

[42] Green 1986, pp. 228–9.   [43] Green 1986, p. 241.   [44] Green 1986, p. 242.

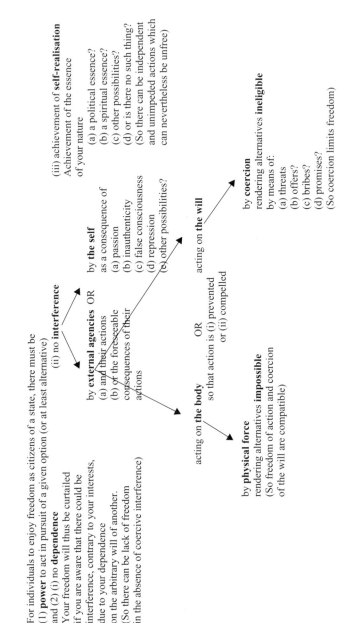

Figure 1

welfare state in which public funds will be used to provide free and compulsory education (because ignorance is a hindrance) in addition to such services as health care (because disease is a hindrance) and state pensions and welfare (because poverty is a hindrance). Furthermore, the state is authorised to protect its citizens not merely from each other and from external enemies, but also from their own baser instincts, thereby leading them towards a higher life of virtue, commitment, fulfilment, and, in a word, freedom.

Having begun my story around the year 1600, I have now arrived at the end of the nineteenth century. By this stage in the narrative, it would be fair to say that all the leading arguments still employed in current debates about the freedom of citizens had been fully articulated. So clearly had the battle-lines been drawn that we can even hope to reproduce them without undue crudity in a diagrammatic form, as I have attempted to do in Figure 1. If this chart traces the story from the early seventeenth to the late nineteenth century, what did the twentieth century find to add to the argument? Within the Anglophone tradition, the first half of the century witnessed an unparalleled enthusiasm for the interventionist state, while in the second half there was a no less vehement reaction against it. By the 1920s, the belief that the state should act to promote the virtue of its citizens had reached such heights that, in the United States, the Constitution was amended to forbid the sale of alcohol, that most notorious hindrance to the exercise of social virtue. By the 1940s, the British state had gone even further in the campaign to hinder hindrances. After the election of 1945, the Labour government imposed what later came to be regarded as confiscatory levels of taxation in order to fund the full-scale provision of health, education and welfare services on which the freedom and self-development of the British people were held to depend.

During the same period, however, repeated and melodramatic warnings were issued against the 'positive' theory of liberty by the exponents of a more in-dividualistic version of liberalism. L. T. Hobhouse, recalling the bombing of London in the First World War, declared that it represented the apotheosis of the Germanic doctrine of freedom by which Green, Bosanquet, and their disciples had been fatally hoodwinked.[45] Isaiah Berlin, writing at the height of the Cold War, similarly denounced the exponents of 'positive' liberty for deforming an ideal of autonomy into a totalitarian creed fit only for 'the latest nationalist or communist dictator'.[46] Little more than a decade later, the so-called libertarians in the United States took a yet further step. They declared that, if we genuinely value our rights, and hence our freedom of action, we must recognise that the very legitimacy of the state is questionable. So argued Robert Nozick.[47] They even warned us that, if autonomy is our fundamental value, the state cannot be accepted as a legitimate institution at all. So argued Robert Paul Wolff.[48] The

---

[45] Hobhouse 1918, p. 6.   [46] Berlin 1969, p. 152.   [47] Nozick 1974.   [48] Wolff 1998.

cordon sanitaire became everything, and doctrines of natural rights began to proliferate with unparalleled exuberance.

The second half of the twentieth century witnessed the widespread triumph of this outlook over the collectivism of the welfare state. With this victory, a number of beliefs about political liberty became so widely entrenched that, in the Anglophone tradition, they now enjoy the status of an orthodoxy. One is the belief that 'positive' liberty is a delusion, and that all coherent theories of freedom must take a negative form. Liberty must be understood as absence of constraint on some interpretation of the concept of constraint, and cannot be understood in any other way.[49] A second and connected belief is that, when we speak about the constraints that take away our freedom, we must be speaking about identifiable acts of interference. Where there is loss of liberty, this will always be attributable to some intervention that has the effect (whether intentional or otherwise) of hindering us in the exercise of our powers.[50] To speak of dependence as a form of constraint is therefore seriously confused. As Isaiah Berlin explains, if we are to speak of a loss of liberty we must be able to point to some act of trespass; the mere recognition that we are living in a state of dependence cannot possibly qualify, since no interference need be involved.[51] Here, as elsewhere, the prevailing orthodoxy recycles the philosophy of Hobbes. In our end is our beginning.

Brief and impressionistic though this survey has been, there are at least two lessons to be learned from it. One is that we cannot usefully ask in a straightforward way which of the various theories of liberty I have outlined is the correct one. Each tradition provides a coherent account of how to think about freedom and the state, and each has at different times answered to important human interests. The neo-Roman claim that dependence constitutes a form of constraint worked well for those whose chief concern was to limit the exercise of arbitrary power. The contention that our freedom is taken away only by identifiable acts of interference worked well for those who wished to insist that contracts are free so long as they are not coercive and that colonisation is legitimate so long as subject peoples are not actively oppressed. The 'positive' ideal of liberty as self-realisation worked well for those who aspired to check the ravages of free markets and to insist on the duty of the state to help those who are unable to help themselves. We may wish to dismiss these social philosophies as misguided, but we cannot do so by pointing to any incoherence in the theories of freedom on which they are based.

The other lesson is that, in the present crisis of our affairs, we might do well to reconsider the merits of the neo-Roman view that dependence involves an

---

[49] See MacCallum 1972, a classic analysis that has been widely taken up. For adaptations see, for example, Day 1983, Narveson 1989, Swift 2001.
[50] Berlin 1969, pp. 122–3.   [51] Berlin 1969, pp. 158–9.

affront to our liberty. Consider, for example, the current predicament of the British people, who have for so long prided themselves on the enjoyment of their liberties. They now find themselves living more and more under asymmetric relations of power and powerlessness. The triumph of free markets, with the concomitant collapse of trade union movements, has left successive governments subject to blackmail by multinational corporations while leaving the work-force increasingly dependent on the arbitrary power of employers. Meanwhile the British people still lack a written constitution, and accordingly remain bereft of any liberties that their Executive cannot decide to take away.[52] Ethnic minorities remain under continuing pressure to conform to a normative account of what it means to be British, an account that devalues much of their culture while undermining their freedom to criticise. The British people as a whole have no power to check their governments, save by changing them at infrequent intervals. Nor does the Legislative, thanks to the unparalleled size of recent parliamentary majorities, have any effective capacity to check the Executive. Any checks constituted by the existence of a second chamber have been made residual, and Britain remains the only country within the European Union to operate with the paradoxical concept of a non-elected representative assembly. The outcome is an unregulated system of Executive power, with the body of the people and their representatives alike condemned to a state of corresponding dependence. With the passing of the latest Anti-Terrorism Act, even the fundamental right of *habeas corpus* has been jeopardised. There is now a power of detention, without charge or trial, on mere suspicion of having committed an offence.

It is partly the acceptance of the view that freedom is undermined only by coercion that allows such systems of power to flourish and seem defensible. The effect has been to shift the balance away from the liberty of citizens and towards increasingly arbitrary forms of state authority. If we believe in democracy, we shall want to shift the balance back again. We could do much worse than begin by reconsidering what it means to enjoy our freedom as citizens of modern states. We have no need to accept the conveniently meagre answer that our rulers and their apologists currently offer us.

BIBLIOGRAPHY

Bentham, Jeremy (1970) [1782]. *Of Laws in General*, ed. H. L. A. Hart, London: The Athlone Press.
Berlin, Isaiah (1969). *Four Essays on Liberty*, Oxford: Oxford University Press.
Bosanquet, Bernard (1910). *The Philosophical Theory of the State*, 2nd edn, London: Macmillan.

---

[52] Nor does the fact that the British government recently adopted the European convention on human rights turn out to make any difference, since it has already claimed the statutory right to suspend its provisions when it judges such a suspension necessary.

Bracton, Henry de (1968–77) [*c*. 1250]. *De Legibus et Consuetudinibus Angliae*, trans. and ed. Samuel E. Thorne, 4 vols., Cambridge, Mass.: The Belknap Press.

Charge of the Commons of England, Against Charles Stuart, King of England, The (1649). London.

Cowell, John (1607). *The Interpreter: Or Booke Containing the Signification of Words*, Cambridge.

Day, J. P. (1983). 'Individual Liberty' in *Of Liberty*, ed. A. Phillips Griffith, Cambridge: Cambridge University Press, pp. 17–29.

Foster, Elizabeth Read (ed.) (1966). *Proceedings in Parliament 1610*, 2 vols., New Haven, Conn.: Yale University Press.

Gardiner, S. R. (ed.) (1906). *The Constitutional Documents of the Puritan Revolution 1625–1660*, 3rd edn, Oxford: The Clarendon Press.

Green, T. H. (1986) [1879]. 'On the Different Senses of "Freedom" as Applied to Will and to the Moral Progress of Man' in *Lectures on the Principles of Political Obligation and Other Writings*, ed. Paul Harris and John Morrow, Cambridge: Cambridge University Press, pp. 228–49.

  (1991) [1881]. 'Liberal Legislation and Freedom of Contract' in *Liberty*, ed. David Miller, Oxford: Oxford University Press, pp. 21–32.

Hobbes, Thomas (1996) [1651]. *Leviathan, Or The Matter, Forme, and Power of a Common-Wealth Ecclesiasticall and Civill*, ed. Richard Tuck, Cambridge: Cambridge University Press.

Hobhouse, L. T. (1918). *The Metaphysical Theory of the State: A Criticism*, London: George Allen and Unwin.

Hume, David (1994) [1741]. *Political Essays*, ed. Knud Haakonssen, Cambridge: Cambridge University Press.

Husbands, Edward, Warren, T., and Best, R. (1643). *An Exact Collection of all Remonstrances, Declarations, Votes, Orders, Ordinances, Proclamations, Petitions, Messages, Answers, and other Remarkable Passages betweene . . . December 1641, and continued untill March the 21, 1643*, London.

James, Susan (1997). *Passion and Action: The Emotions in Seventeenth-Century Philosophy*, Oxford: The Clarendon Press.

Johnson, Robert C. and Cole, Maija Jansson (1977). *Commons Debates 1628*, vol. II: *17 March–19 April 1628*, New Haven, Conn.: Yale University Press.

Locke, John (1988) [1690]. *Two Treatises of Government*, ed. Peter Laslett, Cambridge: Cambridge University Press.

Long, Douglas G. (1977). *Bentham on Liberty: Jeremy Bentham's Idea of Liberty in Relation to his Utilitarianism*, Toronto: Toronto University Press.

MacCallum, Gerald (1972). 'Negative and Positive Freedom' in *Philosophy, Politics and Society*, Fourth Series, ed. Peter Laslett, W. G. Runciman, and Quentin Skinner, Oxford: Basil Blackwell, pp. 174–93.

Mill, John Stuart (1989) [1859]. *On Liberty*, ed. Stefan Collini, Cambridge: Cambridge University Press.

Mommsen, Theodor and Krueger, Paul (eds.) (1970). *The Digest of Justinian*, translation ed. Alan Watson, 4 vols., Philadelphia, Penn.: University of Pennsylvania Press.

Narveson, Jan (1989). *The Libertarian Ideal*, Philadelphia, Penn.: University of Pennsylvania Press.

Nozick, Robert (1974). *Anarchy, State, and Utopia*, New York: Basic Books.

Overton, Richard (1998) [1646]. *A Remonstrance of Many Thousand Citizens* in *The English Levellers*, ed. Andrew Sharp, Cambridge: Cambridge University Press, pp. 33–53.

Paley, William (1830) [1785]. *The Principles of Moral and Political Philosophy* in *The Works of William Paley*, 6 vols., London, vol. III.

[Parker, Henry] (1933) [1642]. *Observations upon some of his Majesties late Answers and Expresses* in *Tracts on Liberty in the Puritan Revolution 1638–1647*, ed. William Haller, New York: Columbia University Press, vol. II, pp. 167–213.

Peltonen, Markku (1995). *Classical Humanism and Republicanism in English Political Thought 1570–1640*, Cambridge: Cambridge University Press.

Pettit, Philip (1997). *Republicanism: A Theory of Freedom and Government*, Oxford: Oxford University Press.

Price, Richard (1991) [1777–8]. *Political Writings*, ed. D. O. Thomas, Cambridge: Cambridge University Press.

Sidney, Algernon (1990) [1694]. *Discourses Concerning Government*, ed. Thomas G. West, Indianapolis: LibertyClassics.

Skinner, Quentin (1998). *Liberty Before Liberalism*, Cambridge: Cambridge University Press.

Swift, Adam (2001). *Political Philosophy*, Cambridge: Polity Press.

Trenchard, John and Gordon, Thomas (1995) [1720s]. *Cato's Letters, or Essays on Liberty, Civil and Religious, and Other Important Subjects*, ed. Ronald Hamowy, 2 vols., Indianapolis: LibertyClassics.

Wolff, Robert Paul (1998). *In Defense of Anarchism*, repr. Berkeley: University of California Press.

2   The concept of the state: the sovereignty of a fiction

David Runciman

Is the state nothing more than a fiction? In one sense, the very idea is somehow ridiculous, given the real consequences we each of us experience at the hands of the state every day of our lives. If what the state does is real – taxation, regulation, prosecution, punishment, war – how can the state itself be unreal? Yet there is also a sense in which the state is constantly disappearing from view, since it is very hard to find anyone or anything in the real world with which finally to identify it, despite the readiness with which many make that claim. Certainly, the state cannot be identified with any named individuals or groups of individuals who may play a part in its ongoing existence, because no individual or group could possibly take onto themselves the entire burden of the state. So, for example, 'state' cannot simply be identified with 'government',[1] because a government is always a collection of named individuals, none of whom could ever sustain the fiscal burden of the state's debt, or the moral burden of the state's acts of violence, as individuals (anyone who did would go bankrupt or mad, or perhaps be bankrupt or mad already). The best those individuals can do is to represent the state in some capacity or other, as all governments in the modern world do in one form or another. Nor can the state be identified with 'the people,'[2] because the people are simply a more numerous collection of named individuals, none of whom are any likelier to assume personal liability for the actions of the state than their governors are. Even if it were morally feasible to make the people pay for the actions of the state, it would be practically impossible, because any list of citizens in any modern state is always out-of-date, and incomplete. Nobody can *be* the state at any given moment, because at all the crucial moments the state is never identifiable with anybody in particular.

Nor, though, can the state be identified with a relation between individuals or groups of individuals, such as that between a people and their government.

---

[1] As it is most often in various forms of utilitarian discourse, particularly the utilitarian jurisprudence of the early nineteenth century (see, for example, Austin 1995 [1832]), p. 190: 'The state ... denotes the individual person, or the body of individual persons, which bears the supreme powers in an independent political society'); and as it is also in newspaper reporting in Britain today, when 'state' and 'government' are used interchangeably.

[2] As it is most often in various forms of republican discourse, including some but by no means all of those emanating out of the French Revolution (see Hont 1994, pp. 192–205).

States may perhaps emerge out of such a relation – for example, out of a contract – and they may be constrained by such a relation – for example, by a constitution. But constitutions do not go to war, nor repay debts, nor punish criminals; states do all of those things. States must therefore be a form of association, rather than a form of relation, because it is associations rather than relations that are capable of action. But the state cannot be identified with the power generated by certain forms of association – say, the legitimate monopoly of coercion,[3] or sovereignty – because that power must attach to something other than itself; sovereignty does not itself possess sovereignty (the sovereign *state* does). Similarly, the state cannot simply be identified with any of the purposes it may serve, whether security, or justice, or freedom, because the purpose is by definition separate from the instrument (if it were not, the purpose would not be served, it would simply *be*). The state is therefore an association that cannot be identified with its members, its constitution, its powers, or its purposes. In law, such associations are known as fictions. But states, surely, are real.

The political theorist who best reflects this ambivalence at the heart of the modern state is also the political theorist who has some claims to having captured the distinctive nature of the modern state best, Thomas Hobbes. In his *Leviathan*, Hobbes makes it as clear as it is possible to be that the state cannot be understood as a relation, or a constitution, or a purpose; it is a person, and it acts.[4] Thus although the state is born of a covenant between individuals, and, in Hobbes's terms, procures thereby 'the safety of the people',[5] the state itself is neither of these things, because neither covenant nor safety is capable of action (both, rather, are the products *of* action). However, Hobbes is also clear that the state cannot simply be identified with any of the persons who inhabit the world of real action. The state cannot be identified with the group of individuals who make up the people, because the people have no unity, and cannot act as a person in their own name. But nor can the state simply be identified with the sovereign power in the state, because the sovereign power is always embodied by an individual or group of individuals ('an assembly') who cannot bear the identity of the state simply as individuals. If the state *is* the king, then the state is a relatively weak, powerless, and absolutely mortal man.[6] The king only enjoys the power of the

---

[3] Weber does not himself identify the state with the monopoly of coercion but with the association that creates a monopoly of legitimate coercion in a given geographical area (see Weber 1994, pp. 310–11); but this distinction is often lost when the Weberian account is used to identify the state with coercion itself, and with the coercers.

[4] See Hobbes 1996 [1651], p. 121.   [5] Hobbes 1996 [1651], p. 231.

[6] It is this problem that led to the identification of the king, and therefore by implication the state, with what was known in England as a 'corporation sole'; that is, a corporate entity which both was and was not distinct from the actual person of the king at any given moment (see Maitland 1911, vol. III, pp. 210–43). This complex and rather obscure conception bears many striking similarities to the complex and rather obscure conception of the 'person' of the state as given by Hobbes in *Leviathan* (see Runciman 1997, pp. 99–102).

state because he is the representative of the people, yet, as we have seen, the state cannot be identified with the people that the sovereign represents, nor with the fact of representation itself. The state is the person that the sovereign bears, but is not the sovereign's actual person, nor the actual persons of the people represented, nor the relation between them (which is not a person at all). So what is it? Hobbes does not say that the state is therefore a person only in some fictitious sense, though it is the conclusion to which his own analysis points.[7] He does not say it, presumably, because he does not want to suggest that the state, and more particularly what the state does both to and for us, is anything other than real.

I do not want to explore Hobbes's account at any length here (though I will come back to Hobbes later). Rather I want to suggest another way of looking at the puzzle of the state's identity, and that is by comparing it with the identity of the only other modern institution which can compete with the state for brute power over people's lives – that is, money. The question of the relation between these two institutions, and of whether one can be said to arise out of the other (either the state out of money or money out of the state) is far beyond my powers to discuss here. I merely want to indicate a number of points of comparison between the most simple question that can be asked of each, which is to ask simply what they are. 'What is money?' is a very similar kind of question to 'What is the state?' Both were, once, central to any investigation into the philosophical foundations of politics and society, and both are to be found side by side in many of the classic texts in the history of political thought (in the work of Aristotle,[8] More,[9] Locke,[10] Montesquieu,[11] Hume,[12] Hegel,[13] and so on). Neither, however, is prominent today. It is rare to encounter a direct attempt to answer either the question 'What is money?' or 'What is the state?' in recent works of political or economic theory; more often the answer to the question is assumed, and assumed to be irrelevant to the task at hand. There are a number of likely reasons for this. One is the ever-increasing professionalisation and specialisation of political and economic science, such that the big, simple questions tend to get broken down and parcelled out into smaller, more complicated ones. Another is the general preoccupation with instrumental over what might be called phenomenological questions: it is generally thought to be more interesting and more important to ask what money can do, or what the state is for, than to ask what either of them are in themselves. But a final reason for the eclipse of this kind of

---

[7] I set out this argument more fully in Runciman 2000.
[8] See Aristotle 1988, pp. 12–13, 16–17.   [9] See More 1989 [1516], pp. 52–3, 109–10.
[10] See Locke 1988 [1689], pp. 292–3, 298–301.
[11] See Montesquieu 1989 [1748], pp. 398–426.   [12] See Hume 1994 [1772], pp. 115–25.
[13] See Hegel 1991 [1821], pp. 93, 337–8.

philosophical enquiry is that in both cases, the phenomenological question, though easy enough to ask, is extremely difficult to answer.

It might seem that, in the case of money,[14] even more than in the case of the state, this ought not to be so. How can something so tangible, and with such extraordinary motive power, be so elusive? 'Show me the money' is a demand we all understand. Could we all understand it if we did not know what money was? Moreover, money, unlike the state, is something you can hold in your hand. But the thing that you hold in your hand is not an answer to the question 'What is money?' The thing you hold in your hand is either paper, base metal, or, if you are very lucky, silver or gold. But money is not, in itself, any of these things. Of course, it has frequently been taken for granted that money is one or other of these things, and it is possible to proceed quite a long way on the basis of that assumption. But if money is identified with paper, eventually (when there is too much of it) you get inflation, to the point where the paper ceases to be money and starts to become paper again (in the end, people will use it as scrap if they have to).[15] Likewise, if money is identified with gold, eventually (when there is too little of it) you will get stagnation, to the point where the gold ceases to be money and starts to become gold again (in the end, people can bury it back in the ground if they want to). Nor can money be identified with some relation between these things, such that one is seen as representative of the other. If money is not simply identifiable as gold, then money is not identifiable as paper masquerading as gold. It says on a British five-pound note that it is not money itself, but a promise of money, or more specifically a promise 'to pay the bearer on demand the sum of five pounds'. But that promise is not strictly true. It is a fiction.

To say that money either *is* paper or gold is like saying that the state either *is* government or the people. It is possible to proceed quite a long way on the basis of such assumptions, but eventually they break down. If the state is identified simply as government there will come a point (in times of political or economic crisis) where government will reveal itself for what it really is, merely a collection of relatively powerless individuals (and in the end, people will kill their governors if they have to). Similarly, if the state is identified straightforwardly with the people, there will come a point (again, in times of political or economic crisis) when the people will reveal themselves for what they are, just a crowd of individuals (and in the end, crowds can run wild if they want to). The state is not a crowd, and when it appears in the form of a crowd

---

[14] The account in this article of the nature of money, and the possibility of its nature being comparable to that of the state, was largely, if indirectly, inspired by Buchan 1997.

[15] During the great inflation in Weimar Germany of 1923, accounting clerks used the blank side of bank notes as scrap paper for their calculations as it was cheaper than buying pads (Brendon 2000, p. 28).

it is no longer a state, just as money, when it appears in the form of paper, is no longer money. Nor can the state be identified with some relation between government and people. If the state is not the same thing as the people, it is not to be identified with a representation of the people. That is an attractive but ultimately unsustainable idea, as Hobbes recognised, and he also recognised that if the state is not a representation of the people, then the government or sovereign must be a representation of something else.[16] That something else, in Hobbes's terms, is the state.

In the end, the demand to 'show me the money', a demand which has (through the fiction of the movies[17]) become part of the discourse of modern American life, though more obvious sounding, is in fact the same kind of request as the much less obvious sounding 'show me the state'. Let us take two examples, both of which might come either from Hollywood or from the real world. A football player is in discussion with his agent, and in exasperation, he exclaims: 'Show me the money!' The agent produces a contract on which a figure is written, and the player signs. A man answers the door in the middle of the night, and is confronted by a policeman who says: 'I arrest you in the name of the state.' The man, who is carrying a gun and is flanked by his two sons, says, in despair: 'Show me the state!' The policeman gestures behind him, where the lights come on two armoured vehicles, each containing six soldiers. The man goes quietly. In neither case has money or the state been revealed for what they are (money is not the figure on the contract, the state is not those soldiers in those vehicles), though each has revealed something of their extraordinary power to make people act.

The naïve identification of money or the state with some physical manifestation of each in the real world has tended to provoke an equally naïve response. Because neither money nor the state are actual people or things, but rather some sort of idea of people and things, there is an obvious temptation to suppose that the idea is simply a 'veil', behind which the real activities of people and things are concealed. Economists have sometimes supposed that, to understand what money is, it is necessary to understand what it is concealing, which is usually taken to be the real workings of the market (the real exchange of real goods and services of real value) over which money is laid like a veil, either (and this of course depends on your point of view) for the purposes of convenience or

---

[16] In Hobbes's famous formulation: 'A Multitude of men, are made *One* Person, when they are by one man, or one Person, Represented . . . For it is the *Unity* of the Represented, that maketh the Person *One*. And it is the Represented that beareth the Person, and but one Person: And *Unity*, cannot otherwise be understood in Multitude' (Hobbes 1996 [1651], p. 114). Because the people are not represented as a multitude, they must be represented as something else, 'the Person of the Commonwealth', which is something distinct from a representation of the people themselves.

[17] The phrase was popularised by its use in the 1997 American film *Jerry Maguire* (dir: Cameron Crowe).

for the purposes of obfuscation, so that the truly exploitative nature of market relations should remain hidden for as long as possible. But to say that money *is* the market that it overlays is like saying that the state *is* (and again this depends on your point of view) either the constitution on which it is founded or the class conflict which it is there to conceal. Most economists, in so far as they trouble to think about it, would now accept that money does not simply reflect real market forces but is itself, in its own terms, a crucial aspect of the working out of those forces. 'Money', in the words of a recent survey of the literature, 'and in particular the cost of acquiring financial resources (the rate of interest), is an integral part of the economic process'.[18] Likewise, most political theorists, in so far as they trouble to think about it, would accept that the state is not simply a reflection of underlying social forces, but is itself, in its own terms, a crucial aspect of the working out of those forces. The state, one might say, and in particular the cost of acquiring the power of the state, is an integral part of the political process. But that does not get us much closer to understanding what the state, which has all this power, actually is.

The difficulty of answering the phenomenological question 'What is money?' has meant that most attention is now focused on the functional or instrumental aspects of the problem, and therefore on the question 'What is money for?' This again has parallels with political theory, where most attention is now focused on trying to understand the state in instrumental terms – as an instrument of justice, law, identity, rights, security, freedom, diversity, and so on. The text-book answer to the question 'What is money for?' has three parts: money serves as a medium of exchange, a store of value, a unit of account. It is perhaps not to stretch the analogy too far to suggest that the state too, in its various guises, serves functions something like these. The state, in the classic liberal account, is a mechanism for reconciling conflicting and potentially incommensurable interests, by means of a common political form into which these different interests can be translated and through which they can be compared. It is a medium of exchange. The job of the state, in these terms, is to enable people with very different wants and expectations to coexist, without flattening out the differences between them, just as money allows people to exchange the different things they have to offer, without prejudging what it is they want or expect from the transaction. Both of these institutions, when they work well, also enable individuals to explore just what it is they do want and expect from their individual situation, and to experiment with various permutations without suffering unnecessary penalties. The liberal state, like money, is thus a vehicle of growth.

Similarly, the state, like money, is also a kind of store of value, in so far as it is the institution that makes possible the continued life of the law. This does not have to mean anything as grandiose as the idea that the state is the repository into

[18] Smithin 2000, p. 2.

which we place all those things we hold most dear for safekeeping, and which therefore represents the best and most considered part of ourselves (although this is of course a view which has often been held[19]). It simply implies that the state is the means by which contingent social arrangements are made secure, and therefore the instrument through which it becomes possible to make plans for the future that have some prospect of being fulfilled. Finally, the state is a unit of account, because it is the state that tells us where we stand collectively in our political endeavours. The state is not itself a collectivity, because (as we have seen) no collection of individuals can be liable for the actions of the state, no matter how those liabilities are distributed. Rather, the state is the institution to which we ascribe liability, precisely so that we can know how we are faring in our great collective projects. This is true in a somewhat literal sense, since it is the state and the state alone that is responsible for the national debt, and it is the state and the state alone that makes the existence of such debts possible; without the state, there would be no way to account for the massive flows of resources on which modern political life depends. But it is also true in a more figurative sense. It is states that go to war, not peoples, and it is the existence of the state that allows peoples to know when they are at war, when the war is over, and whether they have won. Otherwise, war would not be war, but chaos. It is, in other words, the state that enables peoples to know whether they are up or down.

These comparisons and analogies can only be taken so far. The state is a unit of account, but it is not a means of counting, because it is not a numerical system (in the world of the state, the number is always one). Likewise, the state, through its laws, acts as store of value, but it is not a measure of value, because laws are not measurements. The interests that are brought together under the auspices of the state are translated into a single currency (in liberal theory, the currency of rights), but that currency cannot be exchanged at fluctuating rates into any other. Above all, the state is, and remains, an association of human beings, while money is, and remains, an association of things. Human associations are units of action, whereas money is a mediator of human action, and as such is acted upon. Nevertheless, the state does not *itself* act any more than money does. States can only act through their representatives; like money, we only recognise the state's presence in the world when things are done for, or to, it. Moreover, money, like the state, must be understood as something more than simply an instrument of human action, for the simple reason that, however much we might want to think that we act through money, it has a life of its own. Money may exist for the purposes of efficient exchange, prudential planning

---

[19] To give just one example, from a leading British philosopher of the early twentieth century: '[The State] is the ark in which the whole treasure of the individual citizen's head and heart is preserved in a world which may be disorderly and hostile' (Bosanquet 1915, p. 134). The same has sometimes been believed about money, though more often, perhaps, about gold.

and so on, but it can never be reduced to these things, because it has the power
to leave in ruins the most carefully calibrated systems of exchange and the most
prudential plans of action. The state may be the instrument through which we
wage war, raise money to undertake both mundane and heroic projects of social
improvement, and even, when we can, try to make our societies more just. But
it cannot be reduced to these things, because the state has the power to act
in its own interest, and to its own ends, regardless of what the rules of war, or
economics, or moral philosophy might dictate. Those rules constitute important
constraints on how states can be expected to act, but they do not constitute states
themselves, because states too have a life of their own.

This, in the end, is what money and the state have in common. Both have a life
of their own, yet when you strip away the accumulated garb in which that life is
dressed up – all the documents and uniforms and contracts and commands, all
the petty officials and imposing buildings, all the gold and all the government –
it is hard to see anything still there. Both share a quality that is distinctive of
those things we call fictions: they function by having attributed to them as inherent the one thing that they inherently lack. Emma Bovary only functions as a
character in a novel by having attributed to her the one thing that she inherently
lacks – a real life of her own. Money functions by having attributed to it its
own inherent value, even though it has no inherent value, being a way of valu-
ing other things. The state functions by having attributed to it its own inherent
power, even though it has no inherent power, but depends always on the power
that is attributed to it, and exercised on its behalf by its representatives. To call
these things fictions is not to say they are lies, and it is certainly not a question
of undoing what W. H. Auden called 'the folded lie', and declaiming, as Auden
did in the poem he wrote on September 1st 1939: 'There is no such thing as
the State'.[20] Emma Bovary, after all, is not a lie; she is a fiction. Rather, it is
something more like seeing the state as comparable to those individuals who
are described in the British press as being famous for being famous. These
people really *are* famous (hence their appearance in the newspapers), but their
fame rests on the fiction of their fame, and if one was to look too closely behind
the mask one would find very little there worth celebrating (it is therefore important, for all concerned, not to look behind the mask). Money is valuable for
being valuable. The state is authoritative for having authoritative representatives. And so even the most spurious celebrity causes people to gasp and spill
their food in restaurants, and money causes people to work for each other and
to rob, cheat, and kill each other, and the state causes people both to sacrifice
themselves and to make sacrifices, in war and in peace.

[20] 'All I have is a voice/ To undo the folded lie,/ The romantic lie in the brain/ Of the sensual man
in the street/ And the lie of Authority/ Whose buildings grope the sky:/ There is no such thing
as the State/ And no one exists alone;/ Hunger allows no choice/ To the citizen or the police/ We
must love one another or die' (Auden 1979, p. 88).

I said I would return to Hobbes. The second most famous line in Hobbes's *Leviathan*, after the one that ends 'solitary, poore, nasty, brutish and short', is the one that begins: 'For words are wise mens counters, they do but reckon by them: but they are the mony of fooles.'[21] Money, as Hobbes understands it, is something more than mere reckoning, and therefore something more than just the unit of account; it has value, which words lack. Elsewhere, Hobbes argues that the nourishment provided to any commonwealth by the circulation of money is best supplied by silver and gold, which 'have their value from the matter itself'.[22] But Hobbes also recognised that money could not simply be identified with silver and gold, because money could be 'of what matter soever coyned by the Soveraign of the Commonwealth',[23] including such matter as has little or no inherent value at all. Hobbes is therefore ambivalent as to what money actually is: it is both something that has its own value and something that has to have value attributed to it. The same ambivalence attaches to Hobbes's account of the state. The state, for Hobbes, is something more than a mere reckoning up of the individuals who have covenanted with each other in the state of nature. It is a person in its own right, that person in whose name the sovereign speaks and acts. Yet the person of the state is nothing without its sovereign representative; it has no inherent authority, because it has no ability to speak or act for itself. This makes the state a kind of fiction. Another way of putting it (which is close to the way Hobbes himself puts it) is to see the state as a kind of mask.[24] It is important, for all concerned, not to look behind the mask, though there are certain circumstances in which it is impossible not wonder at the whole giant charade. Hobbes accepted, for example, that no-one could be expected to sacrifice themselves in war simply on the word of the state, just as no-one can be expected to work when all they are taking home at the end of the day are pieces of paper. But Hobbes suspected, rightly, that most people would be content most of the time to leave the mask in place, and allow the state to acquire and maintain the power that comes from having power attributed to it.

To talk of masks, and fictions, may suggest that the state, and perhaps money too, are best understood in more open-ended terms than the traditional discourse of politics allows, and incorporated into the discourse of what is usually called post-modernity. But because this is a conception of the state that has its source in the writing of Hobbes, that would be a mistake. The open-endedness of the idea of the state rests on the relatively closed and fixed nature of those other persons and relations whose identity post-modern discourse seeks to open up

---

[21] Hobbes 1996 [1651], p. 28.   [22] Hobbes 1996 [1651], p. 175.
[23] Hobbes 1996 [1651], p. 174.
[24] See Hobbes 1996 [1651], p. 112: 'The word Person is latine . . . [and] signifies the *disguise* or *outward appearance* of a man, counterfeited on the Stage; and sometimes more particularly that part of it, which disguiseth the face, as a Mask or Visard.'

also. These include the identity of the individual, and of the relations between individuals that are mediated by various kinds of individual commitments, including contractual ones. Indeed, this conception of the state is an essentially legal conception, just as money is a conception that relies heavily for its instantiation on the fixed categories of law. The idea that these conceptions are forms of fiction does not mean that they render fictitious or indeterminate the other categories of thought that characterise modern thinking. If anything, it is the reverse: the state, and money, are the institutions whose ambivalence allows us to be reconciled to the inflexibility of modern individualism.

The state, like money, is therefore a modern institution in the true sense. The state, like money, is also an extremely puzzling institution, both immensely powerful and immensely difficult to pin down. It is the coupling of this power and this elusiveness that should make us suspicious of any claims to know what the future has in store for it, particularly any predictions of its imminent demise. It is sometimes said that money is an institution under threat from the forces of technological progress, as more and more transactions take place in cyberspace and on computer screens. But that is to mistake money itself for its physical manifestations. A cashless economy is not a moneyless economy, but rather one in which money has altered its manifest form. Likewise, it would be a mistake to confuse the state with some of its representative institutions, and with the claims to sovereignty that are often made on their behalf. The forces of globalisation will inevitably undermine some of those things with which we identify the state, whether border controls, or parliamentary sovereignty, or even paper currencies. But the state, like money, is a kind of fiction, and it owes both its existence and its power to the fact that it is never to be identified with anyone, or anything, in particular.

BIBLIOGRAPHY

Aristotle (1988). *The Politics*, ed. S. Everson, Cambridge: Cambridge University Press.
Auden, W. H. (1979). *Selected Poems*, London: Faber.
Austin, J. (1995) [1832]. *The Province of Jurisprudence Determined*, ed. W. Rumble, Cambridge: Cambridge University Press.
Bosanquet, B. (1915). 'Patriotism in the Perfect State', *The International Crisis*, 1, pp. 132–51.
Brendon, P. (2000). *The Dark Valley. A Panorama of the 1930s*, London: Pimlico.
Buchan, J. (1997). *Frozen Desire: An Enquiry into the Meaning of Money*, London: Picador.
Hegel, G. W. F. (1991) [1821]. *Elements of the Philosophy of Right*, ed. A. Wood, Cambridge: Cambridge University Press.
Hobbes, T. (1996) [1651]. *Leviathan*, ed. R. Tuck, Cambridge: Cambridge University Press.
Hont, I. (1994). 'The Permanent Crisis of a Divided Mankind: "Contemporary Crisis of the Nation State" in Historical Perspective', *Political Studies*, 42, pp. 166–231.

Hume, D. (1994) [1772]. *Political Essays*, ed. K. Haakonssen, Cambridge: Cambridge University Press.

Locke, J. (1988) [1689]. *Two Treatises of Government*, ed. P. Laslett, Cambridge: Cambridge University Press.

Maitland, F. W. (1911). *Collected Papers*, 3 vols., ed. H. A. L. Fisher, Cambridge: Cambridge University Press.

Montesquieu, C. de S. (1989) [1748]. *The Spirit of the Laws*, ed. A. Cohler, B. Miller, and H. Stone, Cambridge: Cambridge University Press.

More, T. (1989) [1516]. *Utopia*, ed. G. M. Logan and R. M. Adams, Cambridge: Cambridge University Press.

Runciman, D. (1997). *Pluralism and the Personality of the State*, Cambridge: Cambridge University Press.

   (2000). 'What Kind of Person is Hobbes's State? A Reply to Skinner', *Journal of Political Philosophy* 8, pp. 268–78.

Smithin, J. (ed.) (2000). *What is Money?*, London: Routledge.

Weber, M. (1994). *Political Writings*, ed. P. Lassman and R. Speirs, Cambridge: Cambridge University Press.

3 Citizens and the state: retrospect and prospect

Gianfranco Poggi

I

The first part of this chapter looks back on the story of the relationship between citizens and the state; the second points to some recent and current developments in the relationship which render it increasingly problematical. When I speak of the state, I conceive of it in the conventional manner as the polity characteristic of the modern West, a political entity with a claim to sovereignty, a bounded territory and a population which might be more or less plausibly called a 'nation'. Taking this entity as my point of reference, I ask under what determinations, and in what capacities (or incapacities) citizens typically represent themselves to the state. What do citizens (as it were) *look like* when viewed from the vantage point of the state? By way of response, I consider ten aspects of the relationship between states and citizens.

Citizens as subjects. 'Subject' is a tricky word, and at least some of its politically significant meanings do not coincide with the one I am interested in here, which is best conveyed in the Italian expression *suddito* or the German *Untertan*.

That citizens are in the first place, from the state's standpoint, its 'subjects' is on the face of it a paradoxical statement. It is often said that one of the most critical aspects of political modernisation is constituted by the fact that rulers ceased to treat individuals as *subjects* (*sudditi*, *Untertane*) and learned to treat them as *citizens*. This suggests a categorical incompatibility between the two expressions I have emphasised. Yet I would suggest that one gets nowhere if one takes too seriously the subject/citizen transition, for the subject-ness of individuals persists, and their quality as citizens at best sublimates and qualifies that subject-ness. For the state is essentially a system of rules, a set of arrangements and practices whereby one part of a divided society exercises domination over the other part, whether or not the individual components of the population are vested with attributes of citizenship.

This applies also to liberal-democratic states. For, to use a grammatical metaphor, 'state' should be considered as a noun, while 'liberalism' and 'democracy' are as it were adjectives. I mean by this that they are significant but contingent and limited qualifications of a stubbornly asymmetrical relationship, which do not impose upon that relationship a transformation *eis allo genos*. Even under liberal democracy, the rule is exercised *over* a population, so that the key political relationship remains one between those who command and those who obey, and the great majority of citizens, in their routine existence, cannot but experience the state as something different from them, which lies, so to speak, on top of them.

In fact, according to some interpretations – I am thinking chiefly of Foucault, and also of Giddens – political modernisation on the one hand makes the rule milder and more humane, and on the other hand makes it more penetrating and compelling. In particular, according to this interpretation, even in liberal-democratic systems citizens become more and more exposed to governmental surveillance: *citizens as surveillées* might be a way to phrase this particular determination.

If this formulation usefully points up some ambivalences of the modernisation process, I would suggest that there are other ambivalences which, so to speak, run the other way around. Some specific aspects of the original and persistent subject-ness of citizens are considerably modified by the advent of liberal democracy. To illustrate this development, let me turn to a second determination of citizenship.

Citizens as tax-payers. This is a most significant aspect of the political relationship on both conceptual and historical grounds. The conceptual grounds are suggested by the fact that some authors conceive of the polity, indeed of the state itself, as essentially a machine for coercively extracting resources from civil society (envisaged in the first instance as the locus of economic processes). They liken the state to a protection racket, defining its key relationship to society, and to the individuals in their capacity as economic actors, as essentially a predatory one.[1]

Whatever validity this view may have possessed in the past, especially as regards *pre*-state polities, historically the development of the state has witnessed significant modifications of the way in which political 'extraction' takes place. Early on, Western rulers had to take into account that many of the resources they intended to extract were immediately controlled by a privileged stratum of landlords and warriors whose privileges they could not simply do away with. Furthermore, before the establishment of an administrative machinery at the ruler's own disposal, to gather and deploy resources the ruler needed the consent and cooperation of relatively autonomous bodies (estates local and regional, sometimes even 'general', or otherwise constituted corporate entities). Such consent and cooperation had to be negotiated; it could not be simply

---

[1] For a sophisticated and clever contemporary rendering of this view, see the redoubtable book by De Jasay 1985.

compelled. This necessity is the root of a complex institutional development best summarised by a famous English dictum, *no taxation without representation*, and constitutes the early core of representative government and of liberal constraints on state action.

Later, an increasingly expansive and expensive state must find ways of tapping into other forms of wealth, chiefly in the hands of bourgeois and middle-class strata. Typically, such forms are mobile, and if the state is to attain them (without damaging their production and reproduction) its extractive activities must adapt themselves to that mobility, moving towards more and more calculable, predictable, routinised forms of taxation.

As Albert Hirschman argued in *The Passions and the Interests*, this necessity favours – up to a point – the rationalisation of the political enterprise as a whole.[2] More recently, Thomas Ertman[3] has shown the enormous advantage the English state derived from having become, earlier and more effectively than others, complementary to and compatible with a commercial economy. This allowed it, among other things, to finance war through public debt. In other words, the modes of extraction are a significant aspect of the general configuration of the political system, including the place it finds (if any) for the notion and the practice of citizenship.

Citizens as soldiers. Again, this determination of citizenship is both conceptually and historically significant. Conceptually, because it directly addresses the question of organised violence, which most authors conceive as the core of political experience – and of statehood, to the extent that such violence is not only organised, but uniquely legitimate. The historical significance is suggested by too many aspects of Western political development for us to review here. It may suffice to mention that in the Greek *polis* the move away from its institutional design as the exclusive concern of a narrow patrician stratum to one which acknowledged the significance of all individuals – as long as they were male, adult, and free – was connected with the advent of hoplite warfare, which mobilised as soldiers relatively large numbers of individuals armed with relatively uniform weaponry, and trained them to operate in close contact with one another. It is the military empowerment of the common man that assists and to some extent causes his ascent to relatively protected, active citizenship.

Many centuries later, the link between the military and the political capacities of common men was evidenced, at first in the context of the French Revolution – remember *aux armes, citoyens!* – in the parallel between the revolutionary creation of mass armies and the emergence of (at first, relatively) popular suffrage. One might also mention multiple connections between the modernisation and 'totalisation' of warfare and the emergence of particular aspects and moments of the welfare state.

[2] Hirschman 1977.   [3] Ertman 1997.

Both the last two aspects of citizenship, tax-paying and military involvement, point chiefly to the burdens involved in the citizenship relation, and to that extent can be seen as elaborations of their character as subjects. We may counter this emphasis with a very different determination: *citizens as rights-holders*. This relationship has been masterfully (though not uncontroversially) conceptualised by T. H. Marshall.[4] It suggests that the citizen/state relationship is an inter-subjective one; that an entity possessing interests, resources, and capacities of its own lies at each end of the relationship and is accepted and recognised by the other. It is as if every citizen, puny and insignificant as he or she may appear from the viewpoint of the state, were somehow capable of saying to the state itself, 'do not trifle with me'; or even 'I have towards you entitlements you must respect.'

As we shall see below, this capacity not only protects the private interests of all citizens, but authorises them to acquire a certain awareness of the state's doings and even to make some input into those doings – and not *just* as they impinge upon themselves. We owe to George Jellinek one of the most sophisticated statements of this position: under the *Rechtsstaat*, the sphere of legally protected faculties owned and managed by individuals may extend to include '*public subjective rights*'.[5] But one may go further, and assert a more advanced (and, one might say, more counterfactual) position: *citizens as constituents*. This idea is, once more, rooted in the experience of the ancient city, which in some phases, in parts of the Hellenic and the Roman world, saw the population (or rather, the male, adult, free, militarily competent element of it) as responsible for the city's very existence. The city is perceived as a made-up, historically constructed reality, and it is the population which calls it into being, assumes in it and confirms through it a collective identity (generally, with strong ritual and mythical components). The idea is repeatedly echoed, in the medieval West, by the story or the legend of a *conjuratio*, through which formerly discrete and powerless individuals constitute themselves into a new juridically distinctive, politically autonomous, militarily effective entity – the city itself.

But even the subsequent loss of the city's autonomy, discussed in Max Weber's famous essay, does not entirely dispose of the vision of a plurality of individuals who constitute a political entity of their own. By representing itself as a nation or as a people, a population can project itself as the collective protagonist of a state-building enterprise, and as such attribute to each citizen a portion of the authorship and ownership, so to speak, of the resulting political entity. *Qua universi*, the citizens claim and assert the state as their own, and in this sense can be understood as its constituents.

A stronger formulation of this notion might be *citizens as sovereigns* – though in fact sovereignty is more often attributed to 'the people' or 'the nation' rather

---

[4] Marshall 1977.   [5] Jellinek 1905.

than to 'the citizenry'. In any case, I would insist, the hard core of the relation of individuals to the state remains their being the state's *subjects*, and on
this account all formulations which represent the collectivity as self-ruling are
strongly normative in nature. They point to a regulative idea rather than to a
factual relationship.

Citizens as (co)nationals. The state often expects citizens to experience their
identification with a comprehensive and abiding social and cultural entity –
the nation – as more exalting and compelling than most of the commonalities
they construct as they go about the non-political aspects of their existence as
members of marriages and families, as business partners, as co-religionaries,
and so on. This expectation (to which the state seeks to give normative force
through, among other things, its educational activities and its rituals) is markedly
at variance with another aspect of modern citizenship, emphasised long ago
during the *querelle* over 'the liberty of the moderns as compared with that of
the ancients'. This other aspect sees *citizens as private individuals*. Note that
this is perhaps a contradictory concept, for there is an intrinsic tension between
the two terms. Citizenship, under modern conditions, is a qualification or a set of
capacities pertaining to individuals who are not *only*, and indeed not *primarily*
citizens, but who possess resources and interests which do not pertain to the
political sphere, and to which they may well attach higher priority than to those
which do pertain to that sphere.

The young Marx punningly suggested that modern individuals, in order to
become politically aware and involved, must engage in ex-stasis, must as it
were jump out of their own skins, overcome the inertia of often much more
proximate and pressing attachments and sensitivities. Tocqueville emphasised
their reluctance to do this: the great majority of individuals, once satisfied that,
as far as the public order is concerned, each of them is as good as anybody
else – a basic tenet of the democratic condition – may easily lock themselves
into their petty, private cares, and invest in them all their energies and concerns,
neglecting public affairs. This tendency is favoured by a number of aspects
of modern life and culture much 'pushed' by the mass media – particularly
consumerism and narcissism.

This is a troublesome corollary. It is possible *also* for the political involvement and participation of individuals to be motivated and oriented chiefly by
the concern of each with their private condition. The contemporary debate on
state versus market is perhaps misleading: it conceals the fact that state and
market may be considered chiefly as *alternative* ways of securing the *same* result, the maximisation of private welfare across a given society. More generally,
one may view contemporary politics as being to an increasing extent 'economi-
cised'. One aspect of this which much worried Max Weber is that professional
politicians, seeking or exercising leadership, tend more and more to live *from*
politics rather than *for* politics.

The last paragraph points indirectly to a further component of citizenship of great political significance: *citizens as political participants/as partisans*. The link between these two aspects needs to be emphasised. The basic imagery of political participation emphasises the 'vertical' flow of influence between the base and the summit of the political system, where policy is made – a flow carried by the representative system. But one should never forget that, in the liberal-democratic state, that process takes the form of a legitimate but persistent and often bitter 'horizontal' contrast and competition between different components of a society which, like all historical societies, is internally divided. After all, 'to participate' means 'to take sides', to become partisans, to seek to assert some interests of one's own over and against those of others.

The matrix of policy is politics, but the immediate stake of politics is the capacity to take over power positions and to exclude others (however temporarily) from them – *ôte-toi que je m'y mette* – in order to 'reward your friends, punish your enemies'. This reality is masked by the chief ploy of political rhetoric, the presentation of one's partisan interests as general ones – for partisanship is morally dangerous and, one might say, aesthetically unappealing. But the refusal to accept the need for it amounts to a failure of political nerve; and under contemporary conditions it is encouraged by a pervasive tendency which we may label *citizens as spectators*.

Rejecting, or trying to reduce as much as possible, the burden of partisanship – including the cost of acquiring information on complex issues – citizens deem some amount of political involvement justified only if it competes successfully with alternative ways of investing their leisure time, and particularly their attention to the media. Hence the well-known trend toward the spectacularisation of politics, its focus on 'personalities' and other ways of 'packaging' the political game. The danger of this to significant political values is clear: as Rorty suggests, spectatorship is incompatible with agency.

Citizens as equals. This is the critical import of the symbolically laden recourse of revolutionary France to the appellation *citoyen*: individuals address each other, and expect to be addressed, as possessing equal significance and as sharing certain basic entitlements. One of these, perhaps neglected by Marshall, is the entitlement to a certain degree of respect, to a not inconsiderable quantum of recognition. In Durkheimian or Goffmanian terms, all citizens qua citizens are to an extent sacred objects.

II

We have looked back upon a number of ways in which Western citizenship has been institutionally and conceptually defined. I note in passing that this coupling of the institutional with the conceptual mode of definition is a distinctive and significant feature of the phenomenon itself. Perhaps because citizenship was originally an urban phenomenon, and thus presupposed relatively widespread literacy and the possibility of fairly sustained discursive encounters between individuals, its career has mostly been accompanied and counterpointed by rather self-conscious episodes of intellectual justification and debate.

I shall now consider briefly some developments which, as I said at the outset, seriously problematise the whole phenomenon and pose the question, *whither citizenship?* I will assign such developments to three different groupings (even if, as is often the case, the groupings themselves overlap somewhat).

To begin with, the spheres within which some aspects of the citizenship phenomenon inscribe themselves have long been undergoing material and in-stitutional changes which alter, among other things, the significance of those aspects. Let me take two examples. The relationship between citizenship and the military experience has been affected by at least four distinct (and to an extent mutually contradictory) developments. First, contemporary modes of warfare have to a significant extent erased the difference between citizens-in-arms and the rest of the citizenry, particularly as concerns that particular 'risk of war' constituted by the likelihood of being killed or injured by the enemy's military action. Second, over the last few decades armed forces have opened themselves to women. Third, in many circumstances combat can be materially effective only when engaged in by relatively small numbers of highly trained and expen-sively equipped professional fighters; thus the idea itself of a citizens' army has become less and less plausible. However – fourth – the combatants themselves generally need to be supported by larger and larger bodies of civilians: these are expected to be citizens, but they must mostly operate in the capacity of salaried professionals and experts, not citizens as such.

My second example concerns *citizens as equals*. As we have seen, modern social theory has engaged in controversy over a number of problems relating to this aspect of citizenship. According to the late James Coleman, however, it has not been sufficiently aware of a form of inequality particularly significant in contemporary society, and of its impact on citizenship.[6] Advanced societies, Coleman argued, are peopled by two very different kinds of individuals: physical individuals and corporate individuals. Between the two there is a critical and growing imbalance in power. The state can be considered as the largest and on some counts the most powerful corporate individual, but in dealing with it other corporate individuals are generally more capable of asserting their interests than most physical individuals are. Where does that leave all other supposedly *equal citizens*, one may ask?

A second group of developments relates to the emergence of political entities which encompass (and to an extent 'mediatise') states themselves, in respect of which the institution of citizenship, originally established at the level of the state,

[6] Coleman 1974.

needs to be re-thought and re-constructed. To speak concretely, one may ask what is the actual content, if any, of European citizenship as symbolised among other things by the uniform passports currently been issued by the member countries of the European Union (EU), and perhaps even by the existence of the Euro (for twelve of the states of the Union). The point is that many of the determinations of citizenship I have examined in the first part of this chapter simply do not make (much) sense at the European level. I'll give four examples.

The European Union is a political entity with extremely limited fiscal powers and faculties, and its revenues consist largely in contributions from member states. This means that *citizens as tax-payers* does not apply at the Union level. This may be one reason for the equally visible weakness of its representative and properly political institutions. Could it be the case that IF there is *no taxation without representation*, THEN there is *no representation without taxation*? Secondly, whether for this reason or for other reasons, there is as yet little space for *citizens as participants/as partisans* at the Union level. As is often remarked, there are at best only the beginnings, at this level, of a distinct, autonomously institutionalised, party system – one reason (or one consequence?) of the much-discussed 'democratic deficit' of the Union. Thirdly, one barely needs to note that the Union, having no defence policy and no military capacity of its own, has at present no use for *citizens as soldiers*. Finally, it is clear that *citizens as (co)nationals* exist only at the level of the component states (and nations) of the Union.

A similar argument could be made for others among the determinations of citizenship mentioned above. The big exception is possibly that of *citizens as private persons*. The Union originally constituted itself as a Common Market, and its institutional identity to this day is chiefly focused on the sphere of the economy. To that extent, it accommodates and validates most of the private concerns associated with that sphere, by facilitating the mobility of factors of production, by providing uniform regulations for industrial activities, and so on.

On all these counts, we could say that there is a lag between the advances made in Europe towards the establishment of a new political and administrative system, and those realised for the time being in the quantity and quality, so to speak, of European citizenship.

A third set of developments affecting and problematising citizenship relates to so-called globalisation. This complex and controversial phenomenon impinges on citizenship chiefly in two ways. First of all, by weakening the state. As more and more economic resources and processes become 'extraterritorial', those legislative, fiscal, and jurisdictional faculties which states used, through most of the twentieth century, to promote and finance their re-distributive activities, become less and less significant, if not in absolute then in relative terms.

In the global economy, as I have already suggested, corporate economic actors, whose presence had always rendered problematical the presumption of equality among citizens, become ever more significant as aggregations of power and as the sites of decisions of overriding importance for which they are not politically accountable. Since they operate on and through the market, they encourage and indeed compel individuals, from one country to another, to behave in turn towards one another as market operators, and to disinvest (so to speak) from their identity as citizens. Directly or indirectly the great business corporations also sponsor, produce, and benefit from flows of discourse, images, intellectual products, opinions, which delegitimise the centres of political power and undermine their cultural and moral standing within the population.

The second way in which globalisation impinges on citizenship is by a 'reshuffling of the social matter', to use Durkheimian imagery, not just within but between countries. These become more and more permeable to flows of people – among other things. A presumption that to some extent underlay the Marshallian development of citizenship – the presumption that the individuals affected would be nearly all co-nationals, born in a given country of parents also born in it, and destined to remain stably settled in it – is increasingly undermined by massive migration flows. We could say that under these conditions it becomes more difficult to conceptualise *a population* – a purely demographic aggregate – as a *people*. It is implausible to think of *citizens as constituents*, and of the individuals currently active in a country as the cohort within a lengthy sequence of generations, each familiar with the country and committed to its culture and involved in its political fortunes by an immemorial compact. As a result, many immigrants are routinely denied some entitlements of citizenship.

This denial, however, looks more and more arbitrary when it affects substantial and ever-increasing numbers of people, who on other counts tend to become indistinguishable from the native population, and in particular well integrated in its economy. It can be expected to appear even more invidious as immigrant flows become more bilateral and symmetrical – that is, when the probability increases that nationals of a country which denies or restricts the claims of immigrants from another country will themselves migrate to the latter.

The most likely response to this situation is (as is already shown by a number of cases, in particular as concerns social security entitlements) the institutionalisation of a principle of reciprocity between the countries in question. The next step is likely to be in the direction of what has been called trans-national citizenship, understood perhaps as the transposition to the individual level of something like the 'most favoured nation' practice long acknowledged in international law. Or, more ambitiously, an appeal can be made to some understanding of 'human rights' as the ground for a more or less substantial set of portable entitlements, which accompany individuals wherever they are, and which each state must somehow acknowledge and validate.

On a number of counts, such a development may deserve devoutly to be wished, however difficult its implementation. But we should be clear that it contrasts with the notion of citizenship proper, for that notion is intrinsically a particularistic one. It presupposes and substantiates a bond between a given set of individuals and a given political community, broad and internally diverse though it may be. Also, that particularistic bond is always, conceptually, a compound of rights *and duties*. Now, it is not clear, in the 'human rights' vision, which expectations would lie upon individuals as a counterpart to those which individuals themselves would hold *vis-à-vis* states. There is finally the problem of the extent to which rights (or duties) held to be constitutive of the human subject reflect distinctive cultural preferences masquerading as universals.

On all these counts, even disregarding the difficulty of establishing institutions that would validate the new understandings of citizenship, the contemporary situation seriously challenges existing conceptions of citizenship itself, and mandates among other things more serious reflections on its historical career.

BIBLIOGRAPHY

Coleman, J. S. (1974). *Power and the Structure of Society*, New York: Norton.
De Jasay, A. (1985). *The State*, Oxford: Basil Blackwell.
Ertman, T. (1997). *Birth of the Leviathan: Building States and Regimes in medieval and Early-modern Europe*, New York: Cambridge University Press.
Hirschman, A. O. (1977). *The Passions and the Interests*, Princeton, N.J.: Princeton University Press.
Jellinek, G. (1905). *System der oeffentlichen subjektiven Rechte*, Tübingen: Mohr.
Marshall, T. H. (1977). *Class, Citizenship and Social Development*, Chicago: University of Chicago Press.

PART TWO

The medieval background

4   Freedom, law, and the medieval state

Magnus Ryan

As terms in early-modern and modern political theory, freedom, law, and the state are impossible to discuss in isolation from each other, even if they are not the sole terms of enquiry. But as terms in medieval theory, one is virtually absent (state), whilst another is applied in a manner so eccentric by modern expectations as virtually to confound them (freedom/liberty). This means that the third – law – is not obviously concerned either with defending liberty or with giving concrete content to an abstraction as a focus of political loyalty and a source of political obligation. It is, however, the most sharply defined element of this triad of terms, thanks to the explosion of interest in Roman and canon law in the course of the twelfth century. Let us begin, therefore, with law.

It is one of the less frequently noted ironies of scholasticism that a method founded upon synthesis contributed so powerfully to professional specialisation. By the beginning of the period covered by this paper, law was only just asserting itself as a separate discipline. Roman law, if now being taught in isolation from theology and the liberal arts, was still in its first generation. By the 1150s, specialist lectures and monographs on Gratian's *Concordance of Discordant Canons* would give clearer outlines to canon law as an undertaking practically as well as notionally distinct from theology.[1] This is supposed to have cleared the way for a secularisation of other legal studies. As languages of analysis and argument slowly dissociated themselves from each other, so certain terms and concepts acquired technical signification, hard edges. This was true not merely of words but of entire disciplines. In the case of law, that had one vital result. Although the full absorption – in many cases, even the discovery – of Aristotle's works was still in the future, there was a lively sense of law as something other than a speculative discipline. By the later twelfth century this was a commonplace. Gratian (*c.* 1140) had already equated canon law with a norm of right living. Manuals of procedural law such as the *Rhetorica ecclesiastica* would point out that theology was concerned with truths, whereas law had a component of *potestas*, for law was necessarily associated with the power

---

[1] Kuttner 1982.

to command.[2] Law was to be applied, to be lived, and was therefore inherently concerned with the contingencies of the here and now, not the necessary truths of eternity.

All of this will be familiar: the twelfth century as the first age of practical wisdom, of *phronesis*, and as the womb of Lagarde's Birth of the Lay Spirit. However, it is easy to over-interpret such statements. The great canon-lawyer Henry of Sousa (more commonly known as Hostiensis after his cardinal's title) was not expressing anything different a century later when he wrote that legal wisdom 'does not permit us to live in poverty *or die in anxiety*'.[3] Significantly, Henry was discussing Roman law at this point, not canon law. Even at the full flood of the Aristotelian tide, then, law did not just help you live well, it helped you die well, and dying in the right way was far too important to allow the language of liberty to occupy much of a position within the language of law. The basic objective of legislators according to the academic lawyers, whose mountainous works of exegesis on Roman and canon law provide the best guide to ideas about law all over Europe by the end of the thirteenth century, was to keep the peace. The good should be rewarded, the bad punished. Law was the peace-time weapon of the ruler, a counterpart to arms in time of war, as the opening of Justinian's *Institutes* proclaimed.[4] The rigid medium of academic discourse allowed no space for digressions concerning the beneficial effects of law beyond the most basic demands of peace and stability. Freedom under the law was not a phrase to conjure with for the professionals of this period. The normal complement of *libertas* was *ecclesiae*, and the liberty of the church meant the liberty to be ruled by Christ's vicar without secular interference so that as many people as possible could live and die in a manner conducive to their salvation. Lawyers did not, therefore, make any especial commitment to liberty at the beginning of the legal revolution. However, by the mid-fourteenth century, this would begin to change, with results which will occupy us a little later.

To be governed for your own good – whether your good was defined as this-worldly or as your salvation – was, by an irresistible *argumentum a contrario sensu*, constitutive of liberty for some standard-setting theologians, too. For Thomas Aquinas, to be governed for the benefit of your ruler was to be treated as a slave. It followed, with some qualifications, that to be governed for your own good was to be free.[5] Since political life should be governed by reason, and law was univocally taken to be the best means of ensuring the governance of reason, anyone living a political life had at the same time to be living a life circumscribed by law.[6] Questions about the best constitutional order then tended to concern practicalities such as the endurance and stability of constitutions.

---

[2] Wahrmund 1962, p. 17.   [3] Hostiensis 1588, fo. 2vb.
[4] Justinian 2000, introductory Constitution *Imperatoriam maiestatem*, facing p. 1.
[5] Tierney 1995, p. 90.   [6] Thomas Aquinas 1874–89, vol. VIII, p. 590.

Despite occasional hints in Aristotle's writings, constitutions were not judged according to the extent to which they nurtured or limited liberty, but rather by their durability.[7] Liberty or its absence was not, therefore, a concern relevant to the discussion of the best political order for this, one of the most vociferous traditions in the later Middle Ages. It sufficed that governance was directed at enhancing the best interests of the governed for the governed to qualify as free. For the majority of the not-very-numerous theologians interested in the *minutiae* of constitutional discussion, keeping the peace was of paramount importance. Aristotle's *modus operandi* in the *Ethics* and the *Politics* was more than enough to ensure that injustice rather than infringement of liberty was perceived as the main threat to peace.

Negatively, then, we should note that the three anchor-points of this discussion do not have the same intimate relationship in this period as they were to attain later. That does not mean, however, that nothing could be done with them, nor that they were an irrelevance. To see why, we must first stand back from our vocabulary and introduce a little flexibility into the terms of debate. If a generalised, politically applicable concept of liberty was initially lacking, there was certainly a mile or two to be made with *liberties* – specific grants of rights in the shape of privileges, relaxations by rulers of regalian and other kinds of ruling right for the benefit of subjects.

Let us start with the most famous collection of liberties of them all. Magna Carta was a self-styled charter of liberties granted to the kingdom.[8] The barons who forced King John to grant them had become used to granting similar liberties of their own to towns and other communities within their lordships. In 1215 they applied that logic to the king himself and his lordship. Now, in terms of legal logic Magna Carta establishes something new in treating the kingdom not as a collection of subjects, but as the subject of rights, just as churches had been collective recipients of grants and privileges, just as towns had been. Elsewhere, it took most of the twelfth century to turn the town or city into a particular legal territory, a circumscription within which differences in lordship were rendered inoperative by a single, territorial legal order. Before that, a grant of certain liberties had only related to those people within the lordship of the recipient of the grant. We can put it like this, and at the same time escape Angevin England for Northern Italy, an area which will be of some significance later on in this discussion. If I am the bishop of Cremona, and receive a grant from the emperor removing my lands and all who inhabit them from the authority of other public officials such as counts, then the fact that some of those lands and people happen to be within the walls of Cremona is irrelevant: there will be many others within the walls who are not affected by the grant.[9] Once entire cities were brought under one lordship, however, then a grant to

[7] Tierney 1995, p. 90.   [8] Holt 1991, pp. 50–74, esp. pp. 71ff.
[9] Falconi 1979–88, no. 90; Dilcher 1967, pp. 49–50.

the bishop or the count affected everyone in his city, and it is easier to imagine a state of affairs in which the city itself, not the bishop or count, might become the recipient of those liberties.

This was a conceptual shift which both encouraged and was intensified by the wresting of governmental powers from the original incumbent, in this case a bishop, by the inhabitants of the city. By a process of what we might term political metonymy, such a grant of liberties to certain people actually enhanced a sense of locality, with the result that the locality became expressive of the grant, not the other way round. For example, and to return to England for the last time, the liberties accorded by various kings to the abbey of Bury St Edmunds were soon used to describe the geographical area subject to Bury, which became known as 'The liberty of Bury'. When it was the liberty of Bury that was at stake, rather than the liberties of all those people subject for various reasons to the abbot of Bury St Edmunds, a crucial step had been taken towards dissociating liberties from individual lordships, and generalising them as expressions of something more impersonal and territorial, liberty. The overarching authority of the king was never so threatened in England that the abbot of Bury was left to face his tenants and vassals unaided; in Italy, from the mid-twelfth century onwards, it was.

The typical activity of medieval government was to relax or delegate governmental powers so that others might take advantage of them. A medieval government was performing one of its core activities by issuing privileges, exemptions, extraordinary grants.[10] The practice did much to highlight the necessity of an abstract, undying bearer of rights so that those powers could be delegated and exercised with lasting effect. Grants to collegiate churches and to monasteries begged numerous questions concerning legal personality, such that the relationship between bishop and chapter was routinely used in the analysis of papal power in or over the church, and provided the blueprint for the limitations imposed on the power of kings to alienate certain kinds of property thought to belong to the realm.[11] Such associations were so obvious to medieval lawyers and polemicists that they occur without especial emphasis in the course of other, seemingly less important, discussions. But set over every bishop was a metropolitan, over whom presided the pope. Rich as the ecclesiastical corporation was as a source of distinctions by means of which to analyse the relation between rulers and subjects, it was not an inexhaustibly fruitful source. Such a stratified organisation as the medieval church was not a congenial environment for a nascent language of liberty, which is why it took until William of Ockham for liberty to be used as a battering ram against the Avignon papacy.[12]

By contrast, towns prompted the same questions as collegiate churches and more. First, when it came to grants and privileges, they were complex not unitary recipients, just like churches. When it came to managing such prerogatives

---

[10] Boureau 2001.   [11] Kantorowicz 1954.   [12] Tierney 1995, p. 94.

from day to day, however, there were more choices or competitors within a town than in the relatively clear-cut ecclesiastical environment defined by the interplay between bishop and chapter. Moreover, in sharp contrast to churches, towns frequently asserted claims to independence from higher authorities, especially in Italy. Civic politics, both internal and external, imparted an urgency to such questions which issued in some of the most important analyses surviving from the Middle Ages of what constituted a collective. This is why towns, especially Italian towns, bulk so large in modern efforts to delineate the possible paths to later languages of liberty. But as the example of Magna Carta shows, other collectives benefited from the process too. The result was that words like 'kingdom', 'realm', 'patria', and so on acquired non-geographical significance not merely thanks to pressure from above, but also from below. It is true that not every such abstraction which is separable from the ruler and any identifiable group of people forming the ruler is *ipso facto* to be regarded as a state. However, it is equally true that any entity which we describe by that term must at least be such an abstraction, even if it must also fulfil other requirements. This means that the medieval state was not always the servant of authoritarian demands; it was just as frequently a limitation of those prerogatives, in so far as it was the recipient of rights granted by or extorted from a superior authority.

When, for example, jurists of the later Middle Ages sought to explain Italian civic autonomy from the empire and sometimes, although less frequently and with less gusto, from the papacy, the existence of such superior authorities did not render meaningless the effort to ascribe to a given and apparently subordinate city undying legal personality, abstract cohesion, a monopoly of governing powers within its own territory, and so on.[13] This is not to imply that the process under examination here was universal: old political units such as the more durable kingdoms were already endowed with an intuitively obvious if not legally defined personality. The fact remains that even here it was possible to view the relationships between people, especially between inferiors and superiors, from a variety of different perspectives according to the vicissitudes of past and present politics, intellectual trend and, paramount amongst the latter, changing legal languages. In other areas without a history of monarchic rule, or where that tradition had been interrupted, the viability of smaller-scale organisations would be a direct result of their success in establishing themselves as territorial entities. In these cases, the shift from a personally defined relationship between superior and inferior created by lordship – which could take numerous forms and arise from numerous specific considerations – to a generalised, undifferentiated notion of subjection is the converse of the process from liberties to liberty. This is because lordship created discrete groups, and discrete interest-groups enjoyed liberties, whereas subjection on a wider basis

[13] Canning 1987, pp. 93–158, esp. pp. 116–17.

than lordship *ipso facto* created a wider community defined by a monolithic quantity. By the end of our period, that transition had taken place.

The most vivid illustration of this development is a disagreement between two famous thirteenth-century lawyers, both trained in the university tradition of Roman and canon law. For Jean de Blanot, writing in the 1240s, a vassal who is bound to his duke by the feudal bond of liege-homage commits treason if he follows his duke into rebellion against the king of France.[14] This is because the king of France recognises no superior in temporal matters, and therefore enjoys the same rights of command in his kingdom as the Roman emperor (exemplar and type of late-medieval rulership) does in his empire. The king is the emperor in his own kingdom. Now, to rebel against the emperor or to resist his officials in the exercise of their functions is a treasonable act in Roman law. So, for Blanot, you do not need to be an immediate vassal of the king in order to commit treason against him. His authority over you is no longer characterisable as lordship, it is Roman law's *merum imperium*, for the king is the holder of supreme public jurisdiction. That jurisdiction overrides obligations founded on other mechanisms, such as homage. Everybody in France, whether a vassal of the king or not, has in this one respect if in no other a homogeneous obligation to the king. For a second lawyer and thorough-going exploiter of Jean de Blanot, Guillaume Durand (*c.* 1270), the matter is the same, however different it may look at first glance.[15] It is still treason for the vassal to obey his duke, that is, his immediate lord, by going to war against the king of France. The vassal is only bound by homage to the duke, and homage commits you to help your lord against everyone except the king. Only an intense variant of homage called liege-homage compels you to help your lord against absolutely everybody, but – crucially – liege-homage may only be paid to the king. What this shows is that for legal theorists it was of no account, by the later thirteenth century, whether feudal or Roman law was employed, for the results were the same. The personal and affective vocabulary of feudal lordship – never in fact a strong-point of later medieval legal discourse – had obviously become interchangeable with the impersonal, territorially 'flattening' vocabulary of Roman law.

This brings us to a more general point. It is still a reputable opinion that feudal ideas – expressed by the words we have just been concerned with, words such as 'vassal' and 'homage' – were of definitive importance in the acquisition and maintenance of liberty. To modern eyes the classic, mid-twentieth century expressions of this commonplace have a naïve touch. Thus, for Sydney Painter, 'the fundamental features of the feudal system passed into our political tradition'. Enthusiastically developed by Walter Ullmann, this idea emerged in systematic terms as 'The practical thesis' of medieval government.[16] Uncorrupted

---

[14] Feenstra 1965.   [15] Guillaume Durand 1574, fo. 316a.
[16] Ullmann 1966, pp. 63ff; Ullmann 1978, pp. 150–92.

by theoretical speculation, political principles in England grew on the rocky, rugged soil of native feudalism. Following a commonplace of English legal history owed ultimately to Maitland, Ullmann noted that England by 1100 was 'the most perfectly feudalised country in Europe'. This, he maintained, was responsible for the development of the Community of the Realm in the thirteenth century. In contrast to Roman- and canon-law systems, the enjoyment of rights in England in this period did not arise from grant by superior authority, but from membership of the community, itself the offspring of the feudal community of the twelfth century. It was the reciprocity of obligations in the feudal contract which led to an 'equilibrium between lord and vassal'. Because the king was enmeshed in the feudal system as the lord to so many tenants, as a party bound by the legal implications of homage, the English subject was the first in Europe to grow into a citizen. What the Romanist calls private law therefore became public law, constitutional law as we might call it.

Numerous historians of medieval political ideas still subscribe to a diluted version of this thesis. The apparent and often exaggerated abilities of the English parliament to control the king are ascribed to feudal contractarianism. This may or may not be relevant; if so, it is unlikely to be the whole story. More generally, early-modern and even modern ideas of political contract are commonly thought to have an ancestor, if not their direct progenitor, in the medieval relationship between lord and vassal. It is a seductive but flawed idea. It is certainly true that early experiments with ideas of the realm were prompted by anomalies affecting the top echelon of the tenurial hierarchy, at least in England.[17] Detailed analysis of medieval jurisprudence concerning the feudal contract reveals numerous difficulties with this commonplace of modern historiography, however. For clarity's sake it is at least necessary to distinguish between the origins of individual representative institutions on the one hand, some of which have been shown convincingly enough if a little abstractly to have had roots in clienteles of vassals, and transmission of ideas about power on the other. The comparatively few medieval theorists who ratified a right of resistance to abuse or usurpation of power did not ground their comments in feudal law, nor even in contract. Marsilius of Padua – significantly, another thinker more concerned with keeping the peace and government for the common good than with the maintenance of liberty as a good in itself – resorted to a number of justifications for popular sovereignty in his great polemic *Defensor Pacis*, ranging from more or less contentious applications of Aristotle's *Politics* to an argument derived from the formation of the foetus. But contract, let alone feudal contract, is not among them.[18]

Even if we restrict our attention to the lawyers, we can see from the example of Jean de Blanot and Guillaume Durand that there was no discrete category of

[17] Garnett 1985, pp. 113–16.   [18] Marsilius of Padua 1980; Ryan 2002, pp. 51–78.

'feudal political thought', and that feudal language was by the later thirteenth century very easily made commensurate with the *ex hypothesi* more authoritarian language of Roman law. As for English feudalism and political liberty, it is important to realise that what English historians, following the usage of Magna Carta and other contemporary documents, call charters of liberties were in frequent use in other parts of Europe as well, where they were called *privilegia*. The Peace of Constance, concluded in 1183 between Frederick I ('Barbarossa') and the cities of the Lombard League, was the most famous of such privileges.[19] Like Magna Carta, it was revoked, which was the danger with 'liberties' as with *privilegia*. But in both cases the fact of revocation seems to have made no difference to the long-term significance of these documents, each of which became in its own way and in its own region the datum to which future generations looked back when they attempted to identify their own aspirations with a normative and historical locus. Now, no historian has ever tried to explain the extensive concessions made by the emperor to the Lombard League by means of feudal or any other form of contractarianism. That would be absurd. First, the Peace of Constance is couched to a large extent in the language of Roman law. Although some of the precise points at issue concern vassals of the emperor, there is no suggestion from either side that any concessions are owed to the cities of the Lombard League by virtue of a feudal relationship between them and the emperor. All subjects of the emperor, whether vassals or not, owed him *fidelitas* or fidelity. Secondly, it was Frederick I's lifelong, unsatisfied, ambition to get the cities to admit that they held what powers of government they possessed in fief from him, that is, feudally. If the cities had only agreed to this, they would not have fought a war. Yet no historian would feel comfortable ignoring the Peace of Constance when giving an account of liberty, or law, or communal formation in the period.

The same goes, in fact, for the state, and here we reach the point at which all the themes we have been discussing come together. The Italian example is the most dramatic of all, because the passage from city as an episcopal or a comital lordship to city as a territory was so quick. The Peace of Constance is the most important stage in that journey, because in it the emperor acknowledges that cities are primarily defined by their customs, that is, by the fact that each city is an entity in which a law applies to everyone within it by virtue of being in it and for no other reason. Hence the first, most general and most important of Frederick's concessions to the cities were regalian rights and their customs (*consuetudines vestras*). Communities gained liberties a long time before individuals gained liberty. Further, when a community gained *all* the liberties in an identifiable geographical area, such as a city, thanks to extensive grants of regalian right, then territorial conceptions of what it took to belong to a collective were likely to

---

[19] Appelt 1975–90, no. 848.

supersede personal and seigneurial conceptions. When that happened, it became much harder than before to justify exclusion from the community, a community now defined by its exercise of the powers of government, by its immunity or freedom from interference from higher authorities within a definable locality. In an Italian city around 1050, exercise of ruling powers below the rank of bishop or count was defined by one's seigneurial affiliation: if one was a vassal of the bishop or count, the chances are one would have exercised some public functions. It was obvious to those who were not vassals why they did not exercise those same functions. A century later, membership in a particular clientele no longer provided an adequate criterion between participation and non-participation. Everybody lived in the same place, after all, so why did only a restricted circle of people govern? Since it was notoriously the practice of the Italian urban elites to restrict political participation as much as possible, the die was cast for nearly two centuries of civic turmoil.

This is a necessarily sparse analysis, a model rather than a description, but in its very economy it has something to recommend it, because it renders nugatory some questions of forbidding complexity. First, the relevant shift is not from 'feudal' to 'early-modern', nor is it from feudal liberty to state tyranny (for many historians, feudalism and the state are still opposites, a matter made even more complicated by the Germans' faith in the *Feudalstaat*), nor is it a shift from 'medieval constitutionalism' to 'absolutism'.[20] It is from non-territorial lordship to territorial lordship. At this, the most general and abstract level, there is still much sense in an idea first put forward in relation to late-medieval Germany, but later extended to the North Italian principalities as well, which appear to have been built up on an idea of the territory and the ruler's power over it, much more than on the ruler's personal control of specific people.[21] Many qualifications to this simple contrast have been made by subsequent scholars, all of them justified.[22] Notwithstanding such criticisms, however, there is a sense in which the idea can only be right: the territory moves to centre-stage in legal speculation in the course of the fourteenth century. Geography, domicile, spacial relationships dominate even the earliest discussions of citizenship. Statute-law was by definition restricted in geographical scope. The legal mind worried at the relationship between territory and jurisdiction just as it questioned the relationship between one form of circumscription and another, typically the diocese and the *contado*. The result would depend on local tradition, the strength of monopolies over certain vocabularies, the precise mechanisms of rule: monarchy, rural or urban commune, and so on. As we have seen, the stimulus for that could come from above, in the shape of privileges handed out by rulers. Or it could be forced upon the ruler, as it was at Constance and at Runnymede. In both cases, an abstraction was necessary to explain the locus of political obligation and to

[20] Reynolds 1997, pp. xi–lxvi.   [21] Mayer 1939.   [22] Diestelkamp 1970; Chittolini 1972.

identify the beneficiary of rights of ownership, an abstraction which quickly became associated with the place being ruled rather than the person or persons ruling it. The fact that, historically as well as doctrinally in the works of the glossators of Roman law, the original function of these abstractions was to bear the rights called privileges or liberties, indicates that there is nothing by definition authoritarian or anti-authoritarian about an impersonal, abstract source of political obligation. Such abstractions, at least in this period, were a *tabula rasa*. The extent to which they served as the defender or the enemy of liberties depended on what was done with them, on who was allowed to participate, and on what basis. It depended, in other words, on the answer to a series of well-worn Aristotelian questions.

The relationship between liberties and collective organisation was, therefore, a close one, although neither necessary nor general. Territorial concerns came ever further to the fore, partly as a result of the kind of process we have presented in the foregoing pages. There is a loose coherence to these issues, at least. But as far as liberty is concerned, the medieval background really is a background and nothing more. None of the thinkers to whom we owe the most detailed and sustained discussion of law and collective organisation seems to have regarded liberty as a good in itself. Granted, it was not slavery, and therefore a good. Granted, it was necessary to be free in order to live a good life. This was so much elementary Roman law and Aristotle, and as such axiomatic, but there seems to have been little if any stimulus to take the matter further. The clearest illustration of this characteristic of medieval legal thought comes from perhaps the most famous lawyer of the period, Bartolus of Sassoferrato. Bartolus is renowned for squaring a circle in legal theory by maintaining at one and the same time the validity of the universal empire in theory and the validity of autonomous civic government within the empire as a matter of fact. The starting-point for Bartolus is the demonstrable truth that there are such things as free cities, running themselves without reference to their overlord, the emperor. If a city is free, this is because it does not acknowledge the emperor's authority over it. Such a city is accordingly to be treated as its own emperor.

Bartolus is mentioned here because his argument is famous enough to to lead us into a misapprehension. This might appear to be a theory of self-determining political existence founded on the principle of freedom, but it is in fact no such thing. First, for Bartolus the freedom of a particular city is a factual circumstance, an evidentiary concern. Is a given city free or not? The answer depends on whether it recognises the emperor. If it does not, then it is free, and this makes Bartolus's further point relevant, which is that this city is its own emperor. Liberty in this scheme of things is not a desideratum, because it is not especially desirable in Bartolus's eyes that cities run themselves. Where there is freedom so defined, there is a problem, for where there is no emperor there would appear to be no government. So the principle is invoked of the city which is emperor unto itself in order to fill the gap.[23] The opposite of a free city in Bartolus's writings is not an enslaved city, but a city ruled by the emperor. Secondly, when Bartolus turns to the internal arrangements within a city, freedom is not mentioned.[24] A tyrant is unjust, a tyrant rules without right, a tyrant commits all manner of heinous crimes. This is what makes him a tyrant. It is also true that nobody will be free under a tyrant, but this is only one of several consequences of the injustice of his rule, not its defining vice.

What is entirely lacking in this cluster of arguments and vocabulary bequeathed by the lawyers is a sense of cause and effect between, respectively, the internal arrangements within a city and that city's chances of survival against external enemies. The sample of sources is of course a restricted one, in so far as only Bartolus wrote an entire series of monographs on the problems of civic politics from the perspective of a lawyer. Outside the schools, chroniclers frequently drew and emphasised the lesson that a city which cannot unite cannot remain free. It nevertheless took until Machiavelli's *Discorsi* before that cohesion of the citizens was itself identified as the outcome of their own freedom from oppression at the hands of each other within the city.[25] It would be Machiavelli's masterstroke to turn liberty into both the cause and the consequence of a just and durable social order.

BIBLIOGRAPHY

Appelt, H. (1975–90). *Monumenta Germaniae Historica. Diplomata Regum et Imperatorum Germaniae Tomus X Pars I. Friderici I. Diplomata*, 5 vols., Hanover: Hahnsche Buchhandlung.
Boureau, A. (2001). 'Privilege in Medieval Societies from the Twelfth to the Fourteenth Centuries, Or: How the Exception Proves The Rule' in P. A. Linehan and J. Nelson (eds.), *The Medieval World*, London: Routledge, pp. 621–34.
Canning, J. (1987). *The Political Thought of Baldus de Ubaldis*, Cambridge: Cambridge University Press.
Chittolini, G. (1972). 'Infeudazioni e politica feudale nel ducato Visconteo-Sforzesco' in *Quaderni Storici*, Istituto di storia e sociologia dell' Università urbinate, 19, anno VII, fasc. I, pp. 57–130.
Diestelkamp, B. (1970). 'Lehnrecht und spätmittelalterliche Territorien' in H. Patze (ed.), *Der deutsche Territorialstaat im 14. Jahrhundert (Vorträge und Forschungen XIII)*, Sigmaringen-Munich: J. Thorbecke, pp. 65–96.
Dilcher, G. (1967). *Die Entstehung der lombardischen Stadtkommune: Eine rechtsgeschichtliche Untersuchung*, Aalen: Scientia Verlag.
Falconi, E. (1979–88). *Le Carte Cremonesi dei Secoli VIII–XII: Documenti dei Fondi Cremonesi*, 4 vols., Cremona: Biblioteca statale di Cremona.
Feenstra, R. (1965). 'Jean de Blanot et la formule *Rex Franciae in regno suo princeps est*' in *Etudes d'Histoire du Droit Canonique Dédiées à Gabriele le Bras*, 2 vols., Paris: Sirey, pp. 885–95.

---

[23] Ryan 2000.   [24] Quaglioni 1983, pp. 175–213.   [25] Skinner 1984.

Garnett, G. (1986). 'Coronation and Propaganda: Some Implications of the Norman Claim to the Throne of England in 1066' in *Transactions of the Royal Historical Society*, 5th series, vol. 36, pp. 91–116.

Guillaume Durand (1975) [1574]. *Speculum Iudiciale*, Basle, repr. in 2 vols., Aalen: Scientia Verlag, 1975.

Holt, J. C. (1991). *Magna Carta*, 2nd edn, Cambridge: Cambridge University Press.

Hostiensis [= Henricus de Segusio] (1588). *Summa Aurea*, Lyon: Landry.

Justinian, Emperor (2000). *Corpus Iuris Civilis*, ed. P. Krueger and T. Mommsen, vol. I (*Institutiones, Digesta*), 13th repr. of 8th edn [Berlin 1963], Hildesheim: Weidmann.

Kantorowicz, E. H. (1954). 'Inalienability' in *Speculum* 29, pp. 488–502, repr. *Selected Studies*, New York: J. J. Augustin 1965, pp. 138–50.

Kuttner, S. (1982). 'The Revival of Jurisprudence', in R. L. Benson and G. Constable (eds.), *Renaissance and Renewal in the Twelfth Century*, Oxford: Clarendon Press, pp. 299–323.

Marsilius of Padua (1980). *Defensor Pacis*, ed. and trans. A. Gewirth, Toronto: University of Toronto Press.

Mayer, Th. (1939). 'Die Ausbildung der Grundlagen des modernen deutschen Staats im hohen Mittelalter' in *Historische Zeitschrift* 159, pp. 457–87.

Quaglioni, D. (1983). *Politica e Diritto nel Trecento Italiano. Il 'De Tyranno' di Bartolo da Sassoferrato (1314–1357)*, Florence: Olschki.

Reynolds, S. (1997). *Kingdoms and Communities in Western Europe 900–1300*, Oxford: Clarendon Press.

Ryan, M. J. (2000). 'Bartolus of Sassoferrato and Free Cities' in *Transactions of the Royal Historical Society*, 6th series, vol. 10, pp. 65–89.

(2002). 'Feudal Obligation and Rights of Resistance' in N. Fryde, P. Monnet, and O. G. Oexle (eds.), *Die Gegenwart des Feudalismus*, Göttingen: Vandenhoeck and Ruprecht, pp. 51–78.

Skinner, Q. (1984). 'The Idea of Negative Liberty: Philosophical and Historical Perspectives', in R. Rorty, J. B. Schneewind, and Q. Skinner (eds.), *Philosophy in History*, Cambridge: Cambridge University Press, pp. 193–221.

Thomas Aquinas (1874–89). *Summa Theologiae* in *Opera Omnia*, 34 vols., ed. S. E. Fretté, Paris: L. Vivès, vol. II, p. 675.

Tierney, B. (1995). 'Freedom and the Medieval Church' in R.W. Davis (ed.), *The Origins of Modern Freedom in the West*, Stanford: Stanford University Press, pp. 64–100.

Ullmann, W. (1966). *The Individual and Society in the Middle Ages*, London and Baltimore: Methuen.

(1978). *Principles of Government and Politics in the Middle Ages*, 4th edn, London: Methuen.

Wahrmund, L. (1962). *Quellen zur Geschichte des römisch-kanonischen Prozesses im Mittelalter*, 5 vols., Innsbruck 1905–28, Heidelberg 1931, repr. Aalen 1962: Scientia Verlag, vol. I, fasc. IV.

5   States, cities, and citizens in the later
Middle Ages

Almut Höfert

The relationship between historians and their object of research tends to be particularly delicate when they are studying the institution by which they are paid. Although one might claim that the Humboldtanian ideal of free research is not affected by economic dependence on the state, it can be taken for granted that the state will ask for adequate attention as an object of research, although it will not necessarily prescribe the way in which this research is done. The field of historical studies on the state and state formation in different contemporary states is therefore one of the most active areas of historical research. However, the existence of a long, rich, and multiple historiography on states also causes some problems. This is particularly the case for the later Middle Ages. In this chapter, I therefore try to approach the theme of this book – states and citizens – in a double way. On the one hand, I shall problematise the historiography on this topic, which I hope will contribute to more general methodological reflections. On the other hand, I shall try to shed light on some aspects that seem to me especially useful in order to understand political and societal life in the later Middle Ages. In so doing, I shall mainly focus on the medieval city and the question of the degree to which it created institutions and structures that were implemented in the early-modern state.

I

David Runciman has already shown in his chapter how difficult it is to grasp the abstract institution of the state although we deal with it in our everyday life and constantly experience its effects. If it is already problematic to define today's state, historians get into even more trouble when trying to delineate its historical origins. For such an enterprise, it is (or better: it should be) indispensable to make a precise definition of the state the basis for further research. Wolfgang Reinhard, who has recently published a comprehensive history on this topic, defines the state as the owner of sovereignty based on a clearly delimited geographical space as the exclusive sphere of power, with state citizens as its permanent

I wish to thank Doris Hellmuth and Quentin Skinner for their fruitful suggestions on this chapter.

members. As a consequence, he argues that 'Europe invented the state' and that this model was only established at the end of the eighteenth century.[1] Charles Tilly, however, takes a much broader concept as his point of departure by defining states as 'coercion-wielding organizations that are distinct from households and kinship groups and exercise clear priority in some respects over all other organizations within substantial territories'.[2] By this, Tilly can include not only modern European monarchies, but also pre-modern and non-European city-states, empires, theocracies, and others. Reinhard's and Tilly's definitions mark two ends of such a wide spectrum that historians seem to be far from using this term with the same concept in mind. Former problems are raised by the ideological heritage of national historiographies, which still leave their mark in terms like feudalism, territorialisation and others that are central for the period touched by this chapter.

The concept in feudalism shows that national history-writing in the nineteenth century is not the only historiographical tradition that can be blamed for the construction of myths that keep historians from presenting narratives that seem more adequate today. Susan Reynolds has shown how French scholars from the sixteenth century mixed up a twelfth-century source, the *Libri Feudorum*, with elements of the later Middle Ages on fiefs and vassals, thus creating a uniform idea of feudalism that was supposed to have encompassed virtually all aspects of medieval societal and political life. This construction was further strengthened when Montesquieu used the alleged feudal medieval society as a counterpart to Enlightenment thoughts – just in time to give the French Revolution a just cause to abolish *les droits féodaux et censuels*. In contrast to this image, Reynolds offers a differentiated historisation and periodisation of feudalism and argues that from its very beginning it was not only based on interpersonal bonds but included bureaucratic elements as well.[3] The antagonism between feudal personal relations and 'rational' bureaucratic elements therefore has to be reconsidered.

The concept of the territorial state has a long history as well. It can be traced back to the beginning of the seventeenth century, when the scholar Andreas Knichen in his book *De iure territorii* made an early attempt to systematise territorial state law by using Roman law. In the following centuries, this concept was at first used mainly by lawyers. When historians adopted the term *territorial state* as an analytical category in the nineteenth century, it became more and more used not only for the states after 1648 but also for the description of principalities back to the twelfth century. When the first historical maps were designed around 1900, the coloured areas belonging to each principality and lordship suggested a uniformity of medieval 'territories' that did not exist: a prince in the fourteenth century, for instance, could not raise one and the same

[1] Reinhard 1999.   [2] Tilly 1994.   [3] Reynolds 1994.

tax over a whole area but had to negotiate it individually with the nobles and the cities of the different regions. Medieval principalities and lordships were not defined by a geographical space but were rather a conglomeration of different rights of different people. As Ernst Schubert argues, the concept of a territorial state is therefore problematic in two respects. If the term state is implicitly understood as we tend to use it, it wrongly suggests the existence of a medieval rule in the modern sense of being linked to an enclosed area. Furthermore, Schubert excludes nearly all concepts traditionally used by German medievalists such as *Landeshoheit*, *Landesherrschaft*, *Personenverbandsstaat*, and *institutioneller Flächenstaat*. Even the widely respected solution of Otto Brunner, who in a fundamental criticism of anachronistic concepts of legal history had proposed the categories *Land und Herrschaft*, is not spared.[4] However, Schubert himself sometimes cannot escape his own criticism, continuing as he does to use the terms he has disqualified as inadequate for the description of medieval society.[5]

The situation, therefore, is more than tricky and probably will continue to be so for a good while, since almost every analytical category turns out to be burdened by different layers of a long and complex tradition of historiography. Behind these terminological problems, one can figure out a key element: the question how the idea and structure of a state territory was developed. The answer turns out to be difficult in respect of the lordships of princes and kings. But what about another political power that was clearly linked to a geographical space – the city? In contrast to principalities and monarchies, cities had fixed geographical borders. What were the consequences for their inhabitants? Can we speak about a territorialisation within the cities, and if so, in which aspects?

In taking the city as a point of departure, I shall argue that some of the analytical traps concerning the concepts of state, territorialisation, law, and others can be more easily avoided without losing the connection with the general subject of this book. Furthermore, the focus on the city can offer insights on phenomena that tend to be concealed by studies that take the contemporary national state as a point of departure. The study of the cities is therefore an alternative perspective that may be particularly helpful at a time when the traditional structure of the state is in question and the position of cities may well change again. As Wim Blockmans and Charles Tilly have shown in their book on *Cities and the Rise of States in Europe A.D. 1000–1800*, this approach undoubtedly offers a fruitful new axis to a long-term and comparative analysis of state power.[6]

---

[4] Schubert 1996, pp. 52ff; Brunner 1959. For another criticism of Brunner's approach see Algazi 1996.
[5] See for example Schubert 1996, p. 61: 'der unstaatliche Sinn von "Land" . . .'; p. 67: 'patrimoniale(n) Staatsauffassung' and *passim*.
[6] Blockmans and Tilly 1994.

In this chapter, I shall mainly focus on the cities of the German Empire, while taking Dutch and Italian cities as a point of reference. I shall first present the main problems in the historiography of the medieval city (section II). I shall then sketch out some recent findings of historical studies concerned with the legal system of the city (sections III, IV). Finally, I shall raise the question of the degree to which German cities were involved in the development of republican ideas. Since the distinction between imperial, free, and territorial cities was not clearly drawn in the Middle Ages but gained its decisive significance only from the sixteenth century onwards, I have neglected this aspect in this overview without presuming that it was completely irrelevant for the earlier periods.[7]

II

As Magnus Ryan has pointed out, liberty in the Middle Ages was either a liberty conceded by the church or an exemption from the common law, a *privilegium* by which a city could gain the status as a specific territory which was no longer bound to serfdom and seigniorial lordship.[8] The inhabitants of this territory were the burghers. The image historians today draw of the relationship between liberties and burghers within the medieval city can be summed up as follows. Together with increasing commercialisation, the cities could construct a precisely defined space in which peace was guaranteed and the merchants gained a personal freedom enabling them to calculate their commercial activities. In this way, merchants were no longer subject to unpredictable decisions by noble lords. In contrast to principalities and other lordships, the walls of cities seemed to mark their borders in a most significant way. Also, outside these walls the urban district was indicated by hedges and towers. Apart from their geographical distinction, the city was differentiated from its surroundings by its specific legal status: its burghers were free, it had a daily market and a separate court district and was privileged in delivering duties and other contributions. City law was fixed in the town charter, the privilege bestowed by the prince or the king, to which the citizens added their own codifications of the law. When these supplements became more and more numerous, a final synthesis was no longer possible. The cities started to use current books, in which annulled formulas were extinguished and recent resolutions of the city council were integrated. By the end of the fifteenth century, some cities, like Nuremberg, had revised their legal records along the lines of Roman law. The cities thus created the first attempt at a far-reaching legal system.[9] Their

---

[7] Schilling 1992.
[8] There are some hints that urban liberty was first rooted in the *libertas ecclesiae*. Vercauteren 1968, p. 20.
[9] Kroeschell 1993.

well-defined urban space promised personal freedom and offered the possibility of joining the legal community of burghers to everybody who managed to stay there for more than one year: 'Whomsoever shall remain in this city for a year and a day without being reclaimed by anyone shall be secured from others and shall rejoice in their liberty.'[10]

In the nineteenth century, the liberal bourgeoisie saw their own fight reflected in the medieval freedom of the burghers. As Augustin Thierry put it in his famous *Essai sur l'histoire du Tiers Etat*: 'the series of twelfth-century urban revolutions is in some way similar to the movement that has brought a system of constitutional government to so many countries today . . . the bourgeoisie, a new nation with customs of civic equality and labour independence, has risen up between the nobilty and the people, destroying the social dualism of feudal times for ever'.[11] While German historians praised the medieval urban freedom and its legal system, the French Revolution and the resulting power struggles between the *ancien* and *nouveau régimes* made historians project their contemporary dualism back to the Middle Ages, where the already blamed feudalism was seen as opposed to the free world of the burghers.

This construction of an antagonism between the noble and the urban sphere had another historiographical consequence. The cities were studied only during their peak of power. Whereas medieval documents about the cities were published in widespread editions, the German cities (in contrast to their successful Dutch counterparts) of early modern times were ignored as an object of comparative research, since they were the obvious losers in the conflict with the noble territorial state that finally smoothed the path toward modernity.[12] Here, the strong dualism between nobility and princes on the one hand and cities on the other influenced the set of lines of continuity and discontinuity. If the city had not managed to maintain its political power against the principalities and lordships after the middle of the sixteenth century or so, then none of its structures and elements could have survived in the new form of power. The bourgeois myth of the medieval city, therefore, had a high price: precisely because the city was seen as an outstanding island, it was condemned to disappear once its decline was inevitable. It was the successful early-modern state that then could claim to have invented all its institutions.

---

[10] Keutgen 1901, p. 117 (Stadtrecht Freiburg im Breisgau): 'Quicumque in hac civitate diem et annum nullo reclamante permanserit, secura de cetero gaudebit libertate.'

[11] Thierry 1853; Vercauteren 1968, p. 14: 'la série des revolutions municipales du XIIe siècle offre quelque chose d'analogue au movement qui, de nos jours, a propagé en tant de pays le régime constitutionel . . . la bourgeoisie, nation nouvelle dont les moeurs sont l'égalité civile et l'indépendance dans le travail s'élève entre la noblesse et le servage et détruit pour jamais la dualité sociale des premiers temps féodaux'.

[12] Schilling 1993.

III

The fact that the medieval city was idealised by nineteenth-century bourgeois historiography has become a commonplace for urban historians today. Regional studies show that there is no evidence for an alleged antagonism between nobility and the urban burghers. The patriciate of the cities perceived itself as part of the nobility of the surrounding countryside and participated, for example, at their tournaments. Only in the second half of the fifteenth century did the nobility close this circle so that the cities had to organise their own tournaments.[13] The widespread political conflicts between a city and its regional noble opponents did not indicate a fundamental conflict between two different forms of government but was determined by concrete local power struggles.[14]

Within the city, the ideal of equal burghers has long been dismantled. The fights between different factions and corporations against the supremacy of the city councils show that the citizens did not feel that they had the same possibilities for political participation as the urban elites. Apart from this, the urban population was far from enjoying a common legal status. It often contained bondmen and bondwomen, notwithstanding the theoretical guarantee of personal freedom after one year of uncontested residence within the city walls. The clergy and the members of the rising universities were other groups exempt from urban legal status – a coexistence that often ended in conflicts.

Nevertheless, if historians were forced to recognise that there was a conglomerate of different social and legal layers within the medieval city, and that the idea of a community of equal burghers could not be maintained, at least one element seemed to survive this reassessment. Although not every inhabitant of the city had the status of a burgher, and although there were considerable social differences between all those who actually were part of the annual *coniurationes* of all citizens, at least the fact that the urban law guaranteed equal legal status to the burghers could be taken as an extraordinary feature of medieval history. It was no less than Max Weber who had qualified the specific law for the burghers as a rational element of pre-modern society.[15] At least in this aspect, the medieval city with its various rights and regimentations could be regarded as the 'hothouse of the modern constitutional state',[16] and on this basis historians still analyse the city as a legislative government.[17]

As a recent study by Sven Lembke has shown, however, even the dualism of the legal system of noble lordship on the one hand and the burgher's city on the other needs to be fundamentally reconsidered.[18] By analysing court records

---

[13] Zotz 1993.   [14] Schubert 1996.   [15] Weber 1976.
[16] Ebel 1958, p. 1.   [17] Isenmann 2001.
[18] Lembke 1999. I am very grateful to Sven Lembke for putting the manuscript of his PhD thesis at my disposal.

and other sources on crimes, Lembke has identified striking discrepancies between legal prescriptions and the concrete judgements within the city courts. The city council of Freiburg, for example, punished people for committing adultery although there was no corresponding formula in the law. In Basle, there was no law that magic was forbidden, but nevertheless people were accused and condemned for this crime by the court. The sources show that medieval laws were much less clear then modern ones. The legal formulas merely mentioned offences but did not define them in a precise way. The borders between delinquent and accepted actions were not clearly marked. Especially whether violent conflicts between citizens were considered as crimes or not depended very much on how this conflict was interpreted by the judge. Very often it was conceded to a respectable citizen that he had merely defended his honour, a central ethical category. Cities tended to be regulated by an underlying moral law rather than by the provisions of their constitutions.

Even crimes mentioned by the law were persecuted and judged in very different ways. Judgements were made not in respect of the matter, but of the person who was on trial. A decisive criterion for the judgement was closeness to the families represented in the council. The more distant somebody was to the leading patricians, and the less he or she was protected by a group – guild, family – the more likely was an unfavourable sentence. Another important factor was the involvement of lords from outside the city. When an inhabitant of Basle was condemned by a Habsburgian officer for several crimes in the 1440s, the city council first protested against the persecution of one of its citizens but later decided not to proceed with the case. Here, diplomatic interests were finally given priority over communal principles. This case also shows that citizens were often involved in matters concerning different overlapping lordships. The city council did not necessarily fight for a precedence of their citizens' rights when this could cause problems with foreign powers.

Councils exercised a paternal and traditional jurisdiction based not on fixed law but on a common sense of what would be the most adequate judgement in moral terms. Town charters should therefore be read as a *preambula* to an unwritten law which consisted of the council's opinion regarding the *utilitas publica*. The city council did not strive for a correspondence between legal documents and its form of government. The council governed the city in an authoritarian way: not the law established by the commune of burghers, but the council was the sovereign of the city. If the council was restricted in its actions, this did not happen because of the law but on the basis of common values and their interpretation by families, clergy, and corporation. Their consensus was indispensable for the government of the council. It is on this basis that the sources speak of the 'wisdom of the councillors'[19] and that the different groups

---

[19] Lembke 1999, p. 9.

within the city accepted the councillors' decisions not as arbitrary and despotic but as calculable and just.

The constitutions of cities were thus based on social roles defined by models of honour. The council conceded a partial autonomy including the right to act in self-defence to single burghers as well as to families and guilds. As a consequence, it had no means to establish a monopoly on the use of force. Within a coherent system of morality and virtue, the city did not offer the possibility to enjoy an individual and liberal lifestyle nor did it banish violence from the urban space. If a group within the city developed an ethic that did not correspond to the morality of the council, as was the case in the numerous inner-urban rebellions, then, of course, the councillors would fight in order to carry through their version of the *utilitas publica* – partly by integrating the guilds' representatives into their circles. From the fifteenth century onwards, the leading patrician families managed increasingly to establish a monopoly of defining the common good. Within this process, the council could finally establish an authoritarian rule, supported by the increasing use of written documents by a bureaucratic administration. The public space became usurped by an authoritarian government: games of chance were forbidden, public houses with prostitutes were closed, a *Polizeyordnung* was established. The burghers thus became subjects, children in need of protection by their paternal government, and were not longer equal partners. The laws and the numerous recordings of delinquents' acts demonstrate how the authority dominated the urban space with extensive regimentation and control.

If the written law was not the basis for a city's jurisdiction, one might ask why so many scholarly works were written in the fifteenth century dealing with the law for citizens. One reason is that lawyers adopted the language of Roman law in order to represent the rule of the council – this hints at the point Magnus Ryan has made about the way in which Roman law was perceived and conflated with other legal traditions. Lawyers, however, who wrote about the law of the city, acknowledged that the council was not bound to the concrete laws but rather to the criteria of morality. Laws represented rule, but they should not bind the ruler, who was supposed to decide according to *utilitas publica* and moral adequacy. These texts, therefore, have to be read as a general representation and reflection of accepted rules; they do not represent the actual way in which these rules were employed. Jurisprudence was not the discipline we know today, but a branch of moral philosophy that interpreted and strengthened an authoritarian regime.

IV

As Lembke's work shows we cannot analyse the history of law by presuming the modern character of law as a given fact in time and space. The traditional approach of legal history no longer proves adequate to grasp the historically changing significance and realities of laws. This is an important result that puts into question the last bastion of the long tradition of legal and constitutional history of the nineteenth century. It is no longer sufficient to complement legal historical research with the results of political, social, and cultural history. Rather it is indispensable to analyse the very core of legal history, the historical nature of laws, by applying other approaches.

The question whether the medieval city promoted a tendency towards territorialisation has to be answered in more than one way. As we have seen, the idea of a space that determined the legal status of people, instead of feudal personal relationships, is misleading. The burghers continued to be involved in a network of different groups and legal rules because of their personal, not their spatial status. Nevertheless, it cannot be denied that the city *was* a specific territory in which new forms of life developed. The density of people who lived together in the urban space brought forth new elements. With the introduction of paper in the fourteenth century, it was possible to use writing in the practice of lordship. In the principalities, the writing room developed into the chancellery, files were opened, locally fixed archives established. In the cities, however, this process was much more intensive due to the high numbers of people and the complexity of public affairs. The city had also, in contrast to most of the principalities, a central chamber for financial affairs. For the early modern state, this experience and knowledge were indispensable.

The other outcome of the intense use of writing in the city was newly written laws. As we have seen, these legal prescriptions reflected the increasing empowerment of the urban space by the city council. In this way, the urban law did not promote the idea of legally equal citizens, but created, on the contrary, an important element that became central for the early modern state: the subject, controlled and disciplined by its authority. In Jean Bodin's concept of the *civis*, which refers to the urban subject, this authoritarian relationship was transferred from the city to sovereignty of the state. In this sense, the path was smoothed toward the territorialisation of the later state with king or prince on the one hand and the subjects on the other.

V

The medieval city as the cradle of the early-modern subject – with this conclusion, the last element of the nineteenth-century idealisation of the city finally seems to be discredited. However, this is only one half of the story. The history I have outlined is the history of the winners, the sovereign city councils. What about the other side of the coin, the actions and attitudes of the groups in the city that lost power in the fifteenth and sixteenth centuries? As Annabel Brett and Martin van Gelderen point out in their chapters, there was a strong tradition of civic republicanism that affected the idea of citizens' rights and the political theory of the early modern period. In the Italian and Dutch cities, the factions of citizens and corporations that claimed communal participation and republican ideals developed their ideas into coherent political theories. In the German cities, this tendency was much weaker. Nevertheless, even in Germany the efforts of city councils to establish a rule over entirely controlled subjects faced opposition by groups like guilds and other corporations that had formerly had more power, as the widespread communal fights against the seigniorial lordship of the council show. In these conflicts, these groups developed their political ideas. Heinz Schilling has shown that these ideas can be analysed as a form of civic republicanism, although the German cities did not formulate explicit political theories as was the case in Italy and the Netherlands.[20] But in one aspect the developments were similar: as the power struggles in Florence at the end of the fifteenth century brought up a sharper expression of civic republicanism than ever before, so too this happened in German cities in the face of communal liberty. The communal and corporate ideas in Germany, therefore, were not abolished with the reformation, but were strengthened and had a last revival during the sixteenth century. Whereas in the territorial cities this battle was lost until the beginning of the seventeenth century, the imperial cities resisted integration into the territorial states for a much longer time.

One of the most important aspects of civic republicanism in Germany, as analysed by Heinz Schilling, was the focus on personal liberty. By claiming this right, the burghers reacted against the increasing pressure of the city council to centralise urban power and the fact that more and more citizens were being arrested when they protested against the ongoing shift of power. Concerning civic duties and obligations – such as participation in the construction and maintenance of the city walls – the burghers demanded the involvement of all the inhabitants of the city, including clergy and resident officers of the surrounding lordships. Here, the civic principle of equal obligation was indeed defined by the urban territory and not by personal status.

The demand for political participation was, of course, central. It is very interesting that the burghers referred to a communal–corporate original status that had been violated by the magistrates' quest for power. Nevertheless, this demand for power did not question the institution of the city council. The communal–corporate movements did not perceive their claim for political participation as a contradiction of the oligarchic principle of the cities' government but saw only the actual power balance as problematic.

These ideas were also prominent in the fight against the increasing threat to the cities posed by the rising territorial states. Republican principles were

[20] Schilling 1992.

more and more questioned, since they were incompatible with the sovereignty demanded by the princes. The cities found themselves in a position antagonistic to the idea that the prince should be the highest and indivisible authority in the state. In their statements, cities mostly referred to a supposed catalogue of old rights rather than integrating approaches using monarchomach theory or natural law. It is very interesting that one of the few successful fights for urban autonomy was an exception to this rule. This was the case of Emden, where the citizens successfully established their autonomy in the revolution in 1595. Since Emden had not been an autonomous city during the Middle Ages, the burghers could not refer to former rights, but had to formulate their claims within the new framework of the early modern imperial constitution. They claimed a historical-utopian Frisian liberty that could be traced back to the specific, non-authoritarian status of Frisian territory. Some years after the revolution, Johannes Althusius started his service as *syndicus* of the city council in Emden. As Martin van Gelderen indicates in chapter 6, it is certainly not a coincidence that one of the most outstanding German thinkers opposed to Bodin's model of indivisible sovereignty had his roots in one of the few German cities to maintain their autonomy against the early modern state.

VI

As I have tried to show, the analysis of the city can shed light on the question whether and how we can speak about territorialisation in the later Middle Ages. For the principalities, the alleged dualism between territorial lordship and feudal rule has for a long time been discredited. But it is still widely believed that the cities developed a form of political life, which in some aspects could be described as territorialised. Above all, the legal system has usually been mentioned as an indicator for territorialisation. The urban law has been supposed to have been applied not in respect to one's social status, but to his or her actual residence. It is becoming clear, however, that we have to give up the idea of a rational, legally based constitution of the medieval city. Not everything that was called law can be treated as a legal rule in the modern sense. As we have seen, the image of the medieval city that offered equal rights to all citizens is no longer adequate: urban jurisdiction was in fact based on social roles and an underlying code of honour and morality.

If one thinks a bit more about it, this result fits much better with ongoing historical research than the former idea of an urban legal system in the modern sense, which was supposed to mark an isolated island within a world of noble lordship. Charles Tilly and Wim Blockmans have shown that, in the battle of the cities for their autonomy in early modern times, at least the powerful communes did not entirely lose their political weight. The rising territorial state could not ignore urban experience in administration and the successful mastering of public space. In this way, the political elites of the bigger cities managed to implant urban institutions into the state structure.[21] It is now difficult to argue that, within this process, the elites would have given up their legal system that was intertwined with the administration. As we can conclude now, this was not necessary. The urban law was not a system that would have protected the citizen against the rule of the new sovereign. On the contrary, it helped to modulate the new political model of subject and state. With a few exceptions, the other heritage of former urban autonomy, civic republicanism, was no longer a political option in Germany.

BIBLIOGRAPHY

Algazi, G. (1996). *Herrengewalt und Gewalt der Herren im späten Mittelalter: Herrschaft, Gegenseitigkeit und Sprachgebrauch*, Frankfurt and New York: Campus.

Blockmans, W. P. and Tilly, C. (eds.) (1994). *Cities and the Rise of States in Europe, A.D. 1000–1800*, Colorado and Oxford: Westview Press.

Brunner, O. (1959). *Land und Herrschaft. Grundfragen der territorialen Verfassungsgeschichte Österreichs im Mittelalter*, Vienna and Wiesbaden: Rudolf M. Rohrer.

Ebel, W. (1958). *Der Bürgereid als Geltungsgrund und Gestaltungsprinzip des deutschen mittelalterlichen Stadtrechts*, Weimar: Böhlau.

Isenmann, E. (2001). 'Gesetzgebung und Gesetzgebungsrecht spätmittelalterlicher deutscher Städte', *Zeitschrift für historische Forschung* 28, pp. 1–94.

Keutgen, F. (1901). *Urkunden zur Städtischen Verfassungsgeschichte (= Ausgewählte Urkunden zur Deutschen Verfassungsgeschichte 1)*, Berlin: Emil Felber.

Kroeschell, K. (1993). *Deutsche Rechtsgeschichte*, Reinbek: Rowohlt.

Lembke, S. (1999). *Die Souveränität des Rates. Strafen und Urteilen in Freiburg i.Br., Basel und Colmar im Spätmittelalter*, PhD thesis, Freiburg i.Br.

Reinhard, W. (1999). *Geschichte der Staatsgewalt. Eine vergleichende Verfassungsgeschichte Europas von den Anfängen bis zur Gegenwart*, Munich: Beck.

Reynolds, S. (1994). *Fiefs and Vassals. The medieval Evidence Reinterpreted*, Oxford: Oxford University Press.

Schilling, H. (1992). 'Civic Republicanism in Late Medieval and Early Modern German Cities' in H. Schilling, *Religion, Political Culture and the Emergence of Early Modern Society. Essays in German and Dutch History*. Leiden, New York, and Cologne: E. J. Brill, pp. 3–59.

——— (1993). *Die Stadt in der frühen Neuzeit*. Munich: Oldenbourg.

Schubert, E. (1996). *Fürstliche Herrschaft und Territorium im späten Mittelalter*, Munich: Oldenbourg.

Thierry, A. (1853). *Essai sur l'histoire de la formation et des progrès du Tiers Etat*, Paris: Furne.

Tilly, C. (1994). *Coercion, Capital, and European States, AD 990–1992*, Cambridge, Mass. and Oxford: Basil Blackwell.

---

[21] Blockmans and Tilly 1994.

Vercauteren, F. (1968). 'Les libertés urbaines et rurales du XIe au XIVe siècle' in *Les libertés urbaines et rurales du XIe au XIV siècles. Colloque International Spa 5–8 September 1966* (no place given): Pro Civitate, pp. 13–28.

Weber, M. (1976). *Wirtschaft und Gesellschaft. Grundriß der verstehenden Soziologie*, ed. Johannes Winckelmann, Tübingen: Mohr.

Zotz, T. (1993). 'Adel in der Stadt des deutschen Spätmittelalters. Erscheinungsformen und Verhaltensweisen', *Zeitschrift zur Geschichte des Oberrheins* 141, pp. 22–50.

PART THREE

Early-modern developments

6   The state and its rivals in early-modern Europe

Martin van Gelderen

'The most elevated political thought and the most varied forms of human development are found united in the history of Florence, which in this sense deserves the name of the first modern state in the world'.[1] When Jacob Burckhardt published his praise of Florence in *The Civilization of the Renaissance in Italy*, he was not merely expressing his admiration for what he called 'that wondrous Florentine spirit'. His essay represented his main attempt to elucidate the leading features of the culture and spirit of modernity.[2] It was in many ways his answer to the works of Hegel, Ranke, Droysen and their celebration of the absolute monarchy and the modern state as the most elevated and almost divine expression of human rationality. Looking at the state, Hegel saw, in one of his most famous exclamations, 'the march of God on earth', whilst Ranke perceived 'spiritual substances, original creations of the human mind – I might say, thoughts of God'.[3] When Friedrich Meinecke published a special edition of Ranke's *Politische Gespräch* he pointed out that it was possible to turn Ranke's 'brief and yet so swollen and powerful sentences' into 'a full doctrine of the state', connecting it with the fundamental notion of Schelling and Hegel, indeed of Leibniz and Spinoza, 'that all singular things are merely modifications and individuations of one, universal and divine substance'.[4]

In the last decades of his long life Meinecke was torn between Ranke and Burckhardt. With great intensity he explored the differences and looked for connections between the 'two greatest historical thinkers' of German culture. Meinecke was particularly struck by their different appreciation of modernity and the modern state. Whilst both Ranke and Burckhardt saw the rise of the modern state as exemplifying modernity, the latter's judgement was profoundly pessimistic. Indeed, as Wolfgang Hardtwig has put it, Burckhardt's diagnosis

---

[1] Burckhardt 1958a, vol. I, p. 95.
[2] I owe the following interpretation of Burckhardt's work mainly to the studies of Wolfgang Hardtwig. See Hardtwig 1974 and 1990. See also Mommsen 1983; Rüsen 1985 and 1993; Trevor Roper, 1984.
[3] As Ranke put it in *Das politische Gespräch*. Cf. Iggers 1983, p. 82. See also the essays in Iggers and Powell 1990.
[4] Friedrich Meinecke, 'Rankes "Politisches Gespräch"' in Meinecke 1968, p. 79.

of the development was 'pathological'.[5] Burckhardt maintained that the formation of the modern state had unleashed a gruesome and hitherto unknown amorality. It set the forces of evil free in human nature. *The Civilization of the Renaissance in Italy* is full of tales of modern ambition and amorality. In the eyes of Burckhardt the humanists 'are the most striking examples and victims of an unbridled subjectivity'.[6] This is how Burckhardt scorns the humanists and explains their fall: 'Of all men who ever formed a class, they [the humanists] had the least sense of their common interests, and least respected what there was of this sense. All means were held lawful if one of them saw a chance of supplanting another. From literary discussion they passed with astonishing suddenness to the fiercest and the most groundless vituperation. Not satisfied with refuting, they sought to annihilate an opponent'.[7]

In their greed, their egotism, their lust for power, their sensuality, indeed in their unbounded evil, the humanists exemplified the condition of modern man. Modernity set evil free and the cultural beauty and glorious art of the Renaissance were born out of the new forces of evil.[8] Republican Florence excelled not only in humanist learning, but also in the ferocity of power struggles. Florentine humanism was unique because its cultural achievement outshone the darkness of modern politics. Burckhardt greatly admired Guicciardini, Vettori and above all Machiavelli, who was singled out as the greatest philosopher of the state.[9]

Machiavelli's struggle with the passion of power and the demands of morality continued to fascinate the pupils of Burckhardt and Ranke, most notably Friedrich Meinecke himself. As early as 1906 Meinecke recognised the originality of Burckhardt's cultural approach to history. Unlike Ranke, Burckhardt had, as Meinecke saw it, 'not given his heart to the perfection of the state; moreover like Schlosser but in a more comprehensive and striking sense Burckhardt calls power, which is the essence of the state, "evil in itself" '.[10] As a result, as Meinecke pointed out, the Swiss historian took a 'lonely stand'. The German historians of the Wilhelmine era were preoccupied with studying – and glorifying – the formation of first the Prussian and then the newly unified German state.[11] Many Wilhelmine historians were attracted to the history of ideas. They came up with studies of the origins, development, and efficacy

---

[5] Wolfgang Hardtwig, 'Jacob Burckhardt und Max Weber. Zur Genese und Pathologie der modernen Welt' in Hardtwig 1990, p. 195.

[6] Burckhardt 1958a, p. 274.   [7] Burckhardt 1958a, p. 272.

[8] See Wolfgang Hardtwig, 'Jacob Burckhardt und Max Weber. Zur Genese und Pathologie der modernen Welt' in Hardtwig 1990, pp. 194–9.

[9] Burckhardt 1958a, p. 104: 'Of all who thought it possible to construct a state the greatest beyond all comparison was Machiavelli.'

[10] Friedrich Meinecke, 'Jacob Burckhardt, die deutsche Geschichtsschreibung und der nationale Staat', in Meinecke 1968, p. 85. For the reference to Schlosser see Burckhardt 1978, p. 36.

[11] For fine overviews see Iggers 1996 and Blanke 1991, especially pp. 356ff.

of ideas, assuming – but rarely explicating – that ideas 'really' exist and profoundly affect society, politics and state. In a poignant commentary, Ottokar Lorenz observed in 1886 that, surmising the efficacy of ideas, historians simply 'make states rise and fall; ideas appear in history as ghosts, who over here keep the king to his sleeves, whilst over there they push a minister to a fateful course of action and support a general in his operations against the enemy, just before they vanish as quickly as Caesar's spirit at Philippi'.[12]

Meinecke became the most distinguished historian of ideas, not just of the Wilhelmine era but also of the Weimar Republic. As the founding father of the history of political ideas Meinecke opened up a new area of research and gave a strong boost to the study of the idea of the state. His own research culminated in the publication in 1924 of *Die Idee der Staatsräson*, 'the idea of the reason of state', published in 1957 in English under the somewhat misguided title *Machiavellism. The Doctrine of Raison d'Etat and its Place in Modern History*.[13] Meinecke's book is not just a pioneering study of the idea of reason of state, it is above all a study of the struggle of modern man caught between 'Kratos' and 'Ethos', between the drive and lust for power and the fragile bridle of morality. The moral problems of modernity troubled Meinecke as much as they had troubled Burckhardt. Following Burckhardt – and of course Ranke – Meinecke described power as the essence of the state. *Staatsräson* should indeed be the reason of state, that is 'the fundamental principle of statal conduct, the State's first Law of Motion'.[14] *Staatsräson* should teach 'what the State must do in order to reach regularly the optimal condition of its existence'.[15] In this sense Meinecke's study exemplifies his approach to the history of ideas. It should elucidate 'what the thinking man has made of his historical experience, how he has mastered it intellectually, what sort of intellectual conclusions he has drawn'. History of ideas is 'the reflection of the essence of historical experience in the mind, directed to the essence of life'.[16] Meinecke analyses how Machiavelli, Frederick the Great, Hegel, Ranke, and a series of other illuminating philosophers tried to come to terms with the existential tension between power and morality. It is, as Meinecke puts it in a sentence highly reminiscent of Burckhardt, the tragic tale of the 'continuously repeated struggle with the insuperable forces of destiny'.[17] As one of the most distinguished representatives of historicism, Meinecke emphasises that he is not studying 'grey theories', but 'the life-blood of events, absorbed into the life-blood of those men who are called upon to express the essence of their era'.[18] Meinecke argues that in the

---

[12] Lorenz 1886, p. 269, as quoted in Blanke 1991, p. 410.
[13] Meinecke 1976. For the English translation, see Meinecke 1984 [1957]. References are to the German original and the English translation, from which they deviate.
[14] Meinecke, 1976, p. 1; 1984, p. 1.   [15] Meinecke, 1976, p. 5; 1984, p. 5.
[16] Meinecke, 1976, p. 24; 1984, p. 20.   [17] Meinecke, 1976, p. 25; 1984, p. 21.
[18] Meinecke, 1976, p. 24; 1984, pp. 20–1.

study of political ideas the *vita activa* and the *vita contemplativa* come together. Political ideas, as he puts it in one of his more poetic phrases, 'unite the smell of the earth and the perfume of the mind'.[19] Studying the individual tales of political thinkers Meinecke hopes to find – and again this was typical of the historicist approach to the study of history – not so much plain and practical political recipes, but more importantly some fundamental orientation for how to cope with the dark forces of modernity.

At the end of his monumental study Meinecke discards the 'false idealisation of power politics' and 'the false deification of the State, which has continued in German thought since the time of Hegel, in spite of Treitschke's opposition'.[20] It is, however, debatable whether Meinecke succeeded in historicising the political idea of the state. He continued to speak about the 'essence of the state' as an almost transcendental idea, perhaps even, in Michael Stolleis's verdict, as an 'ahistorical mystification'.[21] In 1931 Otto Hintze, a close friend of Meinecke, observed that 'so far we have not succeeded in defining the state in a satisfactory way; indeed it is impossible to settle the question whether the label corresponds to something real at all or whether it merely refers to some thought'.[22] Influenced by recent sociological theory, in particular by the work of Max Weber, Hintze set out to develop a new structural approach based on ideal types. The most important results of Hintze's efforts were typologies of the constitution and the modern state. As national socialists took over German universities, the initial influence of Hintze's new approach was limited, but after the war his work became a source of inspiration for the development of history as a social science in Germany and for the burgeoning study of the formation of the nation-state by social and political scientists. In the seminal collection of essays, *The Formation of National States in Western Europe*, that appeared in 1995, the political scientist Stein Rokkan based his study of 'dimensions of state-formation' amongst others on what he called 'Hintze's classic analysis of variations in state-building in Europe'.[23]

For all their differences with classical historicists such as Ranke, Burckhardt, and Meinecke, the post-war generations of historians and social scientists on the whole continued to see 'state-making' as 'the political dimension of modernisation'.[24] For many, the absolutist state is still the first modern state. Writing from a Marxist perspective, Perry Anderson sees the Renaissance, in his seminal study *Lineages of the Absolutist State*, as 'the historical turning point at which Europe outdistanced all other continents in dynamism

---

[19] Friedrich Meinecke, 'Kausalitäten und Werte in der Geschichte' in Meinecke 1959, p. 88.
[20] Meinecke, 1976, p. 505; 1984, p. 429.
[21] Michael Stolleis, 'Friedrich Meineckes "Die Idee der Staatsräson" und die neuere Forschung' in Stolleis 1990, p. 138.
[22] Otto Hintze, 'Wesen und Wandlung des modernen Staates' in Hintze 1962, p. 471.
[23] Rokkan 1975.   [24] Poggi 1990, p. 86.

and expansion' and he regards the new absolutist state as 'the precise *political form* of the headway of the whole region'.[25]

In much recent work on the formation of the modern state there is little room for the intellectual foundations of the process. The emphasis has been on the forces of coercion and capital, to paraphrase the title of one of the more sweeping studies in the field, in which Charles Tilly takes us, to be precise, from 990 to 1992.[26] There is, at times, the recognition that the concept of the modern state owes much to Jean Bodin's definition of sovereignty. In *Les Six Livres de la République*, first published in 1576, Bodin defines sovereignty as, to quote the first English translation, 'the most high, absolute and perpetual power over the citizens and subjects in a commonwealth'.[27] Bodin's innovative insistence on legislative authority as the 'first mark of sovereignty' entailed a notion of indivisibility. This means that it is impossible to constitute a 'Republique meslée'. Bodin writes: 'To institute the dominion of one, together with that of the few, and also with that of the many, simultaneously, is not only impossible but cannot even be imagined. For if sovereignty is by its nature indivisible . . . how can it be allotted to one and to all at the same time?'[28]

These words had a pervasive impact on political debate across Europe.[29] Bodin's dismissal of the Republique meslée was particularly pertinent to the Low Countries and the old German Empire, which shared the blessings and irritations of the *civitas composita*. Between 1580 and 1650 the history of both the Netherlands and Germany was marked by bitter and long-lasting political and military conflicts. The issues of sovereignty and constitution were at the heart of the debates during the Eighty Years War in the Low Countries and the Thirty Years War in Germany. There were passionate discussions about the strength and weakness of central, federal, and local institutions, about the States-General, the Stadholder, and the towns in the Netherlands, about the Emperor, the Reichstag, the principalities and the Imperial and autonomous cities in Germany.

Responding to Bodin and to the political problems of their times, Dutch and German authors developed a series of new visions for the political community, including the Dutch republican model with Hugo Grotius as one of its main authors, the consociational model of Johannes Althusius and other German Christian thinkers, and the model of the sovereign state as developed by Political Aristotelians from Henning Arnisaeus to Herman Conring. Grotius, Althusius, Arnisaeus, and Conring belonged to the generation of northern *Späthumanismus*. Their ambition was not only to address the political issues

---

[25] Anderson 1974, p. 428.   [26] Tilly 1990.

[27] Bodin 1962, p. 84.   [28] Bodin 1961 [1583], p. 266.

[29] For the importance of Bodin see amongst others the following recent studies: Skinner 1989, pp. 116–21; Franklin 1991, pp. 298–328; and Salmon 1996, pp. 500–22.

of their times and countries, but also to establish new systems and methods of research and education for the humanist disciplines, including politics and law.[30]

As early as 1578, Bodin's definition of sovereignty started to have an impact on Dutch thinking. Bodin was an adviser to the Duke of Anjou, whose military and financial assistance was eagerly sought by the leaders of the Dutch Revolt against the government of Philip II. Anjou had aspirations to succeed Philip, but the Dutch merely wanted him as 'Defender of the liberty of the Netherlands', not as their new sovereign. During the Dutch negotiations with Anjou the prominent humanist Marnix of St Aldegonde rejected the use of the word 'sovereign'. Knowing that on the whole Frenchmen do not speak Dutch, Marnix argued that the word did not exist in the Dutch language. It was a flat lie of the Dutch polyglot, a blunt attempt to avoid the confrontation with Bodin's concept of sovereignty.

The issue of sovereignty was in fact central to the Dutch debates. After the Abjuration of Philip II in 1581, a new generation of humanist jurists tried to clarify and locate sovereignty in the delicate Dutch interplay of towns, provincial States and States General.[31] Hugo Grotius became the most prominent representative of the peculiar Dutch merger of humanist jurisprudence and republicanism. Grotius dealt with Bodin and the issue of sovereignty in a series of unpublished works, including his early *Commentary on XI Theses* concerning sovereignty and *De Iure Praedae*.

In line with the new trends in northern *Späthumanism*, which he studied in Leiden as a pupil of the greatest humanist of the late sixteenth century, Joseph Justus Scaliger, Grotius developed his theory of sovereignty as part of a comprehensive analysis of the foundations of political and legal theory. He opens *De Iure Praedae* with an explication of the *methodus* and *ordo* of his work, before he sets out to formulate the *prolegomena* of his theory. Grotius argues that the topic of *De Iure Praedae*, the issues of war and peace, cannot be analysed 'solely on the basis of written laws'. For a proper enquiry, a turn to the *ratio naturae*, 'to the ordered plan of nature' is needed. Grotius turns to the 'jurists of antiquity', who, 'refer the art of civil government back to the very fount of nature'.[32] Moving from the most general to the more specific, he presents nine axiomatic rules and thirteen fundamental precepts of the law of nature as the *prolegomena* of his theory. Grotius first elucidates – in paragraphs that are now seen as the beginning of modern natural law theory[33] – the primacy of self-preservation (*sui-amor*) and friendship (*amicitia*) as the main characteristics of individuals in the state of natural liberty, where each is 'free and *sui iuris*', before he moves on to explore the origins of civil power. For reasons of

---

[30] For a more elaborate analysis of Grotius's, Althusius's and Arnisaeus's models and of the traditions to which they belonged see van Gelderen 2002.

[31] See van Gelderen 1992, chs. 4 and 5.

[32] Grotius 1868, p. 6. I will also give references to the English translation, Grotius 1950, p. 7.

[33] See amongst others the seminal studies by Haakonssen 1996, Schneewind 1998, Tuck 1993.

demographic growth, better protection, and greater economic convenience, the free individuals of the state of nature start to create smaller societies, which are 'formed by general consent for the sake of the common good'.[34] The *respublica* refers to a multitude of private persons, who have come together to increase their protection through mutual aid and to assist each other in acquiring the necessities of life. At their own free will these individuals unite by way of civil contract – Grotius uses the term *foedus* – in a 'unified and permanent body' with its own set of laws. From *singuli* they turn themselves into *cives*, citizens.

The laws of the commonwealth emanate from its will as a unified body based on consent. Grotius argues that 'civil power, manifesting itself in laws and judgements, resides primarily and essentially in the bosom of the commonwealth itself'.[35] Of course not everybody has the time to devote himself to the administration of civil affairs. The exercise of lawful power is therefore entrusted to a number of magistrates, who act for the common good. By mandate the magistrates have the authority to make laws for the *respublica*, which bind all citizens.

The introduction of the concept of *magistratus* marks the beginning of a distinct rejection of Bodin's theory of sovereignty. By employing this concept Grotius emphasises that those who exercise civil power, be they kings, princes, counts, States assemblies, or town councils, are administrators. Grotius argues that 'every right of the magistrate comes from the commonwealth' and that 'public power is constituted by collective consent'.[36] Grotius has a strong preference for the concept of civil or public power. He carefully avoids concepts such as *maiestas* or *summum imperium* and sticks to the term *summa potestas*. Grotius adopts the old definition of Bartolus and describes *summa potestas* in terms of 'the right to govern the commonwealth which recognises no superior authority among humans'.[37] The power to govern is far from absolute, let alone eternal. When Grotius discusses the most important element of *summa potestas*, the right to declare war, he points out that 'the right to undertake a war pertains to the prince only in the sense that he is acting for the commonwealth and has received a mandate from it'. According to Grotius, 'the greater and prior power to declare war lies within the commonwealth itself'. Generalising this point, Grotius accepts the radical position of Fernando Vázquez that 'the power of the commonwealth remains intact even after the establishment of the principate'. Going back to another Spanish author, Francisco de Vitoria, Grotius endorses the argument of 'the Spanish theologian . . . that the commonwealth may change one prince for another or transfer the principate from one dynasty to another'.[38]

---

[34] Grotius 1868, pp. 19–20; 1950, p. 20.   [35] Grotius 1868, p. 25; 1950, p. 25.
[36] Grotius 1868, p. 91; 1950, p. 92.
[37] Hugo Grotius, 'Commentarius in Theses XI' in Borschberg 1994, p. 215.
[38] Grotius 1868, p. 269; 1950, p. 284. For Grotius's intellectual relationship with Vázquez and Vitoria see van Gelderen 1999, pp. 183–201 (also in Graham Darby (ed.), *The Origins and Development of the Dutch Revolt* (London and New York, 2001), pp. 151–70).

This position enables a subtle play with Bodin's thesis of the indivisibility of sovereignty. When 'the power of the commonwealth' remains intact even after the appointment of one or more magistrates, then the administration of the marks of sovereignty can of course be divided amongst the various magistrates.

The idea that the people as the association of free citizens is the only source of civil power and sovereignty became one of the basic principles of the Dutch Republic. As *majestas realis* popular sovereignty was absolute and indivisible. In terms of *majestas personalis* sovereign powers were administered by magistrates who were fully accountable to the commonwealth. And so the *respublica mixta* was restored to full glory. When he compares the constitutions of these glorious republics, Grotius accepts the pleas of the wisest men for a *respublica mixta*, in the sense that a single *civitas* combines 'the majesty of a prince with the authority of a senate and the liberty of the people'. Grotius has a distinct preference for a *respublica mixta* where the aristocratic element dominates. In the *Treatise of the Antiquity of the Batavian now Hollandish Republic* he argues that Holland has been just such a virtuous republic of optimates since the days of Roman antiquity. The revolt of the Batavians, celebrated by Grotius as the 'authors of liberty', established the Hollanders as a free, self-governing people willing to do the utmost to retain their freedom.[39] Most Hollanders lived of course in towns, and for Dutch Republicans from Grotius to De La Court the *civitas* in the sense of a city of virtue remains the basic unit of political analysis. When Grotius assesses the unity of the United Provinces, he simply – and controversially – describes them as a 'confederation, which is a contract between different sovereigns'.[40]

Whilst Grotius was formulating the most systematic Dutch reply to Bodin, Johannes Althusius (1557/1563–1638) composed the strongest German rejection. Althusius was one of the most important theorists of the *Politica Christiana* which found its origins in the political works of Luther and Calvin. Following the Reformers, *Politica Christiana* starts from the assumption that government is part of the divine order. The study of political institutions and constitutions is intertwined with religion and theology. The Bible contains the guiding principles for secular government, of which the study is therefore marked by a mixture of *recta ratio* and revelation. With authors such as Clemens Timpler and Johann Alsted, Althusius represents the radical monarchomach wing of Christian political thought in Germany. Unlike the other authors of *Politica Christiana*, they emphasise the autonomy of *Politica* as a distinct and autonomous discipline. According to the German Monarchomachs, politics and society rest on the principle of voluntary association, of *consociatio*. Althusius defines *Politics* as 'the art of associating *(consociandi)* men for the purpose of establishing, cultivating, and conserving social life among

---

[39] Grotius 1610, p. 22.   [40] Grotius 1622, p. 5.

them'.[41] According to Althusius the purpose of man, as a symbiotic creature, is to lead a life of 'holy, just, comfortable and happy symbiosis'. By the bonds of association men become able to 'communicate among themselves whatever is appropriate for a comfortable life of soul and body'. As symbiotic creatures, and not as individuals, humans forge the bonds of association. As Clemens Timpler puts it, 'every civil society depends on the will and the legitimate consent of those who join together to create civil life'.[42] Althusius and Timpler use the concepts of citizen and civil society in a novel way to refer to man's social role and status in a widening circle of associations, all of which are based on covenants. As a civil and symbiotic animal, man is part of the web of associations that encompass the fullness of communal, social, and political life. The covenant is the foundation for the natural and private associations of family, households, and guilds and for the wider, more artificial, and public associations of city, province, and *respublica*. Politics is not confined to the level of *civitas* and *respublica*; it covers all symbiotic associations. This means that the republican themes of civic participation and civic virtue do not disappear, but refer to the duties of men as members of associations. In *Civilis Conversationis* Althusius seeks to promote civility and virtue throughout civic life, from conversation to eating. In fact Althusius devotes a whole chapter to the art of civil eating. Apparently Althusius felt that this was a particularly difficult issue for his German readers. He switches from Latin into German in order to argue that a proper dinner has three courses, a *Voressen*, a *Mittelessen*, and a *Nachessen*. Althusius also insists that it is civil to remain seated for all three courses and that eating and drinking require the virtues of temperance and moderation.[43]

So Althusius integrates the themes of civil virtue and citizenship into the analysis of the fullness of social and political roles that humans have as members of various associations. All associations have their own government, and none of these governments wield absolute power. The German Monarchomachs reject Bodin's theory of sovereignty with particular force. In the consociational model all political associations are formed by covenant. The *populus*, defined as the web of corporate associations, is the civil source of sovereignty. Like Grotius, Althusius appeals to Vázquez and Bartolus to defend the claim that 'the people, or the associated members of the realm, have the power of establishing the right of the realm and of binding themselves to it'.[44] The *populus* constitutes the *respublica*, which, following Cicero's classic definition, is therefore literally a *res populi*. Those in government are magistrates, office-holders. The authority of all magistrates, including the *summus magistratus*, is derived

[41] Althusius 1932, ch. I, no. 1, p. 15. The most important recent studies of Althusius include Dahm *et al.* 1988; Winters 1990, pp. 29–51; Dreitzel 1992, pp. 17–32; Duso 1996, pp. 65–126; Duso *et al.* 1997; Duso 1999, pp. 77–94; and Hueglin 1999.
[42] Timpler 1611, Book 1, ch. 4, nr. 5, p. 45.   [43] Althusius 1611, pp. 329–46.
[44] Althusius 1611, XVIIi:16, p. 91.

from the association he serves; the rights and limits of each office are set by the covenant. Alsted puts it in a nutshell: 'Sovereignty is the highest power, which the magistrate has amongst the people by the consent of the people.'[45]

Representation is a central feature of the consociational model. Althusius develops a theory of dual representation, which holds that the body of the *populus* is not only represented by its head, the supreme magistrate, but also by the assembly of its members.[46] In his role of supreme administrator the *summus magistratus* represents 'the person of the entire realm', *personam totius regni*.[47] But the assembly of its members is the true representation of the *populus*. Connecting themselves with French and Dutch theories of resistance, Althusius and other German Monarchomachs label these representatives as ephors. Althusius describes them as 'the representatives of the commonwealth or universal association to whom, by the consent of the people associated in a political body, the responsibility has been entrusted for employing its power and right in constituting the supreme magistrate and in assisting him with aid and counsel in the activities of the associated body'.[48] Althusius emphasises that the authority of the ephors rests on the mandate and consent of the *populus*. A delicate interplay between people, ephors, and supreme magistrate characterises all commonwealths. The recognition of this interplay leads to Althusius's claim 'that every type of commonwealth is mixed and tempered'.[49]

This consociational model of civil and political society put the emphasis on the importance of the towns and the representative assemblies of the German territories as they struggled with the rise of absolutism in the old Empire. Althusius favoured the *respublica mixta* of the city of Emden, which he served as *Syndicus*, and the County of Nassau, where he taught at the new Calvinist university of Herborn. Some authors, most notably Johann Valentin Andreae, even develop blueprints of a utopian commonwealth of Christian associations.[50] These utopian dreams were ridiculed by the main adversaries of Althusius and Andreae, the humanists who prided themselves on being the true followers of Aristotle. Although all German studies of *Politica* are drenched with quotations, concepts, and categories from Aristotle, the Philosopher *pur-sang*, there is a distinct school of Political Aristotelianism.[51] Political Aristotelians not only quote the Philosopher, they adopt a systematic approach modelled on the humanist interpretations of his *Politics*. They argue that *Politica* is an autonomous discipline, the *scientia constituendi et gubernandi rempublicam*, which should be strictly separated from ethics and above all from theology.

---

[45] Althusius 1932, ch. III, Praecepta, p. 1392.
[46] See Hofmann 1988, pp. 513–42; and Duso 1996, pp. 107–14.
[47] Althusius 1932, XIX:98, p. 177.   [48] Althusius 1932, XVIII:48, p. 143.
[49] Althusius 1932, XXXIX:15, p. 405.   [50] See Andreae 1972.
[51] For the study of Political Aristotelianism the work of Horst Dreitzel has been seminal. See Dreitzel 1970; 1988, pp. 163–92; and 1991, pp. 547–66.

Between 1550 and 1650 Political Aristotelianism became the dominant doctrine of politics in the universities of the Lutheran territories. Some of its main proponents, including Henning Arnisaeus and Hermann Conring, were connected with the university of Helmstedt, the creation of the humanist dukes of Braunschweig-Wolfenbüttel. In Helmstedt Arnisaeus wrote his major works, including the massive *De Republica* of 1615, which laid the foundations for the rise of political Aristotelianism in Germany.

Arnisaeus sees the *civitas*, which he defines in traditional Aristotelian terms as a union of households, as the 'material subject' of the study of politics.[52] In a crucial chapter he argues that most of his fellow theorists, including Althusius and Bodin, fail to distinguish between the *civitas* as the material subject of *Politica* and the *respublica*, which Arnisaeus describes in Aristotelian terms as the form (*forma*), end (*finis*), and order (*ordo*) of civil society. To clarify his distinction Arnisaeus uses the Aristotelian concept of *essentia* to define the commonwealth as the 'order of command and obedience'.[53] Politics is the study of government, defined as a separate order where *summa potestas* is located. As Arnisaeus puts it: 'The perfect definition of *respublica* is that it is the order of civil society, not just with some authority (*imperium*), but with exclusive supreme power (*summa potestas*), from which flows the government of the magistrate amidst the entirety of the subjects'.[54]

Arnisaeus fully endorses Bodin's definition of sovereignty but he disagrees with the thesis of indivisibility. As the order of command and obedience the *respublica* embodies and unites sovereignty. However, as Arnisaeus sees it, sovereignty 'is not a simple faculty, [it] is composed of many powers'.[55] As the German Empire shows, these powers can be administered by several different office-holders. At the end of a detailed analysis of the constitutional history of Germany, and of the role of Electors and Emperor, Arnisaeus concludes – after 250 pages – 'in one word that the present state of the Empire is a mixture of Aristocracy and Monarchy, where the Aristocracy preponderates, but where the Emperor has full and highest power over the sovereign rights that remain with him'.[56]

Arnisaeus realises that his redefinition of the *respublica* as the order of command and obedience has important ramifications for the meaning of concepts such as citizen (*civis*) and *civitas*. In the hands and pen of Arnisaeus these concepts leave the realm of politics and lose their connotations with the republican idea that civic participation is the heart of politics. The citizen of the *civitas* becomes the subject of the sovereign government. The emphasis moves from civic participation to the rights and the duties of the subjects.[57] And as citizens turn

---

[52] Dreitzel, Book I, Proœmium, section 4, p. 3.
[53] Dreitzel, Book II, chapter 1, section 1, no. 10 (p. 43); also section 4, no. 22 (p. 77).
[54] Dreitzel, II:1:1:14, p. 44.   [55] Dreitzel, II:6:1:47, p. 881.   [56] Dreitzel, II:6:5:134, p. 1084.
[57] See Dreitzel 1991, p. 557 and Löther 1994, pp. 239–73.

into subjects some of the followers of Arnisaeus start to use the concept of the 'state' for the study of the *respublica* as the order of command and obedience. Authors such as Hermann Conring argue that the *ordo civitatis* has its own rules of civil prudence. Conring and other Political Aristotelians devote hundreds of pages to the detailed study of the practical organisation of government and to the rules of civil prudence. They turn the observation of European states into a separate empirical discipline, the Staatenkunde. The emphasis is often on the monarchy, and many Political Aristotelians are keen defenders of the sovereign rights of monarchs.

With its disconnection between civil society and the order of command and obedience, its endorsement of absolute sovereignty and its defence of monarchy, political Aristotelianism became the most important intellectual foundation for the rise of the territorial, absolutist state in the old German Empire. It was of course not the only intellectual impulse in the process of state-formation. The publication of Justus Lipsius's *Six Bookes of Politics* in 1589 marked the beginning of the rise of Tacitism as the distinct study of political prudence.[58] One of the key elements of Tacitism was what Meinecke saw as the 'essence and spirit of reason of state', the idea that for reasons of political necessity and utility moral and legal rules should be discarded.[59] Lipsius's *Politics* became one of the bestsellers of late European humanism. The book was devoured by the courtiers of Europe's monarchies, as they struggled with the forces of faction, flattery, and corruption. The *Politics* also became a highly popular academic textbook, especially in the old Empire, providing generations of German students with an eloquent starting-point for the exploration of the virtues – and vices – of the Prince, and of the role of counsellors, bureaucrats, soldiers and subjects. In the process of state-formation, Political Aristotelianism and Tacitism fulfilled complementary roles. Whilst the Aristotelians focused on political structures, constitutions, and sovereignty, Tacitists focused on the virtues and vices that were needed to maintain the *status monarchicus*. The connection with the new concept of the state was quickly made. Whilst the earlier translations of Lipsius's *Politica* were still called 'politics', the Dutch translation from 1657 of Lipsius's *Monita et Exempla Politica* was given the title *Admonitions and Examples Concerning the Art of the State*.[60]

Throughout Europe the concept and the word 'state' made increasing headway. The most famous example was the publication in 1651 of what Thomas Hobbes called his study of 'that great Leviathan, called a Commonwealth or

---

[58] This line of research was initiated by Gerhard Oestreich. See Oestreich 1989 and 1982. More recent studies include Burke 1991, pp. 479–98; Stolleis 1990; Münkler 1987; and Weber 1992.
[59] See Meinecke 1976, pp. 14ff; 1984, pp. 12ff.
[60] See p. 357 for the description of Lipsius's, *Politica* from 1589 as 'books about the art of the state'.

State'.[61] Hobbes's theory of the state as an 'artificial man', whose impersonal sovereignty arose out of the passions and rationality of man in the state of nature, changed the political debate across Europe, including the Dutch Republic and the old German Empire. In Holland first the brothers De la Court and later Spinoza used Hobbes to radicalise the republican model of Grotius and his generation. In Germany Samuel Pufendorf's work marked the departure from Political Aristotelianism with the development of a new school of natural law theory that owed much to the work of Hobbes.[62]

Meinecke interpreted *Leviathan* as the celebration of the power of the state and recognised that Hobbes made an important move in portraying the state as a *homo artificialis*. But, as Meinecke saw it, this meant above all that Hobbes's state did not have 'a soul of its own', merely an artificial one. *Leviathan* might appear as the culmination of the absolutist idea of the state, but Meinecke emphasised that in Hobbes's theory the state was merely an instrument to promote 'the welfare, the security and the comfort of individual men'. There was no place in Hobbes's theory for the 'devotion founded on faith and the attachment to the State', that Meinecke deemed vital for the 'truly living and personal State'.[63] Rather Hobbes's philosophy contained the seeds of the Western European idea that the state should be based on notions of individualism and utilitarianism.[64]

In this sense Meinecke saw strong parallels between Hobbes and Grotius. Both failed to develop a 'new empirical doctrine of the State' on the basis of the idea of reason of state; both initiated 'Western European civic individualism and utilitarianism' and both remained, as Meinecke put it, under the 'spell' of the tradition of natural law.[65] Meinecke recognised Grotius as the founding father of the modern law of nations and emphasised that this was the very antithesis of reason of state: 'And so Grotius constructed his system of international law just as if reason of state did not exist; as if there was no force of necessity pushing the States over the frontiers of morality and law; as if it were possible altogether to confine the behaviour of States *vis-à-vis* one another within legal and moral bounds.'[66]

Meinecke paid no attention to Grotius's writings on the Dutch republic. He recognised the importance of Bodin, whose theory of sovereignty he saw as a major attempt to 'determine the legal characteristics of the supreme power in the state'[67] – but not, and that was highly significant, the supreme power *of* the state. But his preoccupation with the idea of reason of state meant that Meinecke did not look at the models of the political community that were developed in response to Bodin. Meinecke ignored not just the republican model,

---

[61] Hobbes 1991, Introduction, par. 1, p. 9.
[62] A comparative Dutch–German study of these shifts is offered by Bödeker 2002.
[63] Meinecke 1976, p. 254; 1984, p. 215.   [64] See Meinecke 1976, p. 255; 1984, pp. 215–16.
[65] Meinecke 1976, p. 246; 1984, pp. 207–8.   [66] Meinecke 1976, p. 247; 1984, p. 209.
[67] Meinecke 1976, p. 67; 1984, p. 57.

but Althusius's consociational model as well. Nor was there any discussion in Meinecke's masterpiece of the Aristotelian model of the sovereign *ordo civitatis*. Whilst Political Aristotelianism can be seen as the major intellectual force behind the rise of the territorial, absolutist state in the old German Empire, Aristotelians certainly did not advocate unlimited sovereignty, let alone a Machtstaat. Following Bodin, they emphasised that divine, natural, and fundamental constitutional laws demarcate absolute sovereignty. Moreover, as Aristotelians observed the practical effects of the forms of government, many of them qualified their preference for the efficiency and sheer power of monarchies and sympathised with the *respublicae mixtae* of the old Empire, the small, temperate monarchies and the independent towns, which somehow left room for moderation and liberty.[68]

Meinecke's fixation on the Machtstaat was widely shared throughout the period of his life – from 1862 to 1954. From Ranke onwards most historians – and not just in Germany – failed to escape from the paradigmatic view that the absolute sovereign state was the political hallmark of modernity.[69] The republican and consociational alternatives of Grotius and Althusius were not seen as forces of modernity but at most as sympathetic examples of the *Ständestaat*, firmly belonging to the old Europe. There were of course notable exceptions. Meinecke's pupil Hans Baron celebrated the Florentine struggle against the threat of tyranny in a series of monumental studies, some of them written and published during the 1930s.[70] It was hard to miss the parallel. In many ways Baron's work was the worthy successor to Burckhardt's celebration of Florence as the first modern state.

In 1948, at the age of eighty-six, Meinecke reassessed the importance of Burckhardt and Ranke. 'With great caution' he now argued that 'Burckhardt had probed more deeply and sharply in the historical essence of his own time' and as a result had been better in foreseeing the future than Ranke.[71] As before, Meinecke pointed to their very different appreciation of the state, contrasting its elevation to metaphysical heights by Ranke with Burckhardt's view that it is at most a useful Notinstitut,[72] an emergency ward. This entailed a very different vision of modernisation. Burckhardt did not celebrate the Machtstaat as the hallmark of modernity. He looked for the forces of modernisation elsewhere in early modern Europe: in Florence, in England, and in Holland. In Burckhardt's view Bacon, Descartes, Bayle, and Spinoza paved the way for a new view of the state, 'no longer founded on divine right, but on reason and expediency and a presumed contract'. Burckhardt found the roots of the values of the Enlightenment not in French or Prussian absolutism, but in Dutch and English

---

[68] See Dreitzel 1970, p. 294.   [69] See also Blänkner 1992, pp. 48–74.

[70] The culmination of Baron's work was of course *The Crisis of the Early Italian Renaissance* (Baron 1955); earlier publications included Baron 1969, pp. 180–211.

[71] Meinecke, 'Ranke und Burckhardt' in Meinecke 1968, p. 94.   [72] Meinecke 1968, p. 100.

revolutions: 'The groundwork for this way of thinking', he argued, 'had been laid by the uprising of the Dutch in the sixteenth century and the English Revolution in the seventeenth.'[73]

BIBLIOGRAPHY

Althusius, Johannes (1611). *Civilis Conversationis Libri Duo Recogniti, & aucti. Methodicé digesti et exemplis sacris et profanis paßim illustrati*, Hanover: Antonius.
(1932). *Politica, Methodice Digesta et exemplis sacris et profanes illustrate*, 3rd edn [1614], ed. Carl Joachim Friedrich, Cambridge, Mass.: Harvard University Press.
Anderson, Perry (1974). *Lineages of the Absolutist State*, London: NLB.
Andreae, Johann Valentin (1972). *Christianopolis* [1619], ed. Richard van Dülmen, Stuttgart: Calwer Verlag.
Baron, Hans (1955). *The Crisis of the Early Italian Renaissance*, 2 vols., Princeton: Princeton University Press.
(1969). 'Politische Einheit und Mannigfaltigkeit in der Italienischen Renaissance und in der Geschichte der Neuzeit', reprinted in August Buck (ed.), *Zu Begriff und Problem der Renaissance*, Darmstadt: Wissenschaftliche Buchgesellschaft, pp. 180–211.
Blanke, Horst Walter (1991). *Historiographiegeschichte als Historik*, Stuttgart and Bad Canstatt: Fromman-Holzboog.
Blänkner, Reinhard (1992). ' "Absolutismus" und "frühmoderner Staat". Probleme und Perspektiven der Forschung' in Rudolf Vierhaus (ed.), *Frühe Neuzeit, frühe Moderne? Forschungen zur Vielschichtigkeit von Übergangsprozessen*, Göttingen: Vandenhoeck and Ruprecht, pp. 48–74.
Bödeker, Hans Erich (2002). 'Debating the Republica Mixta: German and Dutch Political Discourses Around 1700' in Martin van Gelderen and Quentin Skinner (eds.), *Republicanism: A Shared European Heritage*, vol. I: *Republicanism and Constitutionalism in Early Modern Europe*, Cambridge: Cambridge University Press, pp. 219–46.
Bodin, Jean (1961) [1576]. *Les Six Livres de la République*, Aalen [Paris] (reprint edn of 1583): Scientia Verlag.
(1962) [1576]. *The Six Books of a Commonweale*, trans. Richard Knolles and ed. Kenneth D. McRae, Cambridge, Mass.: Harvard University Press.
Borschberg, Peter (1994). *Hugo Grotius 'Commentarius in theses XI': An Early treatise on Sovereignty, the Just War, and the Legitimacy of the Dutch Revolt*, Berne: Peter Lang.
Burckhardt, Jacob (1958a). *The Civilization of the Renaissance in Italy*, New York: Harper & Row.
(1958b). *Judgements on History and Historians*, London: Allen and Unwin.
(1978). *Weltgeschichtliche Betrachtungen*, ed. Rudolf Marx, Stuttgart: Kröner.
Burke, Peter (1991). 'Tacitism, Scepticism, and Reason of State' in J. H. Burns and Mark Goldie (eds.), *The Cambridge History of Political Thought, 1450–1700*, Cambridge: Cambridge University Press, pp. 479–98.

---

[73] Burckhardt 1958b, p. 199.

Dahm, Karl-Wilhelm, Krawietz, Werner, and Wyduckel, Dieter (eds.) (1988). *Politische Theorie des Johannes Althusius*, Berlin: Duneker and Humblot.

Dreitzel, Horst (1970). *Protestantischer Aristotelismus und absoluter Staat. Die 'Politica' des Henning Arnisaeus (ca. 1575–1636)*, Wiesbaden: Franz Steiner Verlag.

(1988). 'Der Aristotelismus in der politischen Philosophie Deutschlands im 17. Jahrhundert' in Eckhard Keßler, Charles H. Lohr, and Walter Sparn (eds.), *Aristotelismus und Renaissance. In Memoriam Charles B. Schmitt*, Wiesbaden: Harrassowitz, pp. 163–92.

(1991). *Monarchiebegriffe in der Fürstengesellschaft: Semantik und der Einherrschaft in Deutschland von der Reformation bis zum Vormärz*, Cologne: Böhlau.

(1992). *Absolutismus und ständische Verfassung in Deutschland. Ein Beitrag zu Kontinuität und Diskontinuität der politischen Theorie in der frühen Neuzeit*, Mainz: Verlag Philipp von Zabern.

Duso, Giuseppe (1996). 'Una Prima Esposizione del Pensiero Politico di Althusius: La Dottrina del Patto e la Costituzione del Regno', *Quaderni Fiorentini per la Storia del Pensiero Giuridico Moderno*, 25, pp. 65–126.

(1999). 'Il governo e l'ordine delle consociazioni: la *Politica* di Althusius' in Giuseppe Duso (ed.), *Il Potere. Per la Storia della Filosofia politica moderna*, Rome: Carocci, pp. 77–94.

Duso, Giuseppe, Krawietz, Werner and Wyduckel, Dieter (eds.) (1997). *Konsens und Konsoziation in der politischen Theorie des frühen Föderalismus*, Berlin : Duneker and Humblot.

Franklin, Julian H. (1991). 'Sovereignty and the Mixed Constitution: Bodin and his Critics' in J. H. Burns and Mark Goldie (eds.), *The Cambridge History of Political Thought, 1450–1700*, Cambridge: Cambridge University Press, pp. 298–328.

van Gelderen, Martin (1992). *The Political Thought of the Dutch Revolt 1555–1590*, Cambridge: Cambridge University Press.

(1999). 'From Domingo de Soto to Hugo Grotius. Theories of Monarchy and Civil Power in Spanish and Dutch Political Thought', *Il Pensiero Politico* 32, pp. 183–201.

(2002). 'Aristotelians, Monarchomachs and Republicans: Sovereignty and *Respublica Mixta* in Dutch and German Political Thought, 1580–1650' in Martin van Gelderen and Quentin Skinner (eds.), *Republicanism: A Shared European Heritage. Vol. I: Republicanism and Constitutionalism in Early Modern Europe*, Cambridge: Cambridge University Press, pp. 195–217.

Grotius, Hugo (1610). *Liber de Antiquitate Reipublicae Bataviciae*, Leiden: Plantin-Raphelengius.

(1622). *Verantwoordinghe van de wettelijcke Regieringh van Hollandt*, Paris.

(1868). *De Iure Praedae Commentarius*, ed. H. G. Hamaker, The Hague: Martinus Nijhoff.

(1950). *De Iure Praedae Commentarius. Commentary on the Law of Prize and Booty* (for English trans.), vol. I, ed. Gwladys L. Williams and Walther H. Zeyde, Oxford: Clarendon Press and London: Geoffrey Cumberlege.

Haakonssen, Knud (1996). *Natural Law and Moral Philosophy: From Grotius to the Scottish Enlightenment*, Cambridge: Cambridge University Press.

Hardtwig, Wolfgang (1974). *Geschichtsschreibung zwischen Alteuropa und moderner Welt. Jacob Burckhardt in seiner Zeit*, Göttingen: Vandenhoeck and Ruprecht.

(1990). *Geschichtskultur und Wissenschaft*, Munich: dtv.

Hintze, Otto (1962). 'Wesen und Wandlung des modernen Staates' in Otto Hintze, *Staat und Verfassung. Gesammelte Abhandlungen zur allgemeinen Verfassungsgeschichte*, ed. Gerhard Oestreich, 2nd edn, Göttingen: Koehler and Amelang.

Hobbes, Thomas (1996) [1651]. *Leviathan*, ed. Richard Tuck, Cambridge: Cambridge University Press.

Hofmann, Hasso (1988). 'Repräsentation in der Staatslehre der Frühen Neuzeit' in Dahm, Karl-Wilhelm, Krawietz, Werner, and Wyduckel, Dieter (eds.), *Politische Theorie des Johannes Althusius*, Berlin: Duneker and Humblot.

Hueglin, Thomas O. (1999). *Early Modern Concepts for a Late Modern World. Althusius on Community and Federalism*, Waterloo, Ontario: Wilfrid Laurier University Press.

Iggers, Georg (1983). *The German Conception of History: The National Tradition of Historical Thought from Herder to the Present*, 2nd edn, Middletown, Conn.: Wesleyan University Press.

(1996). *Geschichtswissenschaft im 20. Jahrhundert*, 2nd edn, Göttingen: Vandenhoeck and Ruprecht.

Iggers, Georg and Powell, J. M. (eds.) (1990). *Leopold von Ranke and the Shaping of the Historical Discipline*, Syracuse, N.Y.: Syracuse University Press.

Lipsius, Justus (1657). *Staatkundige vermaningen en voorbeelden, die de deughden en zonden der vorsten betreffen*, Amsterdam: Pieter la Burg.

Lorenz, Ottokar (1886). *Die Geschichtswissenschaft in Hauptrichtungen und Aufgaben kritisch erörtert*, Berlin: Hertz.

Löther, Andrea (1994). 'Bürger-, Stadt- und Verfassungsbegriff in frühneuzeitlichen Kommentaren der Aristotelischen *Politik*' in Reinhart Koselleck and Klaus Schreiner (eds.), *Bürgerschaft. Rezeption und Innovation der Begrifflichkeit vom Hohen Mittelalter bis ins 19. Jahrhundert*, Stuttgart: Klett-Cotta, pp. 239–73.

Meinecke, Friedrich (1959). 'Kausalitäten und Werte in der Geschichte' in Friedrich Meinecke, *Zur Theorie und Philosophie der Geschichte*, ed. Eberhard Kessel, Stuttgart: Koehler.

(1968). *Zur Geschichte der Geschichtsschreibung*, ed. Eberhard Kessel, Munich and Vienna: Oldenbourg.

(1976), *Die Idee der Staatsräson in der neueren Geschichte*. ed. Walter Hofer, 4th edn, Munich and Vienna.

(1984, repr 1957). *Machiavellism. The Doctrine of Raison d'Etat and its Place in Modern History*, London: Routledge.

Mommsen, Wolfgang (1983). 'Jacob Burckhardt – Defender of Culture and Prophet of Doom', *Government and Opposition*, 18, pp. 458–75.

Münkler, Herfried (1987). *Im Namen des Staates. Die Begründung der Staatsraison in der Frühen Neuzeit*, Frankfurt am Main: S. Fischer.

Oestreich, Gerhard (1982). *Neostoicism and the Early Modern State*, Cambridge: Cambridge University Press.

(1989), *Antiker Geist und moderner Staat bei Justus Lipsius (1547–1606)*, Göttingen: Vandenhoeck and Ruprecht.

Poggi, Gianfranco (1990). *The State. Its Nature, Development and Prospects*, Cambridge: Polity Press.

Rokkan, Stein (1975). 'Dimensions of State Formation and Nation Building: A Possible Paradigm for Research on Variations within Europe' in Charles Tilly (ed.), *The Formation of National States in Western Europe*, Princeton, N.J.: Princeton University Press.

Rüsen, Jörn (1985). 'Jacob Burckhardt: Political Standpoint and Historical Insight on the Border of Postmodernism', *History and Theory* 24, no. 3, pp. 235–46.

(1993). *Konfigurationen des Historismus. Studien zur deutschen Wissenschaftskultur*, Frankfurt am Main: Suhrkamp.

Salmon, J. H. M. (1996). 'The Legacy of Jean Bodin: Absolutism, Populism or Constitutionalism?', *History of Political Thought* 17, pp. 500–522.

Schneewind, J. B. (1998). *The Invention of Autonomy: A History of Modern Moral Philosophy*, Cambridge: Cambridge University Press.

Skinner, Quentin (1989), 'The State' in Terence Ball, James Farr, and Russell L. Hanson (eds.), *Political Innovation and Conceptual Change*, Cambridge: Cambridge University Press, pp. 116–21.

Stolleis, Michael (1990). *Staat und Staatsräson in der frühen Neuzeit. Studien zur Geschichte des öffentlichen Rechts*, Frankfurt am Main: Suhrkamp.

Tilly, Charles (1990). *Coercion, Capital, and European States, AD 990–1992*, Cambridge, Mass.: Blackwell.

Timpler, Clemens (1611). *Philosophiae Practicae Pars Tertia et ultima complectens Politica integram Libiris V*, Hanover: Antonius.

Trevor-Roper, Hugh (1984). 'Jacob Burckhardt', *Proceedings of the British Academy* 70, pp. 359–78.

Tuck, Richard (1993). *Philosophy and Government, 1572–1651*, Cambridge: Cambridge.

Weber, Wolfgang (1992). *Prudentia gubernatoria. Studien zur Herrschaftslehre in der deutschenpolitischen Wissenschaft des 17. Jahrhunderts*, Tübingen: Niemeyer.

Winters, Peter Jochen (1990). 'Althusius' in Michael Stolleis (ed.), *Staat und Staatsräson in der frühen Neuzeit. Studien zur Geschichte des öffentlichen Rechts*, Frankfurt am Main: Suhrkamp, pp. 29–51.

7   The development of the idea of citizens' rights

Annabel S. Brett

I

The idea that the subjects of states are not just subjects, but citizens, and that those citizens hold rights, not just in respect of each other, but in respect of those very governments themselves; these notions – however vaguely defined or understood – are central to the political self-consciousness of most modern Europeans, and a yardstick for the perceived legitimacy of most modern European governments. Associated with other more or less well-defined notions – 'democracy', 'participation', 'the rule of law', and (uncertainly but increasingly importantly) 'civil society' – 'citizen's rights' mark European political organisation off from the 'police state', 'one-party rule', 'military regime', and other political pejoratives that Europeans push to the periphery of their world. By the end of the seventeenth century the ancestor of this division, a similar associative dichotomy marking off legitimate government from tyranny, constitutional from despotic rule, was available for the polemical evaluation of the political formations of early-modern Europe: only this time the perceived antithesis was well within Europe itself, in the form of the monarchies of Spain and, especially, France. Despite the familiarity of these linked ideas, however, and despite their long historical gestation, we ought to begin our enquiry by noticing that the association of 'citizens' with 'rights' – that is, the idea that the citizen is a rights-holder – is not necessarily obvious or self-explanatory at all.

The 'citizen' is ultimately a figure from the Greco-Roman tradition, who, certainly, was equipped with a range of what Wesley Hohfeld, in his seminal work *Fundamental Legal Conceptions* (1920), might have called liberties, privileges, immunities, and powers, and which served to define that citizenship as a status. One might, therefore, suggest that citizens have always had rights, by definition: for what else is the *citizen* as opposed to the *slave*, paradigmatically the human being with *no* rights? But although some have argued that these liberties, privileges, and immunities of the Greco-Roman world can aptly be characterised using the modern idiom of subjective rights, I take my stand with more traditional histories of rights here and argue that our understanding of a right is something quite different, although the word can be stretched to cover liberties, privileges, and immunities as well.

Let me fill that out. Most theorists of rights are indebted to Hohfeld's analysis, which was a *legal* analysis of various abilities and statuses which individuals may hold *under the law*. Hohfeld was concerned to argue that, although in common parlance all these different types may be, and are, called 'rights', only 'entitlements' can be properly so described. In a recent book, however, Richard Primus has concentrated precisely on this aspect of common parlance, or the political *language* of rights.[1] While agreeing with Hohfeld on the technical differentiation between rights, privileges, immunities, and powers – so that, for example, freedom of speech is technically a privilege rather than a right – Primus notes that we cannot, *politically speaking*, substitute 'privilege' for 'right' in the context of freedom of speech without loss of sense (and some political danger to any politician foolish enough to try).[2] Politically speaking, freedom of speech is *not* a privilege – it's a right.

If we are interested in the history of modern European political self-perception and self-description, it is this common political language that we need to try to understand and explain. What is involved in talking about (and claiming) rights in this way? It is clear from the above that when we use the word 'right' to characterise our ability to speak out without fear of persecution or censorship, we are making not a strictly legal, but a moral claim: we are saying not only that the law allows us to speak but that we *ought* to be allowed to speak. We are referring to something that we should have of ourselves, not just be credited with by the law, and we thereby imply – crucially – that there is an 'us' which does not exist only in the eyes of current statute law. The term 'right' thus involves of itself a reference to what we might term a 'zone of non-coincidence' between individuals and the positive legal order of the state.

The early-modern articulation of this moral zone of non-coincidence was primarily in terms of the *contrast* between nature (and its law and rights) and the city[3] (with its laws and rights – understood as liberties, privileges, immunities, and powers). The moral ground, that is, was man as created by God in his original nature, and the positive legal order of the state both stemmed from and could be measured against the natural order of human well-being. Non-coincidence could also be articulated in terms of the contrast between the human city and the city of God, that is, between the spheres of politics and religion. However, the claims of religion were, for much of this period, not primarily expressed in terms

---

[1] Primus 1999.   [2] Primus 1999, pp. 36–7.
[3] I am using 'city' here and throughout as the nearest equivalent to the Latin *civitas* or Greek *polis*, which was understood in the early-modern period to imply a community or association of individual human beings in which there existed a human power of government and of legislation (this distinguished it from other communities such as the household or the village).

of specific religious rights. They tended rather to be assimilated to the natural right of living a moral life within a Christian society (although increasingly the language of rights crept into the sphere of religion *via* the claim of a right to religious freedom). One main argument of this chapter will be that the way in which we use the term 'right' today is parasitic upon (or presupposes) the concept of natural rights that was developed in the course of the sixteenth and seventeenth centuries.

If this is so, however, then there is a question about the attribution of rights involved in the locution 'citizen's rights' – that is, to whom do these rights belong, if the language of rights as we use it today developed in the context of articulating the claims of individuals insofar as they are natural, not civic, beings – that is, men, not citizens? If we turn to look at the heritage of the term citizen, we find that it is a much older notion with its roots in the city culture of the ancient world, and especially of Rome. Although the Roman law used the term *ius* or right to apply to individuals, it did not have the same sense as in the modern concept of rights. Moreover, Roman moral and legal philosophy in their different ways served to disallow the claim of natural man within a civic context. Cicero's *De inventione* suggested that men in their natural state lived scattered and wild and required to be civilised through reason and eloquence.[4] The citizen therefore morally outstripped natural man; or, alternatively, we might say that the best of natural man was already absorbed in the citizen – rendering void any zone of non-coincidence. Roman law with its Stoic heritage conceived of a natural state of man, which might be morally superior to the civil state of man, but which nevertheless did not have any claim upon that civil state which has developed for human advantage. That is, the claims of man as a natural being under natural law had no purchase on his status under civil law (slavery being the prime example of this): the zone of non-coincidence could not provide the grounds for a claim *within the city*. Hence the ancient figure of the citizen is not the bearer of rights in our sense. Furthermore, the ancient citizen as revived in the political discourse of renaissance humanism was not primarily a rights-bearer either. As has been widely discussed, and as we shall see below in more detail, the renaissance humanist discourse of city and citizen focused on virtue, not rights, as the defining mark of the citizen, and its emphasis was on how virtue might be fostered rather than rights guaranteed – the civic perfectibility of humanity and the essential involvement of man within the order of the city.

One might well make a case for saying, therefore, that it is misleading to talk of the *development* of the concept of 'citizens' rights', *per se* and strictly speaking, in the period between 1500 and 1700, in that for much of this period these two locutions were still nested in different ways of talking or idioms of

---

[4] Cicero, *De inventione*, I, 2.

politics. One might almost be tempted to say that the term 'citizens' rights' contains in itself a paradox: a defensive or 'negative' locution ('rights') to fill out a 'positive' concept of belonging ('citizenship'). Nonetheless, these two centuries represent a critical period in any story of the development of citizens' rights. For they are a time when, on the one hand, the notion of 'rights' underwent radical change and enrichment. It is precisely during this period that 'rights' acquire their full modern connotation which, I suggest, tacitly informs our understanding of powers, privileges, and immunities as well (thus enabling us, as Hohfeld noticed, to call them all by the name of 'rights'). On the other hand, they are also a time when the notion of the 'citizen', and the civil philosophy of which that figure is the hero, came under increasing pressure. In the course of this paper I shall try to track these twin developments and, at the end, to offer some thoughts on the outcome of them both.

II

Let us take first the notion of 'rights'. Broadly speaking, the sixteenth century saw the full articulation of two competing concepts of rights. One, inherited from late-medieval scholasticism, elaborated an idea of rights as consonant with law. On this conception, rights are moral faculties which the individual holds to commit certain actions in consonance with the law which governs him (I use 'him' in deference to early-modern sensibilities and somewhat in defiance of ours; later in this paper I shall suggest how early-modern thinkers could worry that the 'him' might after all be a 'her'). The only reason, indeed, why such faculties are rights is precisely their relationship to the precepts of law. The other concept, which I believe stems from legal rather than theological discourse, understands rights as original liberties or freedoms, remnants of an unboundedness that characterises the natural state of all natural things, which is subsequently limited by law.

The primary context for the articulation of both these idioms was the extraordinary political experience of sixteenth-century Spain. The external encounter with the American Indians, the internal problem of analysing the Habsburg empire as a political structure, and the division of Christendom, forced a radical reconsideration of the relationship between nature, city, and God – that is, if we put it in terms of the individual, between natural man, citizen, and Christian. And the important thing about the sixteenth-century Spanish theologians and lawyers was that they *did* frame these issues in terms of the individual.

The Thomist heritage was crucial in furnishing the theologians with the starting-point of their analysis, the individual man as a natural moral agent bound by natural law. Aquinas had conceived of man as able, through his reason, to participate in the eternal law and therefore to *initiate action* towards his natural good, as opposed to being simply *acted upon* like an animal.[5] This capacity for initiating action Aquinas characterised as *dominium* (mastery or command), that by which man is free to determine his own course. Crucially, however, this human capacity for agency or freedom is simultaneously the capacity to understand and to obey the four laws (eternal, natural, civil, and divine) to which man is subject: in Aquinas, freedom or self-direction are never contrary to the direction of the law. The *natural* good of man, to which he was directed by his nature and towards which he (therefore) had the capacity to direct himself, Aquinas held to include preservation, animal well-being, and the moral and religious life of the human being in a political society.[6]

The sixteenth-century Spanish Dominicans Francisco de Vitoria and Domingo de Soto took over this rich articulation of the naturally legitimate human life. But they had available to them not merely a concept of natural law but one of natural *rights*. In the first half of the fourteenth century, the English Franciscan William of Ockham had been decisive in transforming the thirteenth-century concept of *dominium* into a concept of rights understood as juridical capabilities or powers of action, sanctioned either by natural or by human positive law.[7] Importantly, Ockham insisted that neither natural nor human positive rights were held by Christians in their capacity as Christians. They belonged to humanity *per se*, had been enjoyed before the birth of Christ and remained unchanged thereafter despite being held by Christians.[8] All human juridical arrangements, primarily property and civil jurisdiction, were therefore the result of purely human activity. Ockham's highly effective fusion of Aristotelian, canonistic, and Franciscan language had been deployed by the fifteenth- and sixteenth-century French theologians Gerson and Almain in the service of analysing the juridical capability of the community of the church to act against its head.[9] Vitoria and, especially, Soto grafted this idea of rights as marking a capacity for action or agency onto man understood in a Thomist sense. The result of this was a conception of man with natural rights to

---

[5] Aquinas 1966, p. 23: 'it is evident that all [sc. things] share in it [sc. the eternal law], in that their tendencies to their own proper acts and ends are from its impression. Among them intelligent creatures are ranked under divine providence the more nobly because they take part in providence by their own providing for themselves and others.'

[6] Aquinas 1966, pp. 81–3.

[7] Ockham's definition of a right as a power of action is made in the second chapter of *The Work of Ninety Days* (Ockham 1995, p. 24): 'a right of using is a licit power of using an external thing of which one ought not to be deprived against one's will, without one's own fault and without reasonable cause, and if one has been deprived, one can call the depriver into court'.

[8] This position is succinctly stated in the *Short Discourse on Tyrannical Government*, Book III, ch. 8 (Ockham 1992, p. 91): 'This twofold power, to appropriate temporal things and to establish rulers with jurisdiction, God gave without intermediary not only to believers, but also to unbelievers, in such a way that it falls under precept and is reckoned among purely moral matters. It therefore obliges everyone, believer and unbeliever alike.'

[9] See the analysis in Tierney 1997, pp. 207–54 and Brett 1997, pp. 76–122.

self-conservation and self-defence (the goods of animal nature), and to the more specific good of human nature, a moral life in a political community.[10]

Famously, Francisco de Vitoria applied this conception to the question of the American Indians and was thereby able to construe much of Spanish activity in the New World as a violation of Amerindian rights. Equally – or perhaps not so? – famously, he was also thereby enabled to find that if the Indians barred the Spaniards from travelling and trading in their lands, they would thereby violate the natural rights of human communication and travel which belonged to the Spaniards, and so could be the object of a just war. What the concept of natural rights gives with one hand, it can take away with the other.[11]

We are not, of course, talking about the rights of man in this chapter but about the rights of citizens. However, part of my point is to show how it is in the context of *natural* rights that the language of rights *per se* developed. We can see this if we turn from Vitoria to his colleague at the University of Salamanca, Domingo de Soto, and his analysis of the internal structure of the city or commonwealth and, especially, the position of the citizen within it.

Soto belongs with all those within the Aristotelian – and in general the classical – tradition of civil philosophy by holding a strong conception of the necessary integration of man within a political community and of the morally transformative effect of this belonging on the individual.[12] Because of the role of the city in realising the individual's good, the city acquires a power over the citizen to legislate for his moral well-being and to demand the sacrifice of the individual to the common good. But Soto uses the rights idiom which had been articulated by Vitoria in the context of another city – the American Indian city – to argue for a limit to the ubiquitous renaissance political argument from the common good. The citizen, he said, does not stand to the city in the simple relation of hand to body. Yes, the citizen's good is connected with that of the city. But it does not *reduce to* the good of the city and therefore there remains a domain in which the city has no right to legislate.[13]

Soto's critique of the hand–body analogy was acknowledged by his contemporary, the jurist Fernando Vázquez, in his *Illustrious Controversies* of 1564.

---

[10] Soto 1967–8 (vol. II), p. 302 (all translations from these volumes are my own): 'God through nature gave to individual things the faculty of conserving themselves and resisting their contraries: not only with regard to the safekeeping of their temporal well-being, but also through his grace with regard to the prosperity of their spiritual well-being.'

[11] See the *Relection On the American Indians* (1539) in Vitoria 1992, pp. 233–92.

[12] Soto 1967–8 (vol. I), p. 18: 'Aristotle most excellently said that the city is constituted for the sake of being, but exists for the sake of living well . . . For by the same reason whereby man is born to felicity [moral happiness], by the same reason he is a civil animal.'

[13] Soto 1967–8 (vol. III), p. 400: 'a man, although he be a part of the commonwealth, is nevertheless also an individual existing for the sake of himself, and thereby in himself capable of injury, which the commonwealth cannot visit upon him'.

But Vázquez provided an alternative way of understanding the citizen's relationship with the city by positing an original natural state, not of moral faculties
for the pursuit of well-being, but of innocent liberty. In parallel, the city figures not as a moral community necessary for the moral perfection of man, but
as an artificial construct for the sake of convenience.[14] Furthermore, although
citizens might sanction their own servitude to the jurisdiction of a prince in the
interests of their safety, the city's right is always limited by the contingency of
its hold on its naturally unwilling subjects.[15]

During the course of the Spanish 'second scholastic', rights theory in both
idioms thus developed in the context of articulating the *extra*-civic claim of
nature. Whether rights were seen as positive moral faculties to realise objective
goods, or as remnants of an original unbounded liberty, they depended on their
reference to a pre-civic nature for their normative character, that is, their nature
as rights rather than mere abilities. The moral force of asserting a right came
from the individual's moral worth which was conceived not, or not entirely, as
dependent on the city, but as a natural phenomenon. As I suggested at the outset,
this idea of non-coincidence or moral independence is inherent to the language
of rights (as opposed to, e.g., liberties, franchises, privileges, immunities) even
today, and we can see now that it is carried over from the idea of natural rights
to the rights of citizens. It is why we cannot today substitute the language of,
for example, privilege, for that of right without loss of meaning, even in a civic
context and even if that is what the right technically is in legal terms.

So far we have been considering the importance of the extra-civic dimension
in terms of nature and the natural moral agent. What about that other possibly
extra-civic dimension, God and religion? Aquinas had been clear that the ruler
with charge of the human city, while legislating in conformity with natural law,
must also take his cue from him who had charge of ruling towards the higher
end of the heavenly city.[16] In Habsburg Spain, which inherited the intellectual
legacy of the Catholic kings, the School of Salamanca continued to treat the
Catholicism of the prince as a touchstone of political legitimacy, removing the
need for a Catholic conscience to appeal against the city.

Within sixteenth-century scholastic political theory, therefore, the natural
moral agent and the religious subject had found their way into the heart of
the human city. But the course of the later sixteenth century and the early

---

[14] Vázquez 1572, 41v (all translations from this volume are my own): 'for individual citizens with
regard to each other are not like a foot or a hand with respect to the whole body . . . Among
citizens there is only a kind of association of good faith . . . contracted to this end, that each man
might be able to live his life safely, and with every convenience.'

[15] Vázquez 1572, 61v: 'no people can be forced to live under subjection, if it is unwilling and
struggles against it'.

[16] Thomas Aquinas, *De regimine principum* [*De regno*], Book I, ch. 15, translated in Blythe 1997,
p. 100.

seventeenth centuries showed that in practice there was to be no such easy rec-
onciliation between nature, the city, and religion. The civil wars of France
and the Netherlands, and later of England, showed up the uneasy relation
between the city and the religious domain. Theorists and publicists appealed
against the claims of the city on the grounds of those of religion. However, what
was striking about the most radical of the resistance theories of this period was
that the grounds of religion were made part of a much broader appeal to nature
and its law and rights, which prescribed and defended the physical and moral
integrity of the individual against the laws and actions of the city. Within the
scholastic heritage – which was the main intellectual source for this so-called
'resistance theory', whether Catholic or Protestant – the human city had never
had juridical autonomy, being always sandwiched between the law of nature
and the law of God; the wars of religion showed how, under pressure, the city
appeared to lose *any* claim to be a source of rights in itself. Thus although,
on the scholastic understanding, rights are positive moral features of humanity
for positive moral ends *including* the community of the city, nevertheless they
came to have a defensive or negative aspect *against* that city.

The civil wars of the later sixteenth century thus marked a decisive step in
the evolution of rights theory. But at the same time they seemed to indicate that
this penetration of the city by natural man and religious man threatened to lead
to the dissolution of the city. At least, that was the lesson of the civil wars in
France and England to at least some contemporaries. If either the natural moral
agent, or the religious subjectivity, or both, did not feel at home there, they
could appeal against the city to nature or to God in terms of a violation of their
rights.

Faced with this, theorists of sovereignty and the state in the early seventeenth century refashioned rights theory in order to disallow the extra-civic
claim inherent in the sixteenth-century concept. The two major theorists of this
movement started from similar premises but ultimately sketched a different
answer to the conundrum. The work of Hugo Grotius strove to secure the city
against dissolution by minimalising the objective content of both natural morality and religion, thus dramatically reducing the possibility of appealing to either
against the law of the city. Hobbes, by contrast, sought ultimately to integrate
natural morality and religion within the city rather than beyond it; meaning that
man could not coherently make any moral or religious appeal against the city,
as the city contained both within itself.

The basic tool of both Grotius and Hobbes was the exploitation of the legal
device of contract as a device for the exchange or the surrender of rights, together
with a philosophical framework centred around the advantage to the individual
in the surrender of liberty. Drawing on the Vazquezian understanding of right
as liberty in the sense of a lack of limits, Grotius and Hobbes pictured the
individual in the state of nature not primarily as a moral agent in pursuit of the

natural good of man, but as a free agent in pursuit of his own *advantage*.[17] Thus Grotius and later Hobbes were enabled to remove the moral constraint on giving up right provided that a greater advantage, from the individual's point of view, was available. In analysing human advantage, both theorists primarily stressed the *disadvantage* which could accrue to individuals from the presence of other equally free individuals: the lack of limits or exclusion, which rendered the individual and the space around him liable to invasion.[18] Any structure which could limit the rights of all individuals, that is, that could create a kind of 'exclusion zone' around each individual, could therefore be depicted precisely as man's greatest convenience and advantage: and this was the city. The legal device of contract was analysed and deployed in such a way as to allow natural man easy passage into the city but then to bar his way out. Individual right was conceived in an almost commercial vein as natural man's original capital, to be spent on advantage: and the man who bought citizenship with his rights could not then claim those same rights against the city. Citizens' rights were held only against other citizens.[19]

Thus nature and natural rights do not function in these authors as an extra-civic standard by which the city might be judged: nature is a dynamic force that drives man to change his fortune rather than a static moral order framing the city of the world. The extra-civic claim of religion was also neutralised: by Grotius, through a minimalist interpretation of Christianity; by Hobbes, through an insistence that the sovereign's interpretation of Scripture was the only one authoritative in the city. Hobbes's theory was in every way the extreme statement of this case: nature and God in their regulatory roles simply do not exist outside the city, and thus the individual cannot appeal from the city to either nature or God. The juridical sandwich has been flattened into one layer.

III

As we have seen in considering Soto in particular, sixteenth-century scholastic discourse, with its Aristotelian heritage *via* Aquinas, involved the concept of the city as a moral and political community. In this context it deployed the locution of 'citizen' meaning man as a part of the city or *res publica*, a public body made up of individuals in their public aspect. But insofar as Aquinas had refigured Aristotelian activity as subjection to one or other of his four laws,

---

[17] Grotius 1950, fol. 10 (the translation is my own): 'God created man *autexousion*, free, and under his own right (*sui iuris*), in such a way that the actions of each man and the use of his own things lies under his own whim and not that of another.'

[18] Most famously in Thomas Hobbes, *Leviathan* (1651), ch. 13 (Hobbes 1996, pp. 86–90).

[19] Trenchantly, again, in Hobbes 1996, p. 224: 'Every man has indeed a Propriety that excludes the right of every other Subject: And he has it onely from the Soveraign Power; without the protection whereof, every other man should have equall Right to the same.'

the Aristotelian active citizen tended in neo-Thomist handling to slip over into the more passive concept of the subject of civil law (natural law being the only case in which subjection to a law and agency coincided completely).[20] The monarchical tendency of the School of Salamanca confirmed this development even further. The king and his law were responsible for the moral and religious regulation of the citizens; in his capacity as a citizen, man accepted the prudence of the legislator rather than exercising his own.

However, the citizen as active participant in the government of the city had been put firmly back on the sixteenth-century conceptual map through the revival and flourishing of the language of what is still commonly termed 'civic humanism', however contested that idea might be.[21] I take this to be an idiom in which the glory of the city is associated primarily with virtue and with liberty. Virtue is the quality which transforms man from wildness or brutishness to moral humanity, and liberty is articulated not in terms of rights but in terms of autonomy or self-government: the state of not being the slave of another man or subject to a personal superior, which is both the condition of virtue and its natural corollary.[22] Although the key terms of this civic idiom are Latin, the Aristotelian inheritance is critical in filling out the idea of a kind of rule distinct from all other forms, in which the ruler does not rule because of some personal superiority in terms of position or natural virtue, but as part of a community to which the subject of rule belongs equally: this being *political rule* (and indeed, the term *politicum* or *politico* is very much a part of this vocabulary).[23] Famously, Ptolemy of Lucca's continuation of Aquinas's *De regno* distinguished between monarchical and political rule on the grounds that regal lordship imports servitude whereas political government involves not servitude but only subjection to the wise.[24]

In this idiom, the common good was held to be paramount and sovereign over the good of the individual, just as the individual citizen was subordinated to the city, its magistrates, and its law. The sovereignty of the common good did

---

[20] Cf. Aquinas 1966, p. 45 (q. 92, a. 1): 'it is enough for the good of the community if others are so far virtuous that they obey the commands of the ruling authorities. That is why Aristotle remarks that the virtue of a good ruler is the same as that of a good man, but that the virtue of the good citizen and of the good man are not quite the same.'

[21] See Hankins 2000 for a recent survey of the state of the question.

[22] See Skinner 1998, pp. 36–57 and 59–77.

[23] Aristotle, *Politics* I, 7: 'the rule of a statesman [*politikos*] is over free and equal persons'; cf. *Nicomachean Ethics* V, 6: 'political justice . . . is defined by law, and is found in communities where law is naturally accepted: those whose members share equally in ruling and being ruled'.

[24] Blythe 1997, pp. 124–7 (Book, 2 ch. 9). Ptolemy argued that the latter was the form that would have obtained in the state of innocence before the corruption and servitude of sin, i.e. that political rule is preferable as more suited to human nature and to men of virtue. The Augustinian framing of this claim, however, denied any possibility of an appeal to nature from a state of non-political, for example royal, rule.

not, however, detract from individual liberty but in fact enabled and guaranteed it; for subjection to the commonwealth and the common good was the only form of subjection which was not a case of domination or tyranny. The explicitly republican version of this argument held that any form of monarchy was therefore in principle illegitimate. It is important to remark, however, that this idiom was not in fact confined to 'republicanism' in this narrow sense: various versions of 'mixed constitution' theory, in which the law of the commonwealth allows some monarchical element, could also subscribe to this notion of common rather than personal subordination.[25] During the sixteenth century, this 'neo-Roman' figure of the citizen was filled out with that of the Ciceronian orator to form the humanist ideal of the *vir civilis*,[26] a construct which transcended the Italian context to form part of courtly culture throughout Europe. Whether in his republican guise as a member of a self-governing city-state, or in his adapted monarchical form as the trusty counsellor, this vocal humanist hero was the civic *actor*, the counterpart of the natural moral *agent* at the heart of Thomist rights theory.

As with all models indebted to classical political theory, the city within a broadly civic humanist discourse represented and assured virtue – the *perfection* of human nature. It differed from scholastic theory, however, in that its conception of original nature was neither strong nor favourable enough to constitute an extra-civic moral norm against which the city might be judged. The city therefore did not have to refer to *original* human nature for its legitimacy. Machiavelli's *Discorsi* represented the extreme of this understanding, in which the transformative effect of the city is so great as to allow no extra-civic appeal either to nature or to God. Machiavelli emphasised the indifferent stuff of humanity outside good laws, which enabled him to refer the moral virtues and religion entirely to the institutions of the city (hounding the current practice and theology of the Christian religion as inimical to them).[27] But this extreme was very rarely touched upon, let alone explored. Almost all the humanists retained a commitment to natural morality and the theological virtues as part of the city and the virtue of the citizen. The natural moral agent and the civic actor were thus continuous, and an easy rapprochement might therefore seem to have been available between active citizen and moral rights-holder. In fact we find something rather different.

In a development parallel with that within rights discourse, the concept of the active citizen came under increasing pressure towards the end of the sixteenth century and the first half of the seventeenth. Again, a big stimulus to this development was the experience of civil war in France and the Netherlands.

---

[25] As argued in Skinner 1998, pp. 54–7.   [26] Cf. Skinner 1996, pp. 66–74.
[27] Machiavelli 1996, e.g. at p. 15 (I. 3) and pp. 34–49 (I. 11).

Michel de Montaigne, followed by Justus Lipsius and Pierre Charron, formulated a personal ethic of the integrity of the self even if the political world was disintegrating.[28] Sharing the new natural law's perception that most men are motivated not by virtue but by self-interest, Lipsius especially questioned civic *pietas* and love of country as a false or (at best) secondary affection.[29] Theirs was not necessarily an ethic of withdrawal – it was compatible with an ethic of public service[30] – but even in this more political mode, it was not of active, participatory citizenship in the humanist sense, nor did the citizen possess the moral value of autonomy in his aspect as such. Francis Bacon made this distinction clear in *The Advancement of Learning* (1605), when he argued that although it might seem that public duties (*officia*, the subject of Cicero's *De officiis*) belong to the sphere of politics or government, they in fact belong to the private ethical realm of self-government.[31]

Part of the reason for this change was the pressure on the notion of the city itself as a unit of government, that is, the free, sovereign city of the classical tradition which the humanists, again both in their republican and monarchical guises, had tried to revive. This is the story of the development of the *state*, of course, as told by Martin van Gelderen in chapter 6. I advert to it only from the perspective of its impact on the classical notion of citizenship. Where the city or *civitas* had itself been the *res publica* or common wealth, we begin to find the city either distinguished from the commonwealth, most strikingly in Henning Arnisaeus's *De republica*, or both commonwealth and city refigured. The new conception was of an order of government, of command and subjection, held together by *summum imperium* or sovereign power. Hobbes's work *On the Citizen* is once again emblematic here – a conscious refashioning of the city and of the citizen as the subject of civil law, and the polemical excision of any remnants of the republican language of the liberty of citizens.

Before we pause at the middle of the century I want to mention one final aspect of this alteration in the understanding of city and citizenship. This is the worry evidenced by contemporaries about subjection as a *feminine* relationship, succinctly summed up by Miguel de Palacios, that ambiguous Spanish theologian, who tells us that 'the law is as the man, and the citizens as the

---

[28] Cf. Lipsius 1595, p. 79 (I, 4): 'Constancie is a right and immoveable strength of the minde, neither lifted up, nor pressed downe with externall and casuall accidents.'

[29] Lipsius 1595, p. 89 (I, 8): 'Some crie out, These civill warres torment us, the blood of innocents spilt, the losse of lawes and libertie. Is it so? I see your sorrow indeed, but the cause I must search out more narrowly. Is it for the commonwealth's sake? O player, put off thy vizard: thy selfe are the cause thereof.'

[30] As suggested in McCrea 1997, for example at p. xxii and 19.

[31] Bacon 1973, p. 163 (II, xxi, 6): 'that good of man which respecteth and beholdeth society, which we may term Duty . . . This part may seem at first to pertain to science civil and politic: but not if it be well observed; for it concerneth the regiment and government of every man over himself, and not over others.'

woman'.[32] Perhaps more tellingly, Michael Piccart, commenting on Aristotle's *Politics*, posited the whole realm of politics – the sphere in which we are driven to associate with each other in order to alleviate our neediness – as the realm of the feminine side of man.[33] Whereas previously, therefore, the city had transcended the local order of the household, the place of need and of women, and had been inscribed in the cosmic order, the place of virtue and of man: in both commentary on the *Politics*, and in natural law theory in the seventeenth century, we see the city refigured as a *local* order, created out of the universal society of humanity, for the sake of bodily need and want.

IV

By the middle of the century, then, both citizens and rights were being challenged and reworked to the apparent exclusion of any effective notion of what we might recognise as citizens' rights. And yet a combination of arguments served to rescue the citizen and citizens' rights on the one hand from being mere parasites upon natural men with their natural rights or children of God with their religious rights, and on the other from being elided entirely in the state's order of command and obedience.

The new element of crucial importance to the framing of the debate over the rights of citizens within the city was the argument from *history*. During the later sixteenth century and throughout the seventeenth – especially in the context of the English parliamentarian cause – attacks on the current civic state were framed not simply as contravening the natural order or God's will, but as overturning the ancient order of the city itself in which natural rights and religion had been safeguarded. Appeal could be made, that is, not just to nature or to God but to the idea of the true commonwealth – a natural, or at least more natural, less artificial or corrupted state: Francogallia, Batavia, the Ancient Constitution.[34] Historical scholarship and legal scholarship – so closely intertwined in this period – unearthed the remnants of this pristine city in the charters, local laws, inscriptions, and archaisms of language which survived to that day, creating (in the guise of recovering) a civic past of citizens' rights.

---

[32] Palacios 1577, fol. 423: *Sunt enim leges tanquam vir, et cives tanquam foemina.* The possible conflict between virility and citizenship was discussed in some sixteenth-century commentaries on Aristotle: see Maclean 1980, 50.

[33] Piccart 1615, *Preface*: 'That great searcher-out of the most hidden mysteries, Plato . . . says that God in the beginning made man an Androgyne . . . this Androgyne was a compound of mind, as the male, and body, as the female: but because he gave all his concern to the mind alone . . . therefore something was exacted from Man, so that he should remember that he was compounded of body as well.'

[34] See François Hotman, *Francogallia* (1573); for the Dutch appeal to ancient Batavia in justification of revolt against the Spanish and the new Dutch republic, see Grotius, *De antiquitate Reipublicae Batavicae* (1610). For the English argument from the Ancient Constitution, the seminal study is Pocock 1957; by way of recent introduction see Weston 1991, pp. 374–411.

The result was a powerful grafting of an older medieval legal language of the franchises, liberties, and privileges of Englishmen, Frenchmen, or Dutchmen onto the newer moral language of natural rights. Although civil rights therefore took on a defensive aspect much like natural rights, they differed importantly in being a protection not against the city *per se*, but against *present* civil corruption. Giving the city a history meant that there could be a critical perspective on the current civic order which did not come directly from nature or from God. The 'zone of non-coincidence', that is, could be located within the city itself.

This historical, civic bent allowed a rapprochement between natural rights theory and republicanism of the broader, constitutional type. It allowed republicanism to use the argument from nature: it allowed citizens' rights to be vindicated against the state rather than just against each other. But in blurring the distinction between natural rights and civil rights, it equally blurred the figure of the citizen. While the classical understanding had seen him as necessarily integrated in a community of virtue which made him something more than he would naturally have been, the new citizen threatened to become simply the natural man, contingently associated with others in a constitutional arrangement which protected his natural rights. Theorists of this 'naturalised republicanism' thus found themselves once more open to challenge from a Hobbesian perspective.[35]

Written towards the end of the seventeenth century, John Locke's *Second Treatise of Government* exemplified these strengths and weaknesses. The *Treatise* was, from a natural rights point of view, deeply conservative in its reversion to an essentialist notion of extra-civic humanity with rights founded on the possession of reason. This enabled Locke, in very scholastic fashion, to put a natural limit on what kinds of political arrangement were legitimate, so that rights took on the same 'defensive' aspect as they did in sixteenth-century resistance theory. But while this is so, we may nevertheless note several features of Locke's work which make his ultimate political message worlds away from the scholastics and their radical heirs. The first is that natural law functions for Locke as a moral constraint in a purely negative way. It dictates when wrong is done and it provides the means for avenging wrong. But it does not include any prescription of a moral life together with others in society, nor any prescriptions concerning religion (except belief, of some sort, in God). In parallel, Locke's political theory shares with that of Grotius and Hobbes – and is indeed even more explicit in – the 'exclusive' notion of rights and the use of the commercial language of the private company to describe the state; it shares, too, the neutralisation of the extra-civic claim of religion, this time through the demand for toleration. Locke allows for society prior to and distinct from government, and he also deploys the republican language of liberty as a key element in his attack on arbitrary government or tyranny. But this society of citizens or commonwealth

[35] Cf. Skinner 1998, pp. 77–99.

amounts to little more than the common protection of individual private rights.

Hence, although the course of the seventeenth century had found a way to fuse a republican commitment to the commonwealth with the language of natural rights, that fusion was in no sense a resolution of the paradox with which we began. Although the commonwealth, the society of citizens, is indeed seen as a common civic space which could defend itself against the abuses of its government, nevertheless the citizenship of individuals – their *belonging* – is in a city the main purpose of which is to allow them mutually to *exclude* each other from their individual lives and space. Insofar as we are still heirs to this dilemma, the discouraging lesson seems to be that we may need to do yet more thinking, both about the nature of rights and about the nature of citizens. The encouraging lesson for this volume is that to try to think about these two ideas together, the consciousness of a shared civic history is an inescapable necessity.

BIBLIOGRAPHY

Aquinas, Thomas (1966). *Summa theologiae*, vol. XXVIII (1a2ae 90–7), ed. and tr. T. Gilby O.P., London: Blackfriars.
Aristotle (1976). *The Nicomachean Ethics*, London: Penguin Classics.
    (1981). *The Politics*, London: Penguin Classics.
Bacon, Francis (1973) [1605]. *The Advancement of Learning*, London: Everyman.
Blythe, J. M. (1997). *Ptolemy of Lucca. On the Government of Rulers, with Portions attributed to Thomas Aquinas*, Philadelphia, Pa.: University of Pennsylvania Press.
Brett, A. S. (1997). *Liberty, Right and Nature. Individual Rights in Later Scholastic Thought*, Cambridge: Cambridge University Press.
Grotius, Hugo (1950). *De iure praedae commentarius*, vol. II. Collotype reproduction of the original MS, Oxford: Clarendon Press.
Hankins, J. ed. (2000). *Renaissance Civic Humanism*, Cambridge: Cambridge University Press.
Hobbes, Thomas (1996) [1651]. *Leviathan*, ed. R. Tuck, Cambridge: Cambridge University Press.
Hohfeld, W. (1920). *Fundamental Legal Conceptions*, New Haven, N.J.: Yale University Press.
Lipsius, Justus (1939) [1595]. *Of Constancie*, trans. J. Stradling, ed. R. Kirk, New Brunswick, N.J.: Rutgers University Press.
Machiavelli, Niccolò (1996). *Discourses on Livy*, tr. H. C. Mansfield and N. Tarcov, Chicago and London: University of Chicago Press.
Maclean, I. (1980). *The Renaissance Notion of Women*, Cambridge: Cambridge University Press.
McCrea, A. (1997). *Constant Minds: Political Virtue and the Lipsian Paradigm in England, 1584–1650*, Toronto: University of Toronto Press.
Ockham, William of (1992). *A Letter to the Friars Minor and other Writings*, ed. and tr. A. S. McGrade and J. Kilcullen, Cambridge: Cambridge University Press.
    (1995). *A Short Discourse on Tyrannical Government*, ed. and tr. A. S. McGrade and J. Kilcullen, Cambridge: Cambridge University Press.

Palacios, Miguel de (1577). *In tertium librum Sententiarum*, Salamanca.

Piccart, Michael (1615). *In politicos libros Aristotelis Commentarius*, Leipzig.

Pocock, J. G. A. (1957). *The Ancient Constitution and the Feudal Law*, Cambridge: Cambridge University Press.

Primus, R. (1999). *The American Language of Rights*, Cambridge: Cambridge University Press.

Skinner, Q. R. D. (1996). *Reason and Rhetoric in the Philosophy of Hobbes*, Cambridge: Cambridge University Press.

(1998). *Liberty before Liberalism*, Cambridge: Cambridge University Press.

Soto, Domingo de (1967–8). *De iustitia et iure libri decem*, facs. edn in 5 vols., Madrid: CSIC.

Tierney, B. (1997). *The Idea of Natural Rights. Studies on Natural Rights, Natural Law and Church Law, 1150–1625*, Atlanta, Ga.: Scholars Press.

Vázquez, Fernando (1572). *Illustrious Controversies*, Frankfurt am Main.

Vitoria, Francisco de (1992). *Political Writings*, ed. and trans. J. Lawrance and A. Pagden, Cambridge: Cambridge University Press.

Weston, C. C. (1991). 'England: Ancient Constitution and Common Law' in J. H. Burns and M. Goldie (eds.), *The Cambridge History of Political Thought, 1450–1700*, Cambridge: Cambridge University Press. pp. 374–411.

PART FOUR

Citizens, states, and modernity

8   Enlightenment's differences, today's identities

Judith A. Vega

> *To bestow on communities some degree of political freedom, it is perhaps sufficient, that their members, either singly, or as they are involved with their several orders, should insist on their rights.*   Adam Ferguson, 1767

The question of the relationship between the nation-state and the phenomenon of globalisation is usually presented as pre-eminently of topical interest. Where once the nation-state dealt with equality, universal rights, and the erection of a solid civil community, now a world order deals with difference, the call for particular rights, and a fragmented civil society. Current debates on justice centre on tensions between political equality and cultural difference that have ensued from global interactions and interdependencies. Globalisation is cast as the new exemplary situation of citizenship, rights, and publicity, pertaining to a post-modern condition.

The relevant issues are, however, no newcomers to either the political or the cultural scene. In this chapter, I seek to develop a historical perspective on the debates issuing from the confrontation between state and world by discussing their initial context in the Enlightenment. The structuring principle of modernity may be said to have been precisely the relationship between the state and the world – the world as it was opened and represented to Europe, and seeped into Europe's very discussions of equality, difference, and rights. In the eighteenth century, the notions of equal citizenship and human rights were already confronted with several issues of social identity that arose in and from the state's situatedness within and dependence on global exploration and exploitation. The Enlightenment's quest for rights incurred issues of how to discount difference in the civil societies of Europe's nation-states. In the course of their political translation equal natural rights were processed into claims made by different members, different groups of members, of society. On the directly political plane, the existence of colonies loomed above the pursuing of civil rights and made the issue of a 'white democracy' a matter of debate; the demand for women's rights was articulated either through or against idioms inserting it in a scene of globalised political and social concerns. On a more general discursive plane, various new boundaries between politics and culture were drawn which were, so to speak, to split off political and cultural dimensions of social identities.

My argument will deviate from a received feminist idea about the history of women's rights from the French Revolution onwards. I would venture that the idea that the struggle for women's rights centred on pushing for formal equal political rights with men needs to be qualified. I will concentrate on understanding what sort of rights, and what conception of justice, have been involved in the demand for women's rights. The history of this struggle from the Enlightenment until today reveals that from within the modern struggle for rights a specific conception of justice does show up, one that does not coincide with the standard liberal tenet of formal equal rights for all, under the wing of the state's protection.

Below I will discuss a variety of eighteenth-century writings which feature a strong conceptual complicity between the notions of rights and civil society – which eventually gave way to a narrowed location of both the seat and the implementation of rights in the jurisdictional activity of the state. In many texts anxious for political innovation, the explicit demand for political and civil rights is not even the dominant issue, while the ability to live an active civil life is. This suggests an unheeded angle on rights discourse, one in which to be a subject invested with rights, as a specifically modern entitlement or dignity, is a status which originates not in the state and its legislation, but in civil society, in the capacity to live like a citizen. To these authors, the need for rights comes about through the need for civil society. One needs rights not so much because one is a member of this or that state, but rather because one is a citizen, a member of civil society. Rights do not primarily exist in order to confirm an abstract equality, but in order to counter social and civic exclusions.

In this discourse, civil society is not the realm of consolidation of the nation-state, but the domain of difference, contestation, opposition. By way of an excursion to present-day concerns I would suggest that here we find the genesis of what is nowadays loosely termed identity politics. While that term in present-day debate has come to stand for the assertion of some essential cultural identity, its more fundamental motive may be said to consist in the (inevitable) articulation of a difference – and differential position *vis-à-vis* rights – as the ground on which to assert rights, that is, humanity. The political struggle around rights itself effected, and still effects, next to the language of equality and universal humanity, the language of difference, both ascribed and asserted.

This approach to rights finds an elaborated articulation in the work of Adam Ferguson (1723–1816). His *Essay on the History of Civil Society* (1995 [1767]) exemplifies a conceptualisation of civil society as an associational as well as discordant sphere of society. Here justice is to be secured over and against the belligerent tendencies of national animosity, the violence of international commerce, and the 'barbarian' dimensions of the personalities housed by the nation. Ferguson in fact reasoned from the global situation to develop his normative ideas of civil society. He regarded civil society as a necessary device in a world largely defined by opposition, where states exist and act in an international environment – defined by war as well as commerce. This national rivalry forms civil society's context and rationale (1995, p. 24). An interesting upshot of Ferguson's argument is that civil society becomes the counterbid to, or the conscience of, the nation. The nation may be steered by considerations of war or the interests of trade, and 'we would have nations, like a company of merchants, think of nothing but the increase of their stock; assemble to deliberate on profit and loss' (p. 145). Civil society is bound up with notions of public spirit and vigilance in observing and substantiating statutes and recorded rights – whether on a national or international level. 'Political rights, when neglected, are always invaded' (p. 213), he states.

It is not in mere laws, after all, that we are to look for the securities to justice, but in the powers by which those laws have been obtained . . . Statutes serve to record the rights of a people, . . . but without the vigour to maintain what is acknowledged as a right, the mere record . . . is of little avail. (Ferguson 1995 [1767], p. 166)

The foundation of justice is to be found in the egalitarian principles of honour of the savages, 'which save the individual from servility in his own person, or from becoming an engine of oppression in the hands of another' (p. 71), and give them an aversion of being 'obliged to bear with any imposition, or unequal treatment' (p. 88). Ferguson contrasts this savage attitude to honour with the barbarian warrior attitude.

Barbarian societies are to be found all over the world and throughout history. Ferguson's discussion of the ancient republics of Italy and Greece addresses their faulty, bellicose forms of public deliberation at home and their wars abroad as manifestations of their barbarity. Certain aspects of their citizens' zest for civic virtue, their active spirit, and contempt for mere 'moderation' merit praise, but otherwise the ancient republics offer no example for a modern public sphere. 'Quarelling had no rules but the immediate dictates of passion' (p. 198). Moreover, they do not offer any possibility for identification to those not inclined to belong to the rude, loud, pushy horde one encountered in Greek public places. One 'could not understand how scholars, fine gentlemen, and even women, should combine to admire a people, who so little resemble themselves' (p. 197). Neither do they offer an example for international conduct, as in their wars they did not respect the 'rules of humanity' and neither knew 'respect and consideration for individuals': 'they endeavoured to wound the state by destroying its members', and 'they granted quarter only to inslave' (p. 193).

Ferguson's indictment of nations where the military aspect has superseded the civil, and possible internal affection and closeness is matched with a barbarian attitude towards others, is occasionally framed in a censure of their masculine exclusiveness or domination, and a certain defence or apologia of 'effeminacy'.

They may be indifferent to interest, and superior to danger; but our sense of humanity, our regard to the rights of nations, our admiration of civil wisdom and justice, even our effeminacy itself, make us turn away with contempt, or with horror, from a scene which exhibits so few of our good qualities. (Ferguson 1995 [1767], p. 155)

While never touching upon political and civil rights for women, Ferguson instead focuses on the civic composition, culture, and symbolics which exclude them, and deprive them of their honour. He castigates barbarian communities both for their military priorities and their possessive individuals. In contradistinction to savage societies that exemplify, even with respect to women, an egalitarian habitus, the economic exploitation and civic exclusion of women pertain to barbarian societies.[1] These mark women's downfall resulting from the rise of private property and women's semi-rule and semi-property within the domestic sphere. In Ferguson's discussion, the 'other' of civil society, the barbarity that precludes civil society, is masculinity, not femininity.

The epigraph to this chapter succinctly states how Ferguson has civil society frame political society instead of the other way around. Recorded rights are to be backed and substantiated by an active civil society; they are distillates from a pluralistic and agonistic field where an equal right to rights exists of persons who either singly or as members of different 'orders' may, or rather should, press for 'their' rights. Civil society is unlike the nation as it handles difference differently, rescuing it from the warrior's fanaticism; it must be at fault when consisting of a single identity. Civil society must meet the disturbances caused by a hermetic collective identity of the nation: its 'we' only comes about by the identification with justice. Its rationale is counteracting corruption and tyranny, in the grand meaning of the blunt (statist) manifestation of oppression and cruelty, and also in the sense of 'casual subordination'. The latter occurs in every society, 'independent of its formal establishment, and frequently adverse to its constitution', 'possibly arising from the distribution of property, or from some other circumstance that bestows unequal degrees of influence' (p. 133). The detrimental essence of all despotism lies in its suppression of the civil and political virtues, requiring its subjects to act from motives of fear (p. 275). Ferguson deplores the common bias towards a national policy that seldom considers moral effects or seeks 'merely to cultivate the talents of men, and to inspire the sentiments of a liberal mind' (p. 137) as a goal in its own right.

With Ferguson, women's faulty citizenship is related to the problematic identity of a vested civic culture which cannot represent them, and attributed to types of societal and economic organisation which do not further women's civil freedom. Interestingly, women's citizenship is addressed neither in terms of an

---

[1] In the course of the century, views of savages and barbarians arose that eventually reversed the relation, and savage societies became associated with the oppression of women. See Thompson 1987; Rendall 1999.

equality which demands relinquishing difference for sameness, nor in terms of an exteriorised difference.[2]

The concerns of Ferguson's civil society transgress the borders of the state. The observance of justice concerns your own rights, and equally those of others – fellow-citizens and aliens. To Ferguson, rights do not brace possessive individuals, but are the means by which to assert individual or collective claims to civic existence in a not already circumscribed meaning – at least not one identifying it with either property, nationality, or received masculine civic practices. They are instruments for fighting civic and social exclusion.

Ferguson's line of argument illustrates an intuition to be found in many subsequent eighteenth-century texts: women's lack of civic recognition is not presented as a problem to be solved through the mere repair of an exclusion from direct legal equality, but as one to which formal inequality and cultural and economic dominance both contributed. Authors addressing women's citizenship based their demands on two tenets: first, they all presuppose women's equal natural rights, and second, they employ the idiom of women's slavery practically throughout the ages and all over the world. Demands for equal rights were being accompanied by denunciations of the nation that was unjust and barbaric for its proper practice of representation, not just because of the legal inconsistency of not admitting half of its members, but because male tyranny in all areas of social life was being condoned and furthered. Women's political and civil rights as such did become the subject of political struggle, but the most observable focus of concern lay with the actual possibilities for realising women's civic life. Mary Wollstonecraft's famous *Vindication of the Rights of Woman* (1792) was at least in part a response to the new French constitution which excluded women from political rights, if her introductory letter to Talleyrand truly discloses her initial motive. However, as Virginia Sapiro has pointed out, Wollstonecraft hardly discussed women's rights as such, and mainly discussed mind and virtue, duties and social practice, and education in a broad sense. Sapiro's judgement that it is a mistake to believe 'that her writing on women revolved primarily around rights, especially in a strict juridical sense' (1992, p. 118) might pass as an observation about many contemporary discussions of women's citizenship.

The 1790s saw several texts published that touched on the issue of women's rights. These were pressed under the heading of equal human rights, that is, rights to the same political and civil access as men. In the process, occasionally specific women's rights were formulated – under the same heading. The most conspicuous aspect of the demands may be the idiom of slavery and despotism

---

[2] Compare his light-hearted illustration of his admonishment to seek active pursuits: 'The men of this country, says one lady, should learn to sew and to knit; it would hinder their time from being a burden to themselves, and to other people' (p. 43).

in which they were cast. The rhetoric that seconded the pressing for rights of women made the social and domestic 'slavery' of women a prime motive for addressing their want of citizenship. A notable feature of these texts, implicated in the above, is that, far from claiming 'sameness' (as is often presupposed in post-modern critique of 'Enlightenment feminism'), gender identity was hardly neglected or downplayed. I will consider some of the more well-known texts of the eighteenth century that address women's citizenship.

Only two authors treat the subject of the political rights of women at any length: Condorcet and a Dutch author known only as 'P.B.v.W.'. The latter, in 1795, calling for an end to women's slavery and men's tyranny, explicitly demands equality in marriage law, the right to vote for women, and access to public offices in his 22-page pamphlet 'In Defense of the Participation of Women in the Government of the Country' (Vega 1996). Condorcet is in 1788 and 1790 the first author to both systematically discuss and raise the demand for political rights for women, that is, their equal rights to vote and be represented. He argues for political rights for women to be granted on the same grounds as for men. The refusal of rights of citizenship for women he explicitly calls an act of 'tyranny', and its legitimations similar to the pretexts of aristocracy. It is not true that women are not governed by reason, as 'they are governed by their own reason', while the 'more correct' observation that women obey feelings rather than their conscience concerns a difference caused by 'education and social existence', and women's dependence on their husbands is a 'tyranny imposed by civil law'. His celebrated plea for political equality, claiming that the social differences between men and women should have no repercussions on the level of political and civil rights, did not, however, judge such differences as politically innocuous. If Condorcet's wish for a representative political system in general was partly directed by a fear of the disorderly insurrections of the Parisian crowd that he shared with many contemporaries, his wish for representation of women is directed by a similar fear, one equally common: the worn cliché of the dangers of women's informal political power. The vote for women would through public control redress the influence of their power in secrecy. His statement that 'inequality necessarily introduces corruption' regarded the oppressors as much as the suppressed – it leans towards disallowing a political discounting of gender difference in society.

In her 1791 pamphlet on the rights of women, Olympe de Gouges defended general civil rights for women – to be representatives in the Assemblée Nationale, to have admission to all public offices and honours – but not explicitly the right to vote. De Gouges writes to her Queen that women have *lost* rights in society, by which she could mean either the loss of their natural rights, or rights lost during the revolution. She speaks of the 'eternal tyranny of men' that has opposed exercising women's natural rights to liberty, property, and resistance to oppression, while male and female citizens are equal for the law.

She copies the formula of the existing *Déclaration des droits de l'homme et du citoyen* in her title *Déclaration des droits de la femme et de la citoyenne*. Are, then, the rights of men and women simply identical, or does a difference between men, and between citizens, exist? It transpires that, in order for men and women to be equal before the law, an eye to specific interests of women is requisite. She mentions that speaking out about the fatherhood of a child belongs to women's freedom of thought and opinion, and expresses a wish for laws to protect widows and girls who have been duped by false promises by men they were attached to. Thus, human rights are held to admit and sustain specific social interests of women.

Denunciations of women's slavery, male tyranny, and barbaric husbands abound in the *cahiers de doléances*, and some of them address the topic of the rights of women. In 1789 Madame B–B– took the discussion on the liberation of Negro slaves as a starting-point for demanding the admission of women to the *états-généraux*, and granting women who have any form of property their rights to vote. Furthermore, as men cannot represent women, women are to be represented by women. The French constitution will have to generate new laws that are genuinely uniform, and then Europe will look on France as the new Greece. The demand for women representatives in the Assemblée Nationale as well as in the districts and the *communes* is repeated the same year by Madame de M. de la M. Women are equal to men with respect to rights (and to pleasures) and the author has conceived a women's journal for which women are invited to subscribe and to submit articles against unjust men. Some other *cahiers de doléances* were by women asking for protective measures with regard to their occupations, such as florists and laundresses. In her preface to the republished *Cahiers*, Rebérioux writes that, in 1789, the class differences between women activists appear to have been less significant than the similarity in their desire to be recognised as citizens. But after 1792, to women *sans-culottes*, while still perceiving themselves to be citizens without the vote, for defending their rights it hardly appears essential to elect representatives. The idea of direct democracy in the sections seems to exert considerable attraction, and they define their citizenship through their presence in the streets.[3]

Between 1790 and 1795 the Dutch activist in Paris, Etta Palm-Aelders, read or/and published several texts in which rights of women were part of her demands.[4] Her text from December 1790 does state that 'justice demands that the laws have to be common to all human beings like the air and the sun', but is generally a denunciation of women's slave-like existence and a defence of women's equal capacities, and does not enter into the specific rights which should be granted. In June 1791 she read an address to the Assemblée Nationale on behalf of the women citizens of France. Again she claims the equality of

---

[3] See Godineau 1988; Applewhite and Levy 1990; Hufton 1992.   [4] Vega 1989; Kates 1990.

all natural rights for all individuals, without distinction with respect to sex, but stipulates only equal rights to divorce and to education. Only in April 1792 when she addressed the Assemblée Législative did she specify the rights of women that she demanded: equal education for girls; majority for women at the age of twenty-one; equal political liberty and rights for both sexes; the right to divorce. The demand for specific representation, that is, for female representatives for women, is with Palm-Aelders matched by arguing the need for women-only associations. Apart from establishing, and guaranteeing, a specific civic presence of women, these associations were also motivated by the argument that the presence of men may interfere with women's ability to speak.[5]

To recapitulate, women's citizenship in a general sense was a vital topic in all texts on the position of women. But while women's natural rights were clearly presupposed, and time and again insisted upon in almost ritual rhetorical preambles, specific demands for women's political and civil rights followed only occasionally. The insistence on women's participation in social and civic life was frequently accompanied by an awareness of women's asymmetrical functioning within the practices of citizenship. The problem of representation was felt to be acute, not primarily on the level of the state, but on the level of civil society – which encompassed the public, economic, and domestic or marital sphere. Rights were rights to equal participation in all these respects, and the desire to be politically represented or to vote was not as urgent as the mere need to be able to follow the life of an equal citizen.

This does indicate another dimension to the received story of the struggle between two camps for and against women's equality with men, between an anti-feminist Enlightenment failing to extend liberal individualism to women and a few defenders of women's rights. The idea of women's political rights certainly met with forceful resistance, eventually issuing in the explicit exclusion of women from legal equality in the Jacobin constitution of 1793. And rights discourse did, with respect to women, have to compete with Rousseauist separatist notions of female citizenship. A quite other matter, however, is that within the discourse unambiguously favouring women's equal citizenship the demand for the enactment of political rights simply did not figure prominently. One may remark that somehow, the idiom of recorded equal rights must have seemed not as useful, expedient, or attractive as one might have supposed. Secondly, and contrary to received opinion on Enlightenment politics, writings on women's citizenship can be seen to represent a species of political language that testifies to a desire for citizenship hardly identical to a desire for equality. The authors' exertions include recognition of specific occupational issues, unequal

---

[5] Letters on women's associations, to the Dutch paper *Oprechte Nationaale Courant*, 18 April and 6 May 1795, the latter by an author who signs as 'Friend of the truth', and might be Etta Palm-Aelders. I thank Rudolf Dekker for drawing my attention to this.

communicative power, specific interests in view of men's lack of integrity in relationships with women, and wife-beating which made divorce law a women's issue. Onto equal natural rights were engrafted issues that nowadays would fall under the rubric of a gender-sensitive citizenship.

The Enlightenment's humanistic language of progress and equality was sustained by, and mainly expressed in, the two rival vocabularies of slavery and sociability. The trope of slavery was in the eighteenth century applied for various kinds of social critique: the critique of aristocracy, of the market, of male dominance, of absolute power. The concept of sociability stemmed predominantly from the Scottish philosophical quest to civilise and pacify the world through a new morality, one that fitted globalising commerce, and would be the opposite of politics. Both vocabularies made rights idiom incumbent on historical anthropology, albeit in different ways.

The main rhetorical sources for gaining women's citizenship were the thesis of the natural rights of all human beings, and the argument of the inadmissibility of slavery. Whereas the idiom of rights came from systematical political theory, the issue of women's slavery was linked in several ways to the Enlightenment endeavour to situate Europe in a global environment. It could bring off various rhetorical analogies, for example, with citizenship definitions of Ancient Greece (in either positive or negative connotations), or general political practices of barbarity. It was also embedded in the reality of the nation's colonial politics.

It is striking that the conviction of the social oppression of women throughout all ages and cultures was so commonly accepted by progressive eighteenth-century authors addressing the position of women. Laclos and Condorcet are merely two exponents of this position; one more is Sade, whose work may be read as a venomous description of women's social inequality (Vega 2000). Where Ferguson saw a golden age for women with the egalitarian-minded savages before individual property announced their downfall, Condorcet finds women's oppression 'among all primitive peoples', and Laclos is adamant about women's unhappy situation among most peoples. Slavery, barbarity, and tyranny were still characteristics to be attributed to European society. The Ancients, the East, and the West were equally culpable. The likening of women to slaves was a connotation of a political nature rather than the predominantly sexualised connotation of women and foreigners in later, nineteenth-century Orientalism, and potentially could excite a programme of emancipation, justice, and rights.

Abolitionist protagonists of a universal interpretation of civil rights united in French, British, and American associations. Between 1789 and 1791 in the Assemblée Nationale proposals were submitted for the abolition of slave-traffic and slavery, and civil rights for free slaves.[6] But the translation of universal natural rights into political and civil rights was a fundamentally contested matter,

---

[6] James 1963; Davis 1975.

even for authors convinced of the injustice of slavery, whether of women or in colonial society. Choderlos de Laclos's most explicit text on women's social position, *Des femmes et de leur éducation* (1979 [1783]), was a philippic against the enslavement of women and male tyranny, but he never developed his account into an argument for their political or civil rights. This indifference towards rights is repeated in 1791 in his position on slavery in the colonies. He thought the legal distinction between whites and coloured in the colonies a 'barbaric prejudice' and pejoratively employed the term *la démocratie blanche* for the party of those who consent to being democrats, or aristocrats, even to remain French, provided they may keep their slaves. However, he opposed granting civil rights to the coloured, for if subsequently the colonies separated from the metropole and the ports rose against the Assemblée Nationale, this would cause inadmissible social unrest and mass unemployment (Laclos 1979, pp. 644–5). To Laclos, citizen's rights and human rights were indeed irreconcilable, as they were to many contemporaries.

The Enlightenment's anthropology served opposite purposes with regard to women's slavery and black slavery. It tended to discredit the first and legitimate the second. The men of the French Revolution would turn the tables, refusing rights to women and granting them to the freed slaves. But anthropological teachings – creatively and haphazardly employed by authors of the popular pamphlets who often referred to alleged positive examples like women in Celtic society or heroines from Antiquity – did not generally deny, and could as likely inspire and assist the case for European women's rights, whereas they were inclined, together with economic expediency, to undermine the case for even the natural rights of black slaves. Black slavery in the colonies was by certain progressive authors, as well as in many *cahiers de doléances*,[7] used to indict Europe's barbaric urges, but historical anthropology served a variety of theories arguing the inferiority of the Blacks. The respective branches of knowledge pertaining to gender and race partly drew on separate bodies of texts, 'histories of women' constituting a proper eighteenth-century genre disjunct from the scientistic racialisms charted by authors like Poliakov (1971) and Todorov (1993). Historical and comparative anthropology provided arguments on women's slavery not to argue their inferiority, but the inferiority of European society up to the present. Or, more precisely, the accounts of women's inferiority hesitated between its either being inherent in gender-identity and gender difference, or explained by the contingencies of time and place. The nation's history could, subsequently, either be seen as ready for implementing women's political equality, if only as marking a stage towards the final homogenisation of women into universal citizenship, or as being excused from admitting them into the nation's new political identity.

[7] See Davis 1975, p. 97.

Applying the trope of slavery to the position of women in Europe had multiple purposes and effects. One problematic effect is nicely revealed by Condorcet's defence of political equality. Slaves are innocent in respect of any experience and practice of power. As soon as women are *not* outright slaves, but command a power that – at least to men – represents secrecy, danger, and even corruption, the only redress for this aberration of both slavery and sameness is forcing the difference into homogeneity and making women equal on the same formal terms as men. Condorcet supposed that granting women equal rights would counteract women's interest in preserving their 'empire', their presumed informal power over men. Equality here is the recipe for eradicating unwanted female practices from cultural and political life. Secondly, while women's global and timeless slavery could issue in a critique directed at European males, it frequently served a felicitous self-image of European nations that set women in opposition to the barbarity of foreigners. Here, historical anthropology furnished Enlightenment Europe with an 'end of history' image. Normative political theory was severed from history and anthropology, which not only meant breaking away from a disgraceful past, but also from an ethnographical stance with respect to one's proper life-world. In the struggle between Barbarism and the Moderns, barbarism was dispatched to the past and exteriorised from the Europe of the Enlightenment at the expense of the self-critical impulse the idiom had provided.

Eventually, women's involvement in the nation's construction would take intricate shapes of an active social and passive civic nature, with women's representation largely reduced to a symbolic (instead of empirical) presence in culture, psyche, and publicity. Barbarism became – the gender in the phrase is literary – other men's past, instead of men's present, and Europe would represent its identity and future in terms of its modernity. Mme B–B— had had an image of Europe as a judge who would pronounce verdicts on its several nations according to the honourable ideas of citizenship of ancient Greece, which, in her interpretation, would secure women's legal rights and proper political representation. This is an actual attempt to found a self-critical European identity on a common European past. But this idea of Europe as judge of its nations' struggle with their barbarity at home would be superseded by the idea of a modern Europe henceforth setting a standard to the world.

Juxtaposed to, and counterweighing, the discourse on women's slavery is the – mainly Scottish – discourse on women's role in and contributions to the history of civilisation.[8] Together, these discourses show that 'woman as other' was a category as central as it was ambivalent in the eighteenth century, and both fabricated an imagery of womanhood which partook in their respective assessments of the nation's relation to the world. If the trope of women's slavery could serve, next to a self-critical impulse, an 'end of history' self-image of

---

[8] Compare Tomaselli 1985; Tronto 1994; Rendall 1999.

Europe, this latter image was only shored up by the Scottish theory of commercial society. Compared to the 'republican' reception of anthropology on women, the Scottish approach to history, itself the supplier of many of the gendered histories of civilisation, achieved a mirror image of women, or femininity, in contemporary Europe. It represented women as the 'other' within the public sphere, either in terms of their standing for humanity, pragmatic truth, and social norms, or of their mere difference with respect to language, emotion, and rationality. Scottish thinkers would offer various accounts of women's relation to the social, varying from the beneficially conservative to the humane and progressive effects of their influence. These depictions served the Scottish need for a smooth social fabric and polite codes of behaviour that could further international commercial relations. Whatever the normative value of these accounts may amount to from a feminist point of view, the Scottish focus on the social instead of the political and civic precluded the step from their gendered social sphere and their cultural angle to gender difference on to juridical proposals. Sociability's idiom set out to depoliticise femininity, firmly locating it in the social, where it was to benefit economic and moral commerce in a globalising environment. Gender difference had become a social and cultural issue remote from politics, and women's right to rights was simply submerged.

If discounting the relations between politics and culture in the administration of rights is today's problem, this resembles the eighteenth century's problem – one that was not to find juridical solution. The idiom of slavery gave rise to claims of both equality and difference, with the aim in both cases of achieving equal civil participation. But both generally neglected pushing for rights. The idiom of sociability neglected rights in developing a domestic variant of culturalism: approval of women's cultural difference with no consequences in the field of political justice. Eventually, both idioms failed to turn their recognition of woman as *homo*, a naturally equal human being in possession of natural rights, into a recognition of woman as *persona*, as a subject entitled to the encoded rights that fit the expression of her proper sovereignty.[9]

Problems of identity and difference nowadays translate into issues of social and political justice, nationally and internationally. In the international juridical discussion of human rights, the outstanding new concerns in designing and issuing rules bear upon 'culture' and 'difference'.[10] Jürgen Habermas (1992, 1998) traces the competing claims of citizenship and nationality, of human rights and particular rights, to the eighteenth-century concept of popular sovereignty. Constitutional patriotism and nationalism are both legacies of that concept. Charles Taylor (1994) sees a specifically modern desire for recognition emerging at the end of the eighteenth century, from which arose the present opposition

---

[9] For the distinction between *homo* and *persona* see Arendt 1963, esp. pp. 106–9.
[10] A choice from the extensive literature: Cornell 1992; Shute and Hurley 1993; Hoskyns 1996; Askin and Koenig 1999, 2000; Dunne and Wheeler 1999; Zoelle 2000.

between the politics of equal citizenship and the politics of difference. These authors have translated the charge on (both liberal and socialist) politics in the name of culture into a problematic of cultural group differences and their circumscribed 'we's'.

However, if either the concept of popular sovereignty or the desire for recognition prompted the twin birth of human rights and particularist rights, the Enlightenment also generated a 'politics of difference' that appears to elude the categories of liberalism and communitarianism. I would claim that to the complications posed by gender and ethnicity to a universally conceived humanity, not the concept of popular sovereignty, but of natural rights is the quintessential Enlightenment concept. It could simultaneously found the idea of a universal humanity, and elicit a range of dissimilar options on civil and social rights. It challenged the concepts of both citizenship and nation, compromising the 'we's' either concept presupposes.

The impetus of the debate on justice initiated in the last decade by feminist social philosophers arose from the need to address not the competition, but rather the intermingling and contamination of politics and culture – or equality and difference, or citizenship and subjectivity. Women and ethnic minorities recognised that their participation was not interfered with by legal exclusion, but by cultural mechanisms. To the problem of equal participation of culturally different citizens, whether with regard to gender, ethnicity, sexuality, or religion, not the elimination or transcendence but the recognition of difference is the crucial challenge.[11] Iris Young (1990) opened the discussion with her proposal to develop an alternative paradigm of justice. The paradigm of distributive justice, intent on furthering equality through distribution of income and social positions, should be complemented by an approach that includes issues of social and cultural dominance. Such an approach presupposes a broader understanding of what counts as politics, and 'politicizing culture' has been an important goal of several social movements:

Politicizing culture, then, means bringing language, gestures, forms of embodiment and comportment, images, interactive conventions, and so on, into explicit reflection . . . making them the subject of public discussion, and explicitly matters of choice and decision. (Young 1990, p. 86)

Nancy Fraser (1997) has attempted to combine the socialist politics of distribution with a 'postsocialist' politics of recognition. Precisely gender and 'race' are bivalent types of collectivity, and will be confronted with a mixture of cultural and economic suppression. While a double strategy of distribution and recognition will be needed, both distribution and recognition may result in either emphasising or blurring group difference. Fraser opts for abandoning group

[11] The point is explicitly addressed in Phillips 1993.

identities in favour of less dichotomous and massive kinds of difference, and thinks the deconstruction of identity the most desirable candidate for a politics of justice that aims at a transformation rather than an affirmation of the social order.

Judith Butler (1997) examines the relationship between politics and language by relating the two simultaneous political achievements of language: agency and subject-constitution. The problem of sexist and racist language as failures of recognition are discussed within a view of subjectivity as being both upheld and potentially destroyed through language. This 'destruction of recognition' has in the context of the American discussion on 'hate-speech' become a juristic topic, and Butler discusses the problematic of individual ownership of speech acts. If responsibility for the injurious effect rests on repetition of meaning which has come about through history and place, and did not originate in the utterance of one specific speaker, the responsibility is of a cultural and social rather than a juridical nature. Butler's variant of the politics of recognition becomes a politics of meaning, one which should be made a general social (or civic) responsibility, in order to fight ascribed identities which repeat and sustain dominance and suppression. Through Butler's approach, the politics of recognition combines with a politics of mis-recognition – identity being a matter of both self-expression and ascription.

The feminist debate, then, can be said to have established a distinctive angle on the politics of difference. Young's politicisation of culture, Fraser's trans-formative deconstructions, and Butler's attention to the linguistic embedding of subjectivity all point to a newly assessed politics of recognition in which not the expression of essential group identities, but the reflective interpretation of identity and difference becomes the vital object. We have arrived at a concept of justice that alerts us to cultural and economic asymmetries, and to the ways that living and perceiving gender and colour are dependent on a symbolically sat-urated linguistic political universe. This concept of justice will hardly revolve around encoded rights – it will draw largely on regulating practices within the social, cultural, and civil dimensions of society.

In the eighteenth-century texts, representation was perceived as a problem of civil society rather than political society. Slavery of women was an issue that referred not primarily to state power, but to women's domination by their fellow-members of civil society. Their emphasis on access instead of recorded rights squares with several elements of present-day feminist concerns. Present-day feminist political theory explicitly addresses the entanglement of politics and culture. Feminist efforts to influence supranational policies make issues of social exclusion a prime motive for formulating 'gender-sensitive' applications of human rights.

In the eighteenth century, the notion of women's social and civil participation was built upon the idea of natural rights. Again, today, it is the *meaning* of human rights for questions of exclusion and translation into encoded civil rights that is contested. This problematic originates in the Enlightenment and forms the *trait d'union* between then and now. The politics of difference, or recognition, or identity, may be seen to originate in the space where the meaning of natural rights for civil existence came to be contested.

BIBLIOGRAPHY

Applewhite, H. B. and Levy, D. G. (eds.) (1990). *Women and Politics in the Age of the Democratic Revolution*, Ann Arbor: University of Michigan Press.
Arendt, H. (1987) [1963]. *On Revolution*, Harmondsworth: Penguin.
Askin, K. D. and Koenig, D. M. eds. (1999, 2000). *Women and International Human Rights Law*, 2 vols., Ardsley: Transnational Publishers.
Butler, J. (1997). *Excitable Speech. A Politics of the Performative*, New York: Routledge.
Cahiers de doléances des femmes en 1789 et autres textes. Paris: Des Femmes, 1989.
Condorcet (1986) [1788]. 'Essay sur la constitution et les fonctions des assemblées provinciales' in Condorcet, *Sur les élections et autres textes*, ed. Keith M. Baker, [Paris]: Fayard.
    (1976) [1790]. 'On the Admission of Women to the Rights of Citizenship' in Condorcet, *Selected Writings*, ed. Olivier de Bernon, Indianapolis: Bobbs-Merrill.
Cornell, D. (1992). 'Gender, Sex, and Equivalent Rights' in J. Butler and J. W. Scott (eds.), *Feminists Theorize The Political*, New York: Routledge.
Davis, D. B. (1975). *The Problem of Slavery in the Age of Revolution 1770–1823*, Ithaca: Cornell University Press.
Dunne, T. and Wheeler, N. J. eds. (1999). *Human Rights in Global Politics*, Cambridge: Cambridge University Press.
Ferguson, A. (1995) [1767]. *An Essay on the History of Civil Society*, New Brunswick and London: Transaction Publishers.
Fraser, N. (1997). *Justice Interruptus. Critical Reflections on the 'Postsocialist' Condition*, New York: Routledge.
Godineau, D. (1988). *Citoyennes Tricoteuses: Les femmes du peuple à Paris pendant la Révolution française*, Aix-en-Provence: Ed. Alinéa.
Habermas, J. (1992). 'Staatsbürgerschaft und nationale Identität', *Faktizität und Geltung*, Frankfurt am Main: Suhrkamp, pp. 632–60.
    (1998). *A Berlin Republic: Writings on Germany*, Cambridge: Polity Press.
Hoskyns, C. (1996). *Integrating Gender. Women, Law and Politics in the European Union*, London: Verso.
Hufton, O. H. (1992). *Women and the Limits of Citizenship in the French Revolution*, Toronto: University of Toronto Press.
James, C. L. R. (1963) [1938]. *The Black Jacobins*, New York: Random House.
Kates, G. (1990). ' "The Powers of Husband and Wife Must Be Equal and Separate": The Cercle Social and the Rights of Women, 1790–91' in Applewhite and Levy (eds.), pp. 163–80.
Laclos, C. de (1979). *Oeuvres Complètes*, [Paris]: Gallimard.
Phillips, A. (1993). *Democracy and Difference*, Cambridge: Polity Press.
Poliakov, L. (1971). *Le mythe aryen*, Paris: Calmann-Levy.

Rendall, J. (1999), 'Clio, Mars and Minerva: The Scottish Enlightenment and the Writing of Women's History' in: T. M. Devine and J. R. Young (eds.), *Eighteenth Century Scotland: New Perspectives*, East Linton: Tuckwell, pp. 134–51.

Sapiro, V. (1992). *A Vindication of Political Virtue. The Political Theory of Mary Wollstonecraft*, Chicago: University of Chicago Press.

Shute, S. and Hurley, S. (eds.) (1993). *On Human Rights. The Oxford Amnesty Lectures*, New York: Basic Books.

Taylor, C. (1994). 'The Politics of Recognition' in Amy Gutman (ed.), *Multicultural-ism. Examining the Politics of Recognition*, Princeton: Princeton University Press, pp. 25–73.

Thompson, A. (1987). *Barbary and Enlightenment. European Attitudes towards the Maghreb in the Eighteenth Century*, Leiden: Brill.

Todorov, T. (1993). *On Human Diversity. Nationalism, Racism, and Exoticism in French Thought*, Cambridge, Mass.: Harvard University Press.

Tomaselli, S. (1985). 'The Enlightenment Debate on Women', *History Workshop* 20, pp. 101–24.

Tronto, J. C. (1994). *Moral Boundaries. A Political Argument for an Ethic of Care*, New York: Routledge.

Vega, J. A. (1989). 'Feminist Republicanism. Etta Palm-Aelders on Justice, Virtue and Men', *History of European Ideas* 10, 3, pp. 333–51.

(1996). 'Feminist Discourses in the Dutch Republic at the End of the Eighteenth Century', *Journal of Women's History* 8, 2, pp. 130–51. Includes P.B.v.W.'s text translated into English.

(2000). 'Sade's libertijnse republiek. Over pornografische parabels en esthetische politiek', *Jaarboek voor Vrouwengeschiedenis* 20, pp. 109–33.

Young, I. M. (1990). *Justice and the Politics of Difference*, Princeton: Princeton University Press.

Zoelle, D. G. (2000). *Globalizing Concern for Women's Human Rights. The Failure of the American Model*, New York: St Martin's Press.

9 Citizen and state under the French Revolution

Lucien Jaume

I

It is well known that citizenship constitutes a key notion in French revolutionary discourse. However, for the historian of political ideas, citizenship does not appear to have been the object of clear and unequivocal interpretation. There were profound divergences between the different groups that successively took power during the revolutionary period, and at each stage citizenship was linked to a different vision of the state, and to new ways of organising the relationship between the people and their representatives. Thus, in the first phase of the Revolution, amongst the moderate members of the Constituent Assembly, 'man' was more important than 'citizen'. Central in the eyes of these members was the need to protect the rights of the *private individual* and his desire for happiness. The citizen appeared as an intermediary between, on the one hand, the man to be protected, and, on the other, the governors, alone capable of judging the general interest.

From this perspective, if we think of the reflections of philosophers like Aristotle (the theory of deliberation, of *euboulia*), or Rousseau (with regard to the public interest), the formal character of the 1789 notion of citizenship is striking. It was however Rousseau who, speaking of France under the *ancien régime*, had written that the French have, of the citizen, 'no real idea, as can be seen from their dictionaries; and in the contrary case, they would fall [when they use the word loosely] into the error of lèse-majesté' (*Du contrat social*, Book I, note to ch. 6). As will be shown below, according to the electoral system put in place within the framework of the 1791 Constitution, it can be said that citizenship rather corresponds – to borrow Hobbes's concept – to a function of 'authorisation'.[1]

In response to this first vision, two other interpretations will be put forward: Condorcet's attempt to liberate the *rational* capacities of the citizen; and the

---

[1] Hobbes 1991, p. 121: 'Every one . . . shall *Authorise* all Actions and Judgements, of that Man, or Assembly of men, in the same manner, as if they were his own, to the end, to live peaceably amongst themselves, and be protected against other men.'

Jacobins' insistence on an ethical content of citizenship, and on the creation of a *virtuous* civic spirit.[2] Three moments of revolutionary thought will therefore be studied (moments at once successive and in conflict from the first years of the Revolution) in order to clarify, in general terms, the long-term legacy of the French Revolution within political thought.

Our own age, which witnesses growing and multiform challenges to the state (until now, the key actor in French political culture) as well as a crisis of the Republican idea, is also an age where the concept of citizenship seems to be changing its content, meaning, and forms of expression. What, therefore, was the link between the citizen and the state in French political culture – a link that appears recently to have been broken?

II

It is important to remember that one of the great aims of the revolutionaries in 1789 was to *free the individual* from all forms of subservience to social interest or origin. This intention is proclaimed with pride and force at the beginning of the Constitution of 1791. The preamble reads:

> There is no more nobility, nor peerage, nor hereditary distinctions, nor distinction of rank, nor feudal regime, nor patrimonial courts . . . ; nor any chivalric orders; . . . there is no more venality, nor principles of heredity in any public office. There is no longer, for any part of the nation or for any individual, any privilege or exception from the common law of all the French. There are no *jurandes*, or professional, or artistic or working corporations, etc.[3]

The Revolution sought to fundamentally detach the individual from allegiances to all forms of social grouping and hierarchy in order to place him under the sole authority of the law; for a horizontal membership of traditional communities, the Revolution substituted a vertical allegiance to the law, which, as stated in the Declaration of the Rights of Man and of the Citizen, was 'the expression of the general will'.

However, there are considerations of conjuncture, and of political strategy, which prevent these texts from being interpreted as works of pure theory. The revolutionaries who wanted to liberate the individual from – as was said at the time – 'Gothic' limits had, in order to realise this aim, to conquer *sovereignty* from the ex-sovereign: the king, Louis XVI. At the same time, the attempt (that would finally fail) was to keep the king as head of state and to reintegrate him by means of a new Constitution. On 17 June 1789, in what was a veritable

---

[2] The conception of citizenship under the Directory (the Constitution of Year III) could be mentioned. However, this will not be elaborated here in order to avoid complicating the presentation.
[3] The Preamble to the Constitution of 3 September 1791. On the general meaning of this text see Jaume 1989b, p. 187.

'speech act', the Common Assembly affirmed its identification with the nation itself,[4] which enabled it at once to claim sovereignty and to maintain that sovereignty belonged to the nation. As the 1791 Constitution would affirm (Title III, article 1): 'Sovereignty is one, indivisible, inalienable and imprescriptible. It belongs to the Nation; no one section of the people, no one individual can claim the right to exercise it.' Because it is 'inalienable', sovereignty remains the possession of the nation, although representatives exercise it in her name. Likewise, however, simple citizens cannot *exercise* sovereignty. This is the task for those whom Sieyès conceived as the new direction, the professional politicians of the future.

In other words, the citizens' *competence* does not consist of deliberating about public affairs, or of participating in the elaboration and control of laws. Their role is solely to choose the men who can legitimately speak for the Nation, and who can speak for it as a Unity, as a Being that expresses itself with one single voice: that is, as a sovereign in face of the king, or ex-sovereign.[5] It is here that the doctrine of representation was born, a doctrine practised in France until 1958, and employed in particular under the Third Republic. This doctrine gives sovereignty to the deputies, and one of its consequences – soon to be combated by revolutionary radicalism – was that the 'general will' was not formed by the confrontation of opinions within society and did not reside within the public space. The task of formulating and defining the public will fell instead on the organs of power, and therefore in first place on the assembly of representatives. It is within this configuration that the relationship between 'man' and 'citizen', as it was interpreted by the moderates of the Constituent Assembly, may be understood.

These constitutional aspects, which were in part doctrinal and in part a strategy for the conquest of power, played a role in the political policy of the Constituents. In the latter's struggle against the *ancien régime* of monarchy and privilege, the aim was to guarantee and satisfy *particular interests* (the private individual), and also to harmonise these interests in so far as it was possible: the guarantee, satisfaction, and harmonisation were to be the result of a well-made constitution and laws.

From this perspective, the individual-citizen was expected to provide neither knowledge, nor political competence, nor devotion to the public interest. As

---

[4] By calling itself the 'National Assembly' (in response to the question 'who are we?'), the deputies of the Third Estate define the place that the citizens must occupy with regard to them ('who are you?'): they become sovereign. See Jaume 1989a, in the conclusion.

[5] It may be said that the king participates in the elaboration of the general will since, through exercising the right of veto, he is a co-legislator. Nonetheless, the weight of the individual voice of the king as representative of the nation is now balanced. For the king has only a relative (not an absolute) right of veto, and cannot dissolve the assembly of deputies. Moreover, as Necker saw (in *De la Révolution française*), public contributions will be adopted *without royal sanction* (ch. III, art. 8 of the Constitution): a significant material and symbolic inferiority!

Sieyès frankly put it in a pamphlet – *Qu'est-ce que le tiers état?* – that preceded the reunion of the Estates General, and that immediately became famous:

> It would be a misjudgement of human nature to link the destiny of societies to virtuous effort. It is necessary that – even at a time of decadent public morality, when egotism appears to govern all souls – it is necessary, I say, that even during these long intervals, the nation's assembly must be so constituted that particular interests remain isolated, and that the will of the plurality is always in conformity with the general good.[6]

According to Sieyès, therefore, the egotism of individuals is not an obstacle so long as the representative assembly is properly 'constituted'. The assembly's task is, through deliberation and decision, to transcend particular interests and at the same time to isolate those interests which may be dangerous. There is danger only in 'group interests' – in other words, in those where groups (the future 'factions' of revolutionary discourse) try to influence the national will. In another text, this time contemporary with the beginning of the Constituent Assembly, Sieyès wrote that: 'The common interest, the improvement of society itself, demands that we make of government a particular profession.'[7] Given the division of labour that reigns in modern societies, and that is the true basis for the rights of man,[8] political judgement must be the result of education and leisure, and therefore requires specialists. With regard to the representatives, they are a 'particular profession', and the electors need to possess – according to another expression of Sieyès – 'interest with capacity'.[9] Hence the two-tier, tax-based electoral system established in 1791, a system that was not far from Sieyès's views.

'Active citizens' participate at the first stage of voting in the primary assemblies – that is, 4.3 million individuals, out of 6 million male adult citizens. These are the veritable electors who, according to the tax criterion, correspond (but in an exaggerated way compared to what Sieyès had demanded) to the idea of 'interest with capacity'. Deliberation begins here, although at this stage it only involves the choice of candidates; and those eligible – theoretically chosen from all active citizens, including citizens within the primary assemblies – will deliberate, as deputies, about the general interest.[10]

---

[6] Sieyès 1789c, p. 86.　　[7] Sieyès 1789b, p. 35.

[8] For Sieyès, the rights of man are the judicial translation and guarantee of the relations of exchange by which man is useful to man: see Sieyès 1789a. Cf. the manuscript where Sieyès expresses the same ideas: 'The rights of man to man come from the same source: necessity; they are only an exchange. They can be reduced to one sole right: to not oblige the other, to leave him free, to determine his will by offering him something he prefers to that which you are asking of him' (reprinted in Fauré 1988, p. 320).

[9] *Reconnaissance et exposition raisonnée des droits de l'homme et du citoyen*, Sieyès 1789a.

[10] In 1789, a relatively low tax rating was envisaged (ten working days, depending on local value), which would give 2,670.000 electors, but a very high tax of eligibility (the famous 'silver mark'), involving 430,000 people. In 1791, in the 'revision of the Constitution', the number of great electors was reduced (to 500,000), and as compensation the tax of eligibility was removed. In fact, the silver mark was moved towards the secondary assemblies. See Gueniffey 1993, pp. 102 and 61.

This system of electors electing great electors excluded 'passive citizens' from the vote. The latter were presumed, because of their poverty (from destitution or seasonal work), to lack both the interest and the capacity necessary to give *confidence* according to solid criteria. Passive citizens were considered as a virtual category of full citizenship, a group of individuals who, through the progress of public instruction and work, would rise in the social scale. Not enjoying the function of 'authorisation' towards a superior category, they received the rights and protection accorded to man – as distinct from the citizen. It is important to note that *women*, despite the demands of Sieyès and Condorcet (far in advance of common opinion), were not even passive citizens: only male individuals – as some said, the 'heads of family' – could give an opinion on the social interest.

To liberate the individual whilst specialising his political functions: this was the general aim of the moderates of the Constituent Assembly. Very much as in Montesquieu's conception, the citizen (as 'active citizen') is the individual who procures legitimacy, who can assert his demands through publicity and petition, but who cannot exercise power.

Still in the name of the liberation of the individual, the moderates insisted that there must be nothing between the individual and the state – and thus their fear of *associations* and, *avant la lettre*, political parties. Le Chapelier, in the last days of the Constituent Assembly, clearly expressed this obsessive fear, directed especially at the Society of Jacobins.[11] Le Chapelier explains that, in popular clubs or societies, certain individuals capture the recognition of the people, obtain a 'popularity' (that he designates as 'usurped') and, finally – thanks to the collective force of the club – succeed in rivalling the assembly in what must be its monopoly: to represent the people as a unified entity. 'The Revolution is over. There are no more abuses to combat', Le Chapelier affirms. There is no place, therefore, for the *organised expression* of opinion within society, for what, today, is called the associative life of democracy. Full of the individualist spirit of 1789, Le Chapelier maintains that clubs replicate the destroyed *corporations* and that they exert an intolerable pressure on the single legitimate will: the will of the nation as expressed through the assembly.

The conflict between the assemblies and the popular societies continued throughout the Revolution, and weighed heavily on freedom of association in France, severely compromised by article 291 of the Napoleonic Penal Code.[12] The citizen of the French Revolution therefore represents a remarkable paradox in the eyes of today's observer: he is liberated from all social attachments only to be restrained, if not forbidden, in his relations with other fellow citizens. In effect, freedom of association is not part of the Rights of Man and of the

---

[11] See Jaume 1989a, pp. 59 ff.

[12] Article 291, which demands governmental authorisation for all reunions of more than twenty people, has in fact existed until the law of 1901. Even the Third Republic (out of fear of religious congregations) hesitated for thirty years before voting the law of 1901. On this, see Jaume 2001.

Citizen – and this is in no way an oversight: it is a deliberate choice. The same may be said for the Constitution of 1791 (1st Title), where the right of 'meeting peacefully without arms' is recognised, but not, properly speaking, the right of continued association.

It may be observed that, when considering the act of deliberation, the revolutionary has the tendency to reduce the process to its *result*, in other words, to the taking of a decision on a precise point. The reproach that the revolutionary clubs substitute themselves for the representatives of the nation, elected to make the laws, undoubtedly originates here. Take, for example, the denunciation made by the deputy Delfau, himself an ex-Jacobin from the provinces, against the Jacobins of Paris, in June 1792:

Messieurs, what would you think if one day in the street, or in some public place or other, a group of citizens is deliberating on political matters and voting, by seat or by hand, projects of decree? Doubtlessly you would immediately dissolve this new type of national assembly. So then, this is exactly what happens every day a short distance away from the legislative body.

This speech by Delfau reveals the difference – as seen by the moderates – between a 'citizen' and a member of the assembly, between the function of authorisation and the function of deliberation. The principal idea is the following: when the rights of man have been declared, when the constitution has been well built, and when all laws conform to it, everyone is protected – and this constitutes the essential goal of political society. Citizenship is certainly not an end in itself. It is not even the realisation of the potentialities of man, for the latter is much more a being of needs and economy than a political animal. It may therefore be said that citizenship is simply a pure means, the form of articulation – indispensable, in this sense – between society and power, between the private sphere and the tasks of public order.

However, this conception was to be violently shaken by the dynamic of conflicts between the king and the assembly, and between the clubs and the Legislative. In this light, the Parisian insurrection of 10 August 1792 marks a turning point, forcefully restarting the debate on citizenship.

III

In the eyes of Condorcet, who at the moment of insurrection was an important member of the Legislative, 10 August represented a double failure: a failure of legality, because the constitution was overthrown by an insurrection, at the same time as the power of the king which was the target of the uprising; a failure of citizenship, because, once again in the Revolution, the avant-gardes had taken the upper hand (the forty-eight sections of Paris, and the clubs – including those of the Jacobins). For Condorcet, it is inadmissible that an organised minority can stand for the entire people, and 10 August is therefore an opportunity to draw lessons, and to attempt to put into action an audacious reform: that of semi-direct democracy. In February 1793, the project of a new constitution, presented by Condorcet in front of the convention, materialised this new hope.

Comparing the first ideas of Condorcet in 1789 with those expressed in 1793, a number of theses can be seen not to have varied.[13] On the one hand, the citizen cannot claim competence in technical aspects of legislative work, which still require a specialisation of tasks. However, every citizen may judge, through the use of his reason, and even without instruction, on the respect or the violation of *natural* rights in a draft bill. Condorcet proposes that in the future large preliminary consultations should be organised for the elaboration of laws. It may be remarked that, in this philosophy of judgement founded on natural right, Condorcet takes seriously – or literally – one of the goals affirmed in the Declaration of 1789: 'to expose in a solemn declaration the natural, inalienable and sacred rights of man . . . so that the complaints of citizens, now founded on simple and incontestable principles, are directed towards the maintenance of the Constitution and the happiness of all'. According to a formula close to that of Locke, Condorcet writes on many occasions that the political rights of human beings 'derive essentially from their quality as beings sensitive and susceptible to moral ideas, and capable of reasoning'.[14] Quite quickly, in the revolutionary process, Condorcet rallied to the idea of universal suffrage (that was decreed, in a two-tier form, after the events of 10 August), that he hoped would be truly universal, that is to say also including women. From the judgement on legal bills through natural right, Condorcet moved on to demand the extension of the vote as an act of the citizen's judgement – all the more so as he became a republican after the king's flight to Varennes.

Similarly, in his reflections on the political use of reason, Condorcet never ceased to insist on the need to form *judgement*, principally through free public instruction – a project that he would unfortunately present to the assembly on the very day of the declaration of war! According to this conception, the citizen is someone who has the capacity to examine the general interest and who has the duty to do so, even if, contrary to demagogues, it is necessary to recognise that the talents and faculties of individuals are not equal amongst them – a fact that schooling cannot ignore. The formation of intelligence (according to the distinction between 'instruct' and 'educate', that opposed Condorcet to the Montagnards) provides access to the *universal*: even conceived as a professional aim, knowledge that has been correctly instilled enables man to break through

---

[13] Among my studies on Condorcet, see Jaume 1989c and 1992. See also Le Cour Grandmaison 1992.

[14] Citation from the discourse presenting the Project for the constitution, *Archives parlementaires*, vol. LVIII, p. 594.

his closed world of private interest. The former conception of the moderates was clearly surpassed.

The constitutional project of February 1793 tried to put into practice this democratic credo; notably through the mechanism called 'people's censure on acts of national representation',[15] *a single citizen* could mobilise, thanks to a system of tiered votes (from the electoral assemblies to the National Assembly), the procedure of revising a law that had formerly been voted. The same procedure was applied to laws that 'would be contrary to the Constitution', or to a referendum of popular initiative (to a question that had been submitted to the assembly for priority examination). The preoccupation expressed here was the respect for *minorities*, which had to be protected according to a procedural logic, and at the same time the need to combat the principle of avant-gardes, those other minorities that had led the events of 10 August in Paris. Through these mechanisms of initiative and control, Condorcet believed that 'the active portion of citizens will cease to appear as the entire people',[16] a confusion that activists encouraged to their own advantage. It may be added that when Condorcet proposed mechanisms for revising the constitution according to the same principle – that is, through an initiative led by the citizens – and when he insisted that the constitution was also ratified by the citizens, he was demanding what was refused when elaborating the first French Constitution of 1791.

In the final analysis, Condorcet's project sought to introduce means of arbitration and negotiation within the contradictions that had appeared during the first four years of the revolution: contradictions between particular interests and the general interest, between 'private' opinions and public deliberation, between democratic aspirations and the elitism of representative government, between competence and common sense, etc. However, his project was violently opposed by the Montagnards and the Jacobins, whilst Condorcet's Girondin allies only weakly supported him.[17] What the Montagnards reproached Condorcet with, above all, was his attempt to implement legal means of rationalising the famous right of 'resistance to oppression' that had enabled the combined actions of revolutionary minorities in the clubs and street demonstrations, where the people were supposed to be present in person. The 'right of complaint' was conceived as becoming a device internal to the constitution itself, therefore avoiding the need for force. According to a tradition that would remain strong on the left and in republican associations, Jacobin anti-legalism[18] and the panegyric of the people at arms would render suspect all attempts to constitutionalise the sovereignty of the people: the citizen, in other words, became

---

[15] This system responds predominantly to a specific problem: the 'guarantee of the rights of man'. I have retraced the revolutionary debate on this question in 'Garantir les Droits de l'homme: 1791–1793', Jaume 1993. See also Jaume 1997.

[16] Project for the constitution, *Archives parlementaires*, vol. LVIII, p. 600.

[17] See, notably, Badinter 1991.   [18] On this aspect see Jaume 2000a.

fundamentally a militant element. Condorcet was therefore accused of intellectualism, of complacency towards the spirit of the salons.[19] It is important to note that in the spring of 1793, whilst the Montagnards led their offensive against the Gironde (which would culminate in the violent coup against the Convention of 31 May–2 June 1793), it was not so much the citizen that the Montagnards were championing, as the People – an entity at once indivisible, virtuous, and all-powerful. For the Montagnards, they were the 'true representatives' of the People; and the avant-garde of the People (as a speech-made entity) was supposed to be located in the forty-eight sections of Paris, those sections which would effectively lead the revolutionary *journées*. What was created here, was the third revolutionary notion of citizenship – and the legendary image of the *sans-culotte*.

IV

After the month of June 1793 – which saw the elimination of the Girondins from the Convention – the project of the Montagnard and Jacobin left was to lead a 'new revolution' (the second or the third according to some). From now on the former revolution was relegated to the past – that is, to the *ancien régime*. Saint-Just summarised in an abrupt formula the new meaning of the revolutionary idea: 'What makes a Republic, is the total destruction of all that is opposed to it.' From this perspective of the eradication of the 'old' (which is sometimes quite recent) and the *regeneration* of man, the citizen is a central figure. In revolutionary discourse he is exalted – as, for example, in the slogan posted in the meeting-places of certain popular societies: 'Here, we honour the title of citizen.'

However, the citizen – it is apparently a paradox – must accept his subordination to society, to the great All that is 'the people'. The Montagnard declaration of rights (June 1793) underlines, from its first article, that collective and social happiness comes before individual happiness, whereas the latter was the goal of 1789: 'The aim of society is the common good. Government is instituted so as to guarantee man's enjoyment of his natural and imprescribable rights.' Certainly, it can be remarked that the reference here is to 'man' and not to the 'citizen'; however, the citizen has no other choice than to follow the aim of society, which is to revolutionise man. The citizen will be civic, or he will lose his very quality as citizen, and thus become one of the various 'enemies of the people'.

Whilst the moderates of 1789 had a relatively formal view of the citizen, reduced to a function of authorising power, the Jacobin idea had an ethical content, which could only prove itself through militant action – denunciation,

---

[19] Characteristic, in this sense, is the discourse of Saint-Just, *Sur la Constitution de la France* (April 1793), in *Archives parlementaires*, vol. LXIII, pp. 200ff. See my analysis in Jaume 1990, pp. 64–6.

and the periodic 'regeneration' of societies and organs of power.[20] In 1789 the notion of citizenship supposed a separation between society and the seat of power (coming close to the fiction of identity through representation). The revolutionaries of 1793 wanted to recognise citizenship as present in the very seat of power – hence the use of organic metaphors: the Convention and its organs of government *incorporate* the people as Hobbes's Leviathan incorporated individual members of the 'multitude', transforming them into a united 'people'. For example, the Committee of Public Safety developed this concept of citizenship through its great circulars that accompanied the founding decree of the revolutionary government (December 1793). The citizen is therefore an atomic element of the totality that encloses him, of a political body that rejects the 'gangrened elements' (using the image commonly employed).

The Jacobins' moralistic rhetoric came from here, calling – with strikingly religious over-tones – for a 'new man'. This man was to be such that in him the citizen had eliminated egotism and the seduction of particular interests. Robespierre presented this programme with lyricism in his great discourse of 18 Floréal, Year II, in favour of the Supreme Being:

> The idea of the Supreme Being and of the immortality of the soul is a continual appeal to justice; it is therefore social and republican . . . The *chef d'œuvre* of society would be to create [in man], for all moral questions, a rapid instinct that, without the slow help of reason, will lead him to do good and to avoid evil; for the particular reason of each man, led astray by passions, is often only a sophist who pleads their cause.

Whilst Condorcet criticised *enthusiasm* as a political means and as an educational procedure at school, Robespierre contested the utility of reason for civic life: devotion to the *Patrie* (France was at war) and sacrifice for the general interest required a 'rapid instinct' that the 'mercenary rhapsodies'[21] of Condorcet and other academicians sought to suffocate.

The paradox is that the same Robespierre, who in the summer of 1789, and then in the spring of 1793, had fought the notion of the *duties* of man and citizen, should now give a list of duties in his project for a new cult. State force (supposedly exercised by the people), in which the virtuous citizen is called to co-operate, was also translated into a Spartan project for education, that took the opposite course to that proposed by Condorcet. This project, created by Michel Lepelletier, described a passionate utopia, opening onto 'a new, strong, laborious, organized, disciplined race, a race that an impenetrable barrier will have separated from impure contact with our old species infested by prejudices'.[22]

---

[20] See, for example, the *Essai sur la dénonciation politique*, by Etienne Barry: Jaume 1989a, pp. 203–5.

[21] The expression is from the discourse of 18 Floréal. See Jaume 1986.

[22] Lepelletier, *Plan d'éducation nationale*, reproduced in Robespierre 1974, vol. II, pp. 157–96.

The project for a regenerated humanity is at once what justified the launch of the Terror, and what was born from the practice of the Terror – the latter being a means of eliminating the political enemy, in the context of war, by developing, in the very interior of the country, the logic of war: so to say, 'citizenship or death'. However, as is well known, the militant voluntarism to which the citizen was called finished by aggravating the contradictions that it was supposed to resolve. Factions tore each other apart within the Convention itself, and Saint-Just ended by writing: 'Everyone wants to govern, no-one wants to be a citizen.'

As can be seen, the heritage of the Revolution is at once rich and ambiguous: despite the strong echoes raised by the Declaration of the Rights of Man and of the Citizen in 1789, the interpretation of what it actually means to be a citizen demands an effort of clarification that still merits research today.

Firstly, amongst the general traits that can be extricated from the ten years of revolutionary upheaval, one image, or utopia, that stands out is that of the *tabula rasa:* the desire to reconstruct a society from the bottom to the top, to found an authority based on liberty, to give to the legislator the certitude that the *law* is the sole source of right, against all historical principles derived from usage, or custom, or, as common lawyers put it, 'precedent'. The radicalism of the Revolution, from the very first moments of 1789, is a characteristic trait of the French case. Inevitably, in these conditions, the citizen is an abstraction; and it is this abstract character that gives him the force to wrest himself free from all sense of identity (geographic, linguistic, religious, and social) and that enables him to conceive the nation, not as an ethnic entity, but as a *project* of common life directed by the three famous values (liberty, equality, fraternity). As Burke well realised (and as scandalised him too), the French Revolution attempted to speak for all humanity, instead of defending only the 'rights of the French' – even though the French Revolution was leading a combat firmly inscribed within a particular context. It is Tocqueville who would go on to clarify this particular French context: a centralised state administration, an absolute monarchy supported by the Gallican Church, a privileged class that, in contrast to the British aristocracy, was at once closed in on itself (the 'noble blood') and forbidden, by royal will, from contributing to social utility. It is understandable that the most abstract equality, notably translated on a juridical level, but just as powerful in men's minds, became the arm that was appropriated to achieve a *tabula rasa.* Moreover, the idea is in conformity with the taste for great *principles* enjoyed by a group of intellectuals, a group that was excited by the philosophy of the eighteenth century and that, according to Tocqueville, had until then only experienced a purely 'ideological' participation in politics. The moderates put into action a 'machine' that would surpass them through its own dynamics.

The revolutionary heritage was strongly felt in French politics throughout the nineteenth and twentieth centuries. How could society in its diversity be represented, when the revolutionary discourse – whether moderate or radical – had so valued the symbol of unity? How could political, or even religious pluralism be conceived, when freedom of association appeared to carry such a seditious potential? Finally, the haunting question of executive power[23] had shown that the great failure of the Revolution, the fear of 'bringing back the king', had led to oscillations between regimes of authority and regimes of assembly – up to the present, fifteen constitutions have been attempted.

The Third Republic confirmed the influence of the French Revolution (or of the revolutionary doctrine of representation) in its refusal of all forms of direct democracy, and in its embrace of the principle of 'absolute representation' (Carré de Malberg) that gave sovereignty to parliament, refusing the practice of referendums, any revision of the constitution by the 'sovereign people', as well as any control of the constitutionality of the Republic's laws. The Third Republic further confirmed its ancestors' influence by engaging officially in free and obligatory lay education, still considering that without proper intellectual instruction the citizen was at risk from religious or regionalist obscurantism. The same may be said of female suffrage, obstinately refused by the Senate of the Third Republic.

Today, when the state is challenged by globalisation and European unification, many other citizens' demands are being raised that challenge the abstract model of citizenship propagated by the French Revolution. Such new demands include, for instance, business rights, the rights of women and of territorial, religious, or sexual minorities, the civic and political rights of non-nationals, etc. To those claims the American model has prompted suggestions, revealing also the danger whereby a formerly exalted (sometimes hypocritical) universalism can be brutally inverted into a collection of uncontrollable and anarchic particularisms. What is sure, however, is that the current explosion of 'plural citizenships' confirms, *a contrario*, that the citizen of the French Revolution was powerful only to the extent that he had the support of the state and of the force of law.[24] The present questioning of the state and of the Republic obliges us to ask a question that the Revolution addressed with confusion: *what is a citizen, if he refuses to sacrifice either liberty or equality?* The answer surely lies in the conciliation of two poles, those of unity and plurality.

Summary

To determine the nature of the citizen during the ten years of the French Revolution (1789–99) is not a question that can receive a simple response, for

---

[23] It has not been closed under the Fifth Republic, as can be seen in the recurrent debates on the function of the President of the Republic.
[24] See my recent clarification, Jaume 2000b.

the diverse revolutionary forces were in conflict over this point. This chapter distinguishes the moderate perspective of 1789 (the citizen is a means of protecting the private individual), Condorcet's opinion (citizenship must be a rational function), and the point of view of the Jacobins and Montagnards (the citizen is part of the People, and under the standard of virtue). The citizen *à la française* is characterised by its abstraction and allegiance to the law. Today such characteristics are placed in question.

BIBLIOGRAPHY

Andrieu, C., Le Béguec, C., and Tartakowsky, D. (eds.) (2001). *Associations et champ politique*, Paris: Publications de la Sorbonne.
Archives parlementaires de 1787 à 1860, 1ère série (1867–), Paris: Dupont, then CNRS.
Badinter, R. (1991). 'Condorcet et les Girondins' in Furet et Ozouf: 1991.
Bart, J., Clère, J.-J., Courvoisier, C., and Verpeaux, M. (eds.) (1997). *La Constitution du 24 juin 1793. L'utopie dans le droit public français*, Dijon: Editions Universitaires de Dijon.
Berstein, S. and Rudelle, O. (eds.) (1992). *Le modèle républicain*, Paris: PUF.
Châtelet, F., Pisier, E. and Duhamel, O. (eds.) (1986, and 2001). *Dictionnaire des œuvres politiques*, Paris: PUF.
Crépel, P. and Gilain, C. (eds.) (1989). *Condorcet mathématicien, économiste, philosophe, homme politique*, Paris: Minerve.
Fauré, C. (1988). *Les déclarations des droits de l'homme de 1789*, Paris: Payot.
Furet, F. and Ozouf, M. (eds.) (1991). *La Gironde et les Girondins*, Paris: Payot.
Goyard-Fabre, S. (ed.) (2000). *L'Etat moderne, 1715–1848*, Paris: Librairie philosophique Vrin.
Gueniffey, P. (1993). *Le nombre et la raison. La Révolution française et les élections*, Paris: Editions de l'EHESS.
Hobbes, T. (1996). *Leviathan*, ed. R. Tuck, Cambridge: Cambridge University Press. French edition 1991, Paris: François Tricaud.
Jaume, L. (1986). 'Robespierre', in Châtelet, Pisier, and Duhamel 1991.
    (1989a). *Le discours jacobin et la démocratie*, Paris: Fayard.
    (1989b). *Les Déclarations des droits de l'homme (Du débat 1789–1793 au Préambule de 1946)*, collection Garnier-Flammarion, Paris: Flammarion.
    (1989c). 'Individu et souveraineté chez Condorcet', in Crépel and Gilain 1989.
    (1990). *Echec au libéralisme. Les Jacobins et l'Etat*, Paris: Kimé.
    (1992). 'Condorcet: des progrès de la raison aux progrès de la société', in Berstein and Rudelle 1992.
    (1993). 'Garantir les Droits de l'homme: 1791–1793', *The Tocqueville Review – La Revue Tocqueville* (Toronto), 14, no. 1, pp. 49–65.
    (1997). 'La souveraineté montagnarde', in Bart *et al.* 1997.
    (2000a). 'L'Etat jacobin ou le constitutionnalisme en procès', in Goyard-Fabre 2000, pp. 205 ff.
    (2000b). *La liberté et la loi. Les origines philosophiques du libéralisme*, Paris: Fayard.
    (2001). 'Une liberté en souffrance: l'association au XIXe siècle', in Andrieu *et al.* 2001, pp. 77 ff.

Le Cour Grandmaison, O. (1992). *Les citoyennetés en Révolution (1789–1794)*, Paris: PUF.

Robespierre, M. (1974). *Textes choisis*, ed. J. Poperen, Paris: Editions Sociales, 3 vols.

Sieyès, E. (1789a). 'Reconnaissance et exposition raisonnée des droits de l'homme et du citoyen', in *Archives parlementaires*, vol. VIII, pp. 256 ff.

   (1789b). *Observations sur le rapport du Comité de constitution*, Versailles: Baudouin.

   (1789c). *Qu'est-ce que le tiers état?*, Paris: PUF, 1981.

10   A state of contradictions: the post-colonial state in India

Sudipta Kaviraj

I

No story of the European state can be complete if it does not take into account its effects outside Europe. Francois Guizot's classic history of the European state requires a supplement.[1] His magisterial account presents the picture of the state inside Europe's own history, but the story of the European state has an equally significant counterpart, a history that happens outside. Outside Europe the modern state succeeded in two senses – first as an instrument, and second as an idea. First, the organisation of European societies produced by the modern state was an essential factor in Europe's ability to bring the rest of the world under its colonial control. Here the state functioned as an immense and unprecedented enhancement of the European societies' capacity for collective action – in raising military resources, producing the economic resources which undergirded its military success, focusing on clearly defined stratagems of control and conquest. In fact, when other peoples began to reflect on the reasons for this astonishing success, they often settled on this as its intangible but indispensable instrument. Pre-modern forms of political authority were utterly inadequate in dealing with the power of the modern European state. It could be restrained and eventually effectively opposed only through a movement that organised the power of entire populations against European colonial regimes.

The European state also succeeded a second time as an idea. Successful nationalist movements, after de-colonisation, enthusiastically accepted the idea of a modern society centred upon the state's sovereignty – a principle of social construction entirely different from traditional ones. Except for a few odd individuals like Gandhi and Tagore, nationalists did not object to the presence of the modern state, only to its being in the European's control. With independence, they did not wish, except in a few cases like Gandhi, to 'abolish' the state, but to use it for their own purposes. After two hundred years of colonialism, the European state receded from India, but the idea of the state brought in by colonialism continued its triumphant career. Eventually, the gigantic transformations of third-world societies after de-colonisation, for good or for ill, were

[1] Guizot 1997.

145

driven through by this modern instrumentality of the state. In the absence of other forces – such as great revolutionary social classes like the bourgeoisie or the proletariat that played such an important role in European social transformations – it was the state which almost entirely arrogated to itself the power of proposing, directing, and effecting large-scale social change. There might be great debates about judging what the state has done; but there is no doubt that it has been the single most powerful collective agency in the recent history of these societies. That is why the state is central to the story of non-Western modernity, and Western colonialism is central to the story of the non-Western state.

This chapter is not about the post-colonial state in general, only the historically specific form it assumed in India. It is thus necessary to spell out what can be generalised from the Indian case and what cannot. First, although India is a single country, its numerical significance is obvious: what happens to its people politically represents the collective experience of about one-third of the non-Western world. Second, as there is little dispute today about the desirability of democracy, the Indian case is particularly important. It is one of the most successful cases of democracy outside Europe. But the 'success' of democracy is an ambiguous idea, it is possible to give it a minimal or an expansive interpretation. The narrow and minimalist reading is simply the continuance of a competitive electoral system of government: if this system continues uninterrupted over a long period of time, that draws applause as a success of democracy. But there can be an alternative, Tocquevillian reading of democracy's success – which is not just a continuation of a system of government, but the capacity of this government to produce long-term egalitarian effects. In India, democracy has been a remarkable success in both these senses. First, in a highly diverse society, divided by religion, caste, classes, languages, the democratic system has functioned without interruption or popular apathy for nearly six decades. Second, and more significantly, this institutional continuation of democracy has produced a fundamental social transformation which is in some respects startlingly different from the European social processes. Thirdly, if democratic institutions spread and achieve success in the non-European world, these will produce historical results depending on the forms of sociability available in each historical context. Such cases of possible democratic success are likely to follow trajectories closer to India's than to modern Europe's. To understand the prospects of democracy in the future, the story must include the Indian case alongside the Western narratives of the nineteenth century.

This chapter interprets 'post-colonial' as indicating not the trivial fact that this state emerged after the colonial regime departed but in the stronger sense to mean that some of its characteristic features could not have arisen without the particular colonial history that went before. I also believe, unlike some other political scientists, that political change in modern India cannot be studied fruitfully except in a long-term historical perspective. To understand the unfolding story of politics and the state today, it is thus essential to start with the historical transformation of political power in the age of colonialism.

Modernity in India, and perhaps also in other European colonies, was largely a political affair. All commentators on European modernity point out the significant, if not originary role that transformations of the production and economic processes played in the making of European modernity. I wish to suggest that in India by contrast the causal powers of economic change were far more limited. The type of capitalist development that eventually took place was determined to a large extent by political imperatives of state control. The colonial state created the conditions for early capitalist development, rather than the other way round. Modernity came to India by the political route, through the introduction of a new activity called 'politics'. Indeed, the activity was so new that in many vernaculars it is still colloquially referred to by the English-derived word 'politics', rather than by an orthogenetic term. This new activity assumed primarily three forms in successive stages of modern Indian history. Initially, it entered with the establishment of new institutions of colonial rule, eventually crystallising into a colonial state/regime. Sociologically, 'politics' was an activity which involved British rulers and Indian elites who engaged in transactions of power with them. In the second phase, its scope was extended through the popular nationalist movement from the 1920s when Indians from other social groups and classes took part in this as a large, encompassing transformative activity. Although most Indians were affected by this form of politics, their participation and capacity to behave as actors depended on class and education. Nationalist politics, in spite of its wider appeal, remained more the politics of the wider educated elites, much less of the ordinary Indian peasantry. Curiously, even after independence, this structure continued unchanged for about two decades. Since the 1970s, in another serious transformation, the business of 'politics' has become much more expansive, with lower-caste and lower-class politicians bringing the concerted pressures of their ordinary constituents into the life of the state.

What were the central processes in this transformation? Why has politics of a discursive, representative, democratic character succeeded in India? The basic argument of this chapter is controversial, but fairly simple. There can be no doubt that in the last two hundred years Indian society has undergone a most fundamental transformation. The central point of this change, in my view, is the transformation of a society in which 'imperative co-ordination', to use Weber's inelegant but useful phrase, was achieved through a religious system based on caste, with comparatively little role of the state, to an order controlled by the state – its institutions, its laws, its resources, its functionaries, and its place in the ordinary people's imagination. In pre-modern times, control over the state was relatively marginal to the narratives of significant social change. The most significant upheavals in traditional Indian history were not dynastic or regime changes, but the challenges to the religious organisation of society through the reform movements of Buddhism and Jainism against ritualistic Brahminism in ancient India, or the rise of the bhakti cults against Hindu orthodoxy in late-medieval times. By contrast, from the middle of the nineteenth century the state's role has been absolutely central in the passage of social change. The colonial state ended in 1947, but the new way of organising social life through 'politics', making the society state-centred, has not merely continued, but expanded its jurisdiction over all aspects of social life. The 'European' state thus still dominates modern Indian life in those two senses. The institutional apparatuses introduced into Indian society by British colonial power have not been dismantled, but massively extended. Secondly, the idea that to be modern is to live through the state, to organise society through this central institution of power, has had a great vindication – ironically through the demise of colonial power itself.

Following this main idea, I shall present my argument in three parts: the first will offer a brief outline of the arrangement of social power in traditional (pre-colonial) India, the second will describe the changes brought in by colonialism and the Indians' transaction with its initiatives, and the final section will analyse what has happened to this state after independence – by its becoming a 'nation-state', and the manner in which principles of democracy have been interpreted by social forces in India.

II

Colonial power came to an Indian society which already had a long-standing and intricate political organisation. Much of northern and central India had been under an Islamic empire for nearly six centuries.[2] Yet the presence of Islam in India was special. In most other societies, a conquering Islamic power had converted the people and transformed indigenous social practices and religious doctrine. In India the irresistible military power of Islamic dynasties learnt to coexist with the immovable social structure of the Hindu caste system. Indian society thus had a dual structure of power, composed of a strange crossing of Hindu and Islamic principles. From very early times, 'Hindu' society (an anachronistic description for a collection of different sects united by a single sociological order[3]) had an explicit and intricate arrangement of social power

---

[2] See Bayly 1989. For a different argument, and based on a different regional perspective, Dirks 1998.

[3] Al Biruni, the great Islamic scholar, despaired of discovering any doctrinal singleness in the Hindu sects, but decided, brilliantly, that the key to their unity lay in a sociological order of Brahminism. Al Biruni 1914.

structured in a caste order. Caste represents a peculiar structure of social power which tends to circumscribe the jurisdiction of political authority. Caste, as is generally known, has two forms – the formal, ritualistic structure of the four *varnas*, and the effective sociological structure of much more numerous *jatis*. Social anthropologists usually give less importance to the formal *varna* structure, but it is significant for one central reason. It shows that at the centre of the caste order is a scheme of an *asymmetric* hierarchy, which separated the goods that ordinary human beings seek and value in mundane life, and segregated groups according to these. The underlying theory behind the caste order implied that the primary values/goods of human life were ritual status/ religious prestige, political power to rule over society, and the economic power to control wealth. The central logic of the *varna* version of the caste system was to separate the social groups which exercised monopolistic control over each of these human goods. The social order of castes ritually separated the fields of intellectual authority, political and military supremacy, and commercial wealth.

These arrangements meant that, by contrast with the aristocratic societies of pre-modern Europe, political pre-eminence, economic wealth, and cultural prestige did not coincide in a single social elite. Occupational separation by birth ensured that social groups lived in three types of relations to each other: segmentation, interdependence, and hierarchy. Occupationally divided social groups could not seek the same goods; and therefore, it reduced, if not entirely excluded, competition for wealth and power. Secondly, the caste order was based on a generally recognised *social* constitution, an authoritative allocation of social roles, rewards, and therefore life-trajectories which governed the conduct of social groups in minute detail. Significantly, this authoritative allocation did not originate from political authority. Political rulers could not alter the rules of this social constitution, but were expected to uphold and administer its 'immutable' norms, and crucially, were themselves subject to its segmentally relevant rules. Consequently, in this social world, the power of political rulers was limited to 'executive' functions: that is, to protect the social constitution, punish infringements, and return it to its order of normalcy. In this sense, the political rulers did not have the 'legislative' authority to reconstitute this order, except in marginal ways. The idea of modern sovereignty therefore did not apply to the power of the political authority in this society.

However, there is an obvious objection at this point. Is this not an excessively Hindu view of political power? Since large parts of Indian society had been continually governed by Islamic rulers since the eleventh century, does this model apply to those areas? One of the most interesting historical questions about India's political past is the precise relation that Islamic imperial power established with the predominantly Hindu society over which it exercised control. Although Islamic religious doctrine was fundamentally different from Hinduism (e.g., about idolatry, monotheism, egalitarianism, etc.), in sociological terms (i.e., in the relation between *political* authority and the *social* constitution) Islam in India observed very similar principles, and tacitly accepted the restrictions the caste society placed on the 'legislative' functions of rulers. Thus, the coming of Islam was highly significant in other ways, but not in terms of the fundamental structure of the relation between political power and social order. It required a state of a very different sort, animated by very different intellectual principles of self-organisation and endowed with new types of cognitive-statistical appliances, to alter this stable social constitution. The modern state is, by definition, the state which, because of its self-interpretation in terms of the principle of sovereignty, considered this invasive transformation of society possible.

III

Although the colonial system of states meant a subordination of other societies to some metropolitan European powers, the actual transactions of colonialism were extremely diverse. First, the European states themselves came from vastly different cultural and institutional contexts, and these differences were reflected in the system of political power each of them brought into their colonies. Secondly, much depended on exactly when a territory was brought under European control. Third, European powers followed entirely different projects in different colonies, and though experience of colonial rule in one part of the world often informed decisions about another, British rule in Africa, for instance, was very different from what it was in India. Finally, the exact nature of colonial rule depended not merely on what the colonial power was ideologically intent on doing, or instrumentally capable of achieving, but also the manner in which the colonised society deployed its own cultural and political resources in this encounter. Focusing on India therefore gives us a single story out of many diverse ones of European colonial rule, and because of the strange intimacy that developed between India and Britain, it might portray European colonial domination in general in a misleadingly benevolent light. Not all groups in colonised countries responded to the arrival of European power and culture with the initial enthusiasm of the modern Indian elites. European powers did not direct the same amount of attention and energy towards the moral and social transformation of all their dominions. The sharing of at least abstract common political principles between the colonial rulers and the nationalist elite to produce an effective framework of political conflict was also rather unusual, as was the negotiated nature of the eventual withdrawal of British power.

The state established by British colonialism was an historical force of an untraditional kind. Even though its immediate instrument was a commercial company, the dominion established by British power occurred in an intellectual context which presupposed sovereignty as a definitional quality of state-power.[4] Thus, when the British eventually turned India into a crown colony in 1858, the colonial state explicitly assumed the rights of sovereignty as understood in European discourses of the nineteenth century. Interestingly, as British colonial power did not enter India in the shape of state authority the initial conflict was not in the form of a struggle between two states – the declining Mughal empire and the British crown. It is the peculiar constitution of society, and the relative externality of the state to the orders of caste practice which allowed this to happen. By the early nineteenth century, British authorities already controlled much of commercial activity, military power, and quasi-political administrative apparatuses and had a substantial influence on cultural life in several parts of India. When they finally ended the fiction of Mughal rule after the rebellion of 1857, Mughal authority was already purely nominal. But this first, and rather peculiar stage in the establishment of British power, stretching over a century, is critical for an understanding of the special dynamics of British colonialism in India. In this stage, we must try to sketch out the contours of advancing colonial *power*, rather than describe the structure of the 'colonial *state*'.

British power, established initially through control over channels and instruments of commerce and revenue-collection, and at the second step, through the introduction of modern cultural apparatuses, slowly turned into a state of the modern kind – though its actual institutions were quite different from nineteenth-century European models. The most significant implication of this is that Indian opinion was always internally deeply divided about colonial rule. Older aristocracies that lost their power to the British were understandably hostile to the gradual entrenchment of British authority. Similarly, traditional Hindu holders of social authority and prestige, like conservative Brahmins, often looked at the new influences with hostility. Recent historical research has strongly underlined the fact that the British could establish their control over a large and diverse territory like India, partly because they went along with historical trends that had already started in India in the eighteenth century, and for this reason they also drew substantial support from indigenous groups. Powerful commercial interests, aspirant political groups, and relatively modern professional elites produced by new educational institutions strongly supported the establishment of British rule. Eventually, this allowed British government in India to become an interesting arrangement administered by large groups of

---

[4] One of the most interesting accounts of this underlying connection between the commercial and political impulses in the Company's India was given in Burke's famous indictment of Warren Hastings before the House of Lords. Edmund Burke, 'On the impeachment of Warren Hastings, 15–19 February 1788', in Burke 1998, pp. 31–8. The question of 'sovereignty' also figured prominently in discussions among British utilitarians and their critics about economic policy. For an excellent analysis, see Stokes 1959.

Indian elites who collaborated with British authority and ran the colony under British supervision.[5]

In the long term, the colonial state altered Indian society in two ways. The establishment of a new kind of state, with formal legal claims to sovereignty, was itself a major transformative project, which reversed the logic of limited political authority in the segmentary caste civilisation. It established and familiarised the idea that the apparatuses of the state, especially its legislative organs, in British or Indian hands, could, in principle, judge social institutions critically, and formally alter them by law. Some of the most fateful and long-lasting effects, however, were not introduced through political policies of the state, but through more indirect cultural changes it induced through its administrative habits.[6] Administrative procedures, like the great statistical enterprises of the colonial regimes, though not political in themselves, nonetheless caused fundamental changes in social identities and their preparation for a new kind of politics. Surprisingly, the colonial administration changed identities by implanting cognitive practices which objectified communities, changing them from an earlier fuzzy or underspecified form to a modern enumerated one. Processes of enumeration of the social world, like mapping and census, irreversibly altered social ontology by giving groups a new kind of agentive political identity.[7] This was not political agency in itself, but a precondition for the development of a political universe in which political agency could be imparted to large impersonal groups – like castes, ethnicities, or religious communities.

However, the colonial state was subject to contradictory impulses. It set in motion large information-gathering processes under the rationalist belief that, in order to rule such a large and complex society, officials had to know it accurately and exhaustively. This statistical project was not part of a state-directed agenda of wholesale social reform. One strand of administrative thinking advocated a state of deliberate inactivity, which would not meddle in social affairs which colonial rulers did not understand fully, and which might unwittingly create disaffection. Even in the case of a barbaric practice like Sati (suttee) – the burning of widows on the funeral pyre of their deceased husbands – the initial response of the colonial regime was extremely cautious. Only the righteous indignation of the native reformers eventually pushed it into legislation banning it.[8] Apart from cultural scruples, the colonial state also mistrusted over-expansion of its

---

[5] For the new historical arguments suggesting this 'indigenous' force in favour of British success, see Bayly 1989, Washbrook 1988, and Stein 1985. Parallel arguments are advanced in Subrahmanyam 1990. For an excellent analysis of the contradictory impulses that shaped the early colonial state, see Washbrook 1999.

[6] Recently, much work has been done on how the information order of colonial India was created, and how it underpinned colonial administration. See, for instance, Irschik 1994 and Bayly 1996.

[7] I have discussed this in greater detail in Kaviraj 1994. Cf. Appadurai, 1996.

[8] For a detailed account of the intellectual debates around sati, see Mani,1998.

activities on purely prudential grounds. British policy oscillated between an urge towards reform, which wanted to restructure Indian society on rational lines, and a policy of restraint, which wanted to leave social affairs of Indians alone. The self-limitation of the colonial state, justified at various times by arguments of financial prudence or cultural relativism, allowed a wide space for the development of a distinctive elite associational politics in nineteenth-century India. This initial ability to form associations, exercise group solidarity, pursue their economic interests, and transact business with the colonial state gave the modern Indian elite the confidence to develop eventually larger projects of self-government, and led to the growth of Indian nationalism.

Ironically, the specific ideological culture in which the British colonial state operated played a part in the eventual growth of nationalist arguments in India. The time of the greatest expansion and power of British colonialism in India coincided with the time when principles of modern liberalism were being established in British political culture. The Indian empire thus witnessed all the internal contradictions of an imperialism which also sought to subscribe to liberal doctrine.[9] Liberal political theorists were arguing passionately against the substantial remnants of despotic power, and advocating dramatic expansion of citizens' freedom. Such principles sat uneasily with the demands of the expanding empire. In the colonial context, liberal writers were often at pains to oppose precisely such extensions of freedom to colonial subjects. Educated Indians by now had gained considerably fluency in the theoretical arguments of liberalism and looked with interest at the practical extensions of suffrage. They were quick to convert to universalist liberal doctrines and demand their instant extension to India.

Liberal imperialism also produced a peculiar dynamics through the exchanges between Indian and British authors on the question of political morals. Indian intellectuals quickly realised that the best form of injustice was the injustice administered by liberals. The philosophical anthropology and procedural universalism of liberal doctrines required that political principles of liberty and equality should be declared as universal truths. Liberalism enunciated its principles in an abstract, impersonal, and universal form, but often made ungainly attempts to avoid their realisation in practice. This was done in one of two ways – both unwittingly allowing nationalists to develop compelling counter-arguments. In some contexts, the 'universal' principles were simply ignored in practice, which made it easy for nationalists to accuse the British of dishonesty, and to embarrass the administration by comparing the stated principles with actual practice. In other contexts, theorists like John Stuart Mill tried to produce a more serious intellectual argument using a stage theory of history, similar to

---

[9] For an excellent general treatment of this particular dilemma of liberal theory, see Mehta 1999. For the ideology of the British Empire, see Armitage 2000.

that of the Scottish Enlightenment thinkers.[10] His writings argued that representative institutions were incontrovertibly the best form of government, but incongruously counselled an indefinite postponement of their conferment on Indians. Although liberal institutions were, in the abstract, best for all mankind, they were not suitable for most of human societies until they had attained a required stage of civilisation.[11] This ingenious argument saved the abstract universality of liberal ideals, but justified imperial rule for an indefinite future. Not surprisingly, this line of reasoning appeared more persuasive to the British than to the Indians. Yet this particular ideological configuration contributed subtly to the surprisingly amicable nature of the central political conflict in colonial India. The intellectual form of the British arguments subliminally acknowledged that denial of self-government was not right in principle, and could not be continued indefinitely. It also created a subtle sense of defensiveness, if not guilt, in the ideological defence of the empire. Interestingly, in their critique of British imperial rule Indian nationalists could appeal to the same principles. This sharing of principles, admittedly at a very abstract level, contributed to the slow but steady sequence of constitutional shifts, which eventually led to the transfer of power to Indians in 1947.

IV

After 1947, the defining structures of the Indian nation-state were produced by a combination of structural pressures and conjunctural openings. The state after independence had a double and in some ways contradictory inheritance. It was a successor both to the British colonial state and to the movement of Indian nationalism. To combine the two sets of attributes – ideals, institutions, aspirations – that emerged from these contradictory legacies was not an easy task. Broadly, the legal institutions and coercive apparatuses of the state remained similar to the last stage of colonial rule – to the disappointment of those who expected a radical overhaul of the state. During its nationalist agitations, Congress had identified education, the police and the bureaucracy as the three pillars of colonial domination, and made repeated promises to introduce radical changes in their functioning. In the event, when they assumed power, especially after the panic of the partition, they left these three apparatuses of persuasion and control entirely unreformed. On one point, however, a major transformation took place – though its full effects became apparent only after a certain historical interval. From the early decades of the twentieth century, the British authorities had

---

[10] Mill's arguments about India can be found in his *On Liberty*, introduction, especially p. 73 and his *Considerations on Representative Government*, chapters XVI and XVII. His detailed comments on Indian government are collected in Mill 1990.

[11] One of the most famous cases of such arguments in J. S. Mill are in *On Liberty*, chapter 1 and *Considerations on Representative Government*, chapters 10 and 12.

cautiously introduced partial representative institutions.[12] Despite apprehensions about widespread illiteracy, the new state introduced universal franchise in a single dramatic move of inclusion.[13] The ideological discourse of nationalism had also created vast popular expectations from the state once it was taken over by the Congress, in sharp contrast with the rather limited objectives of the colonial state. Apart from the conventional responsibilities of the state in law and order, it was expected to play an enormous role in the ill-defined and constantly expanding field of 'development'.

The entire story of the state for the half-century after independence can be seen in terms of two apparently contradictory trends. Paradoxically, the Indian political world saw the simultaneous strengthening of two tendencies that can be schematically regarded as the logic of bureaucracy and the logic of democracy. The antecedents of both these trends can be found in the history of colonial rule. Since the middle of the nineteenth century, a process of gradual domination of the society by modern state institutions had brought all significant social practices under its surveillance, supervision, and control. The colonial state also began a slow and cautious introduction of practices of representation – so that this increasing control could be seen not as imposition of external rules of discipline, but imposition of rules and demands generated by the society itself. Both trends became more extensive and powerful after independence.

Under British rule, the extension of bureaucracy was mainly sanctioned by a rhetoric of state efficiency; under nationalist leadership, this was replaced by the rhetoric of 'development'. For entirely fortuitous reasons, at the time of the state's foundation, Jawaharlal Nehru came to enjoy an extraordinary degree of freedom in shaping its institutions and basic policies. The death of Gandhi and Patel, who had very different ideological inclinations, left the conservative sections of the Congress without effective leadership. Unopposed temporarily, Nehru imbued this state with a developmentalist and mildly redistributivist ideology. According to this political vision, the state was seen as the primary instrument of development, with extensive responsibilities in the direct management of production and redistribution.[14] In part, this was because the massive industrialisation programme undertaken after independence could not be financed

---

[12] Major institutional changes were introduced several times in the first half of the twentieth century. The Montagu–Chelmsford reforms of 1919 began the processes of institutional change; further changes in the structure of government with Indian parties in the provincial legislatures and executives were introduced by the Government of India Act of 1935. The first elective governments took office in 1937. This act formed the main legal template for certain parts of the constitution adopted in 1950.

[13] Austin 1964, chapter 2, section 4 analyses the discussions about universal suffrage. More detailed treatment can be found in Rao 1964. An excellent analysis of the theoretical bases of the democratic institutions can be found in Bhargava 2000.

[14] Chakrabarty 1987 provides a clear exposition of the economic objectives of the developmental state. Its historical development is analysed concisely but acutely in Bardhan 1985. Two careful, detailed analyses of the state's role in development can be found in Frankel 1978, and Rudolph and Rudolph 1987.

or managed by private capital; in part, because private capitalist development was expected to worsen income inequality, while state-managed development could simultaneously contribute to redistribution of wealth. Eventually, this led to a massive expansion of the bureaucracy without a corresponding change in its culture. Rapid over-extension of the bureaucracy intensified its inefficiency, reduced observance of procedures, and this produced large zones of corruption and malpractice. By the late sixties this led to the familiar paradox of the over-extended state. It was expected to supervise all aspects of activity, from managing the army and running the administration to running the railways and the postal system and providing schools and hospitals. Its vast reach and responsibility resulted in a reduction of the reliability of social services. The state in contemporary India became ubiquitous, but also universally unreliable.

However, over the half-century of its existence, subtle changes took place in the character of the developmental state itself; since the 1970s, its structures and practices have changed imperceptibly. Initially, during the Nehru years, the developmental state was seen primarily as an engine of production, specially active in the production of essential industrial capacities and in creating infrastructure. But the ideological justification of this constantly expanding state machinery was in terms of arguments of distributive justice. If the state managed heavy industries, the argument went, existing inequalities of income would not increase; and it would also act against the concentration of resources in a few private hands – classical Marxist arguments for socialist politics. In the first two decades after independence, state institutions with the responsibility of establishing and running heavy industries performed with reasonable efficiency. They helped set up and run a considerable heavy industrial base driven by the current economic theory of self-reliance and import-substituting industrialisation. By the early 1970s, a certain change in the character of state enterprises was discernible, and a corresponding change in their relation with political authority. 'The state sector', as it was called in India, came to control vast economic resources – through its gigantic, interconnected networks of financing, employment, and contracts emanating from both the productive and welfare activities of the state enterprises.

Nehru's government accorded to these enterprises a relative decisional and managerial autonomy to ensure technical correctness of decision-making. With the vast increase of their resources, however, political leaders and ministries began from the 1970s to seek more direct control of their operations. The government leadership under Indira Gandhi slowly abandoned the earlier Nehruvian aspiration of giving serious direction to the economy through directive state planning. Instead of being seen as segments of an internally coherent policy of development planning, these enterprises sank into uncontrolled bureaucratisation, which increased unproductive activities, pushing them deeper into inefficiency. Anxiety over inefficiency made managements more dependent for their survival on the support of political leaders. The price the political class extracted for this support was indirect access to the use of these resources for political ends – for example, raising funds for the parties in power or distribution of patronage. The huge economic bureaucracy of the developmental state increasingly had little to do with realistic redistributive objectives, but became utterly dependent on a disingenuous use of that rhetoric. The sizeable economic surplus under the state's control came to be used for illegitimate purposes by elected politicians who developed a vested interest in defending this large, over-stretched, inefficient state.[15] From 1991, successive Indian governments have rather reluctantly begun some re-structuring of the state under the general slogan of 'liberalisation' of the economy. But compared to the swift and large-scale structural reforms carried out in other parts of Asia and Africa, the liberalisation in India has been remarkably slow. The logic of bureaucracy still pervades and dominates Indian political life.

The second undeniable historical feature of Indian political life has been the irresistible expansion of democracy. But the lines of its movement were at times surprisingly different from the history of European democracy in the nineteenth century. First, unlike the gradual, incremental development of the suffrage in most European states, democracy was introduced to India in a single, dramatic gesture of political inclusion. Although the colonial administration had slowly introduced representative institutions from the early twentieth century, the electorate at the last election under colonial administration was about 14 per cent of the adult population. The constitution adopted in 1950 installed universal adult suffrage in a country that was still 70 per cent illiterate. The new entrants into the arena of politics thus instantly outnumbered social elites already entrenched in representative institutions. This was likely to result in a conflict over representation, with entrant groups contesting the claim of elite politicians to 'represent' the entire nation – an eventuality that did happen, but after a considerable lapse of time. The probable reason for this comparatively placid introduction of an electoral revolution was that poor people showed traditional habits of deference towards socially dominant groups. Similarly, it also took time for lower classes in a caste society, used to social repression, to understand the historic possibilities of the strategic use of the right to vote. For about two decades, although the poor and the disprivileged in Indian society had the formal right to vote, they actually left the arena of institutional politics entirely in the hands of the modernist elites. Paradoxically, the institutions of democratic government seemed to function with impeccably formal propriety precisely because levels of participation were low, and popular expectations from democratic government were limited. The usual problems of electoral politics – resource allocation on the

---

[15] For a serious attack on the basic principles of the developmental state, and an argument that it has slowed down economic growth, see Bhagwati 1993.

basis of electoral pressure, which makes rational long-term decisions particularly difficult – did not affect Indian democratic government in the Nehru
years.[16]

By the 1970s, however, the situation had changed significantly in two ways.
Politicians of all parties had lost the inexhaustible fund of legitimacy that
Nehru's generation had from their leadership in the national movement. The
new generation of leaders, including Congress leaders like Indira Gandhi, had to
acquire support in the short term by electoral promises of resource distribution.
It was also clear that ordinary voters, especially the urban poor and the lower
castes in the countryside, had learnt strategic use of the vote. They made greater
demands on the political system, and politicians from these under-privileged
groups began to emerge first in state assemblies, and later in parliament and
national government. This somewhat delayed but decisive entry of the common people into the life of the state utterly transformed its character. Politics
came to be practised increasingly in the vernacular – in two senses. Literally,
much of political discourse was carried on in the vernacular, in contrast to the
first decades when English was the mandatory language of high politics. But
more significantly, after the 1970s, the political imagination of major social
groups came to be shaped by a kind of conceptual vernacular as well, used by
politicians who did not have the conventional education through the medium of
English and whose political thinking was not determined by their knowledge
of European historical precedents.

Nationalist leaders who had devised the constitution had expected democracy
eventually to have wider social effects; but their expectations followed the familiar trajectories of European democracy. The introduction of modern democracy
in Europe made the stark class inequalities of nineteenth-century capitalist society increasingly unsustainable. Radical leaders like Nehru had accordingly
anticipated that, as ordinary Indians acquired a democratic consciousness, they
would cease to identify themselves through traditional caste categories and
demand greater economic equality. Democratic institutions would thus lead,
in the long term, to modernist movements for reduction of poverty. But what
happened through half a century of democratic politics defied and confounded
such expectations.[17] Democracy certainly led to vast revolutionary effects in
the Indian context as well – but that historic change resembled Tocqueville's
'revolution' more than Marx's.[18] Democratic politics produced a fundamental

---

[16] The dialectic between government's ability to take long-term decisions and the insistence of
electoral pressure is discussed in extensive detail in Rudolph and Rudolph 1987.

[17] I have sought to analyse this surprising turn in caste politics in 'Democracy and Social Inequality'
in Frankel 2000.

[18] In fact, one of the major weaknesses of Indian Marxist writing about politics has been its
reluctance to take the democratic upsurge seriously as a process of real, not illusory social
change.

transformation of Indian society – but not in terms of class. By contrast with Europe, the logic of democracy did not force changes of policy encouraging greater equality of income, but led to a real redistribution of dignity. The deep European influence on India's intellectuals made them subtly predisposed, irrespective of ideology, to underestimate the social presence of caste, and to underestimate the adaptive fecundity of traditions. Both liberals and socialists, who dominated the discourse of India's political world in the decades after independence, expected that traditional forms of belonging and behaviour would disappear under the twin pressure of the economic logic of industrialisation and the political logic of electoral democracy. Historically the actual unfolding of modernity has proved enormously more complex.

The most comprehensive defining principle of India's social life before the coming of modern influences was undeniably the caste order. That order determined the individual's life chances, and its structural principles governed the relation between the collective bodies of castes in the social system. In all parts of India, despite regional variations, the expansion of economic modernity – urbanisation and industrial development – led to a decline of caste observances in daily life. Hindu rules forbidding intermixture in marriage, social intercourse, and commensality lost their former ability to constrain individual behaviour and private lives. Ironically, in the public arenas of political life, by contrast, caste identities seem to have become much more assertive, defying modernist expectations. Caste affiliations have not broken down or faded in political life under the impact of electoral politics; the order of caste life has simply adapted to the operation of parliamentary democracy to produce highly effective large caste-based electoral coalitions.[19] Paradoxically, the historical demand of this form of caste politics is not the end of caste-identity, but a democratic recognition of equality among self-recognising caste groups – a state of affairs unthinkable according to the traditional grammar of caste behaviour.

The new caste politics therefore defies characterisation in terms of the easy dichotomy of modernisation theory.[20] It is not a wholly modern practice, since it is based on caste; equally, it is not wholly traditional, as it puts caste to an unprecedented modern use. An anomalous accompaniment of this development is the peculiar translation of the language of rights in contemporary Indian culture. In Indian society, despite pressures of modernity, the process of sociological individuation has not gone very far. Consequently, although the universe of political discourse is ringing with unceasing demands for recognition of rights,

[19] M. N. Srinivas, the eminent Indian sociologist, who did pioneering work on the operation of caste practices in modern conditions, called these new configurations 'monster castes' to indicate that they are vast coalitions in size, but also that they defy the traditional segmentary logic of the caste system. Srinivas 1986.

[20] Scholars have pointed out these trends and their theoretically unsettling implications since the late 1960s. Cf. Rudolph and Rudolph 1968 and Kothari 1970.

rarely have these advocated the rights of atomistic liberal individuals. In a world made of very different principles of sociability – marked by the primacy of castes, regions, and communities – the strident new language of rights has sought to establish primarily rights of contending groups. Most major radical demands in Indian politics are now for group equality rather than income equality between individuals – leading to a strange fading from the discourse of one of the poorest societies of the world of the distinctive arguments of socialism. The largest numbers of the Indian poor themselves seem to be more intent on removing degradation rather than poverty.[21]

It is not surprising that elite groups, who have most to lose from the assertion of demands of lower castes, have given large-scale support to an historical counter-move through a reassertion of religious identity. Hindu nationalist parties were relatively unsuccessful electorally in the period of Congress's hegemony. The Jana Sangh, the party of Hindu nationalism, had stable support among some social groups in particular regions of northern India, but it never came near threatening Congress dominance.[22] But in a climate of intensifying lower-caste assertion, their insinuation against the muddled secularism of the Congress – that it discriminated against the Hindus in return for secure voting support from the Muslim minority – attracted substantial upper-caste backing. Assisted by an inflammatory rhetoric of restitutive justice, centred on an old mosque allegedly built on a destroyed temple in the sixteenth century, the Hindu nationalist Bharatiya Janata Party (BJP), the successor to the Jana Sangh, made dramatic electoral gains in the elections in the 1990s. It finally emerged as the largest single party in parliament, and has been ruling India for the last five years with the support of volatile coalitions.[23] What is remarkable in this contest is that the BJP has sought to fashion a response to the politics of lower caste groups by appealing to the emotions of another form of community. Communitarianism in Indian politics takes complex and at times extremely unpleasant forms.[24]

But democracy is a complex ideal which appeals equally to two types of political principles. On the one hand, it claims its legitimacy from the pursuit of conflict through established, transparent procedures, which ensure that no group loses out finally and irreversibly, so that they continue to follow their objectives through recursive electoral contests. On the other hand, it appeals

---

[21] Communist parties in India had been traditionally reluctant to take up the cause of caste indignity as a central issue, preferring to focus on poverty and economic inequality. In the last decades, they have sought to adapt their agenda to the politics of the lower castes.

[22] For an excellent analysis of Hindu nationalist politics till the late 1960s, see Graham 1990.

[23] The fact that the BJP has come to power only as part of a coalition is highly significant: since some of its coalition partners do not share its strong anti-Muslim programme, it has imposed some moderation on its administration.

[24] There are several excellent studies of the recent growth of Hindu nationalism. See especially Jaffrelot 1994 for a detailed history. Hansen 1999 links the Hindu upsurge with a Tocquevillian understanding of democratisation. Rajagopal 2000 analyses the associations between creating collective emotions and the use of semiotics and the media.

to the principles of participation in both the deliberative and expressive forms. The politics of community assertion in India has created a potential conflict between these two principles. Political parties representing large communities, with a strong sense of grievance, have often regarded the procedures of liberal government as unjustified obstacles in their pursuit of justice. Procedures, which are central to the successful operation of democracy, can, as Indian experience shows, be threatened by some forms of participatory politics.

Another peculiarity of the story of modern politics in India is the simultaneous power of democracy and bureaucracy. Although theoretically, bureaucracy and democracy seem opposing tendencies, as the increased power and reach of the state seems to conflict, in principle, with democratic demands against it, this apparent paradox is not difficult to resolve. Democratic participation has increased ordinary people's expectations about conditions and quality of life. In a society which does not generate enough wealth to enable interest groups in society to pursue their institutional aims with their own resources, all demands for amelioration – for hospitals, schools, roads – are directed at the state, which is the only possible source for creation of collective goods. Thus the rise of democracy has reinforced the tendency towards a constant extension of the bureaucratic state.

For an understanding of how Europe affected the history of other cultures over the long term, the Indian story is significant for two reasons. A common pessimistic argument asserts that the 'export' of the state, with bounded territories and modern institutions of governance, to other parts of the world through European colonialism has largely failed, ending in most cases in disaster. It has forced people to live their lives, unsuccessfully, under unintelligible institutional frames, leading to increased tensions and expanded capacities for violence. Eventually, the argument runs, such historical experiments have failed, leading in most cases to the common experience of state collapse. The Indian case encourages a more optimistic conclusion.[25] It shows that a country comprising nearly a fifth of the world's population has successfully mastered the techniques of establishing a modern state. Despite the complex demands on its ideological and material resources, India has not seen a collapse of its institutional structure leading to a breakdown of minimal social order. Interestingly, although its state has been overstretched, it has managed to avoid bankruptcy and failure to provide basic services. India has avoided both the economic and the political forms of 'state collapse'.

Perhaps the most astonishing part of the Indian story has been the relative success of democracy. There are some familiar arguments in political theory

---

[25] In comparisons of this kind, size matters. The pessimistic argument that states have failed in hundreds of cases should be weighed carefully against the fact that India, although representing a single state, accounts for a very large proportion of the non-Western world. Although one state, it is a powerful counter-argument to the claim that modern states have failed outside the field of modern Western culture.

which stress the economic or cultural 'conditions' for the success of democratic government. Either a certain level of prior economic growth, or an underlying cultural common sense which accords equal value to individuals, has been re-garded as a necessary condition for the success of democratic institutions. The relative success of Indian democracy defies both arguments. In the politics of one of the poorest countries of the world, with a traditional order based on the pure principle of hierarchy, democracy has for half a century been a universally uncontested ideal. But the 'success of democracy' in India can mean two differ-ent things. In much of Western journalism, and in a part of academic analysis as well, the success of democracy simply means the uninterrupted continuance of electoral politics. Actually, however, the 'success' of Indian democracy ought to be viewed in Tocqueville's terms – as the historical development of a social force that has transformed fundamental social relations of everyday lives. It is true that the historical outcomes, the political trajectories of this story of democ-racy have been quite different from the great European stories of democratic transformation. But that is hardly surprising. Formal institutions of democracy operate on the basis of a template of the specific sociabilities available in each society. If democracy achieves success in other non-European societies in fu-ture, their trajectories are more likely to resemble the Indian narrative than the European ones. It is impossible to predict the exact direction this narrative of political transformation of a hierarchical society might take; but, despite the fact that it has happened in relative historical silence, without the spectacular violence that accompanied the American or French revolutions, it will rank as a story of one of the great transformations of modern times.

BIBLIOGRAPHY

Al Biruni (1914). *Al Biruni's India*, transl. and ed. E. C. Sachau, London: Routledge and Kegan Paul.
Appadurai, A. (1996). 'Number in the Colonial Imagination' in *Orientalism and the Post-colonial Predicament*, Philadelphia: Pennsylvania University Press.
Armitage, D. (2000). *The Ideological Origins of the British Empire*, Cambridge: Cambridge University Press.
Austin, G. (1964). *India's Constitution: The Cornerstone of A Nation*, Oxford: Clarendon Press.
Bardhan, P. (1985). *The Political Economy of Development in India*, Delhi: Oxford University Press.
Bayly, C. A. (1989). *Indian Society and the Making of the British Empire*, Cambridge: Cambridge University Press.
  (1996). *Empire and Information*, Cambridge: Cambridge University Press.
Bhagwati, J. (1993). *India in Transition*, Oxford: Clarendon Press.
Bhargava, R. (2000). 'Democratic Vision of a New Republic: India 1950' in Francine Frankel *et al.* (eds.), *Transforming India: Social and Political Dynamics of Democ-racy*, Delhi: Oxford University Press.

Burke, E. (1998). 'On the Impeachment of Warren Hasting, 15–19 February 1788', in B. Harlow and M. Carter (eds.), *Imperialism and Orientalism*, Oxford: Blackwell.

Chakrabarty, S. (1987). *Development Planning: The Indian Experience*, Oxford: Clarendon Press.

Dirks, N. (1986). *The Hollow Crown*, Ann Arbor: University of Michigan Press.

Frankel, F. (ed.) (1978). *India's Political Economy*, Princeton: Princeton University Press.

Graham, B. (1990). *Hindu Nationalism and Indian Politics*, Cambridge: Cambridge University Press.

Guizot, F. (1997). *The History of Civilisation in Europe*, transl. and ed. L. Seidentop, Harmondsworth: Penguin.

Hansen, T. (1999). *The Saffron Wave*, Princeton: Princeton University Press.

Irschik, D. (1994). *Dialogue and History*, Berkeley: University of California Press.

Jaffrelot, C. (1994). *The Hindu Nationalist Movement and Indian Politics*, New York: Columbia University Press.

Karivaj, S. (1994). 'The Imaginary Institution of India' in G. Pandey and P. Chatterjee (eds.), *Subaltern Studies*, vol. VII, Delhi: Oxford University Press.

(2000a). 'Democracy and Social Inequality' in F. Frankel (ed.), *Transforming India*, Delhi: Oxford University Press.

(2000b). 'Modernity and Politics in India', *Daedalus*, winter.

Kothari, R. (ed.) (1970). *Caste in Indian Politics*, Delhi: Orient Longman.

Mani, L. (1998). *Contentious Traditions: The Debate on Sati in Colonial India*, Berkeley: University of California Press.

Mehta, U. S. (1999). *Liberalism and Empire: A Study in Nineteenth-century British Liberal Thought*, Chicago: Chicago University Press.

Mill, J. S. (1962). *Utilitarianism, Liberty, Representative Government*, ed. A. D. Lindsay, London: J. M. Dent.

(1990). *Writings on India, Collected Works of J. S. Mill*, vol. XXX, ed. J. M. Robson, M. Moir, and Z. Moir, London: Routledge.

Rajagopal, A. (2000). *Politics After Television*, Cambridge: Cambridge University Press.

Rao, B. S. ed. (1964). *The Making of the Indian Constitution*, 4 vols., Delhi: Indian Institute of Public Administration.

Rudolph, L. and Rudolph, S. H. (1968). *The Modernity of Tradition*, Chicago: University of Chicago Press.

Rudolph, L. and Rudolph, S. H. (1987). *In Pursuit of Lakshmi*, Chicago: Chicago University Press.

Srinivas, M. N. (1986). 'Caste in Modern India' in his *Caste in Modern India and Other Essays*, Delhi: Oxford University Press.

Stein, B. (1985). 'State Formation Revisited', *Modern Asian Studies*, 19, no. 3, December.

Stokes, E. (1959). *English Utilitarians and India*, London: Oxford University Press.

Subrahmanyam, S. (ed.) (1990). *Merchants, Markets and the State in Early Modern India*, Delhi: Oxford University Press.

Washbrook, D. A. (1988). 'Progress and Problems: South Asian Ecomomic and Social History, 1720–1860', *Modern Asian Studies*, 21, no. 4.

(1999). 'India, 1818–1860' in A. Porter (ed.), *Oxford History of the British Empire: The Nineteenth Century*, Oxford: Oxford University Press.

PART FIVE

After the modern state

11   The state and its critics: is there a post-modern challenge?

Bo Stråth

In the 1930s, after a century or so of bargaining on 'the social issue', the state became the locus of social responsibility and welfare provision. Social contention had begun in the 1830s over the question of poverty; and it had ended in the 1930s as a response to mass unemployment. Throughout, the main issue at stake was responsibility: did responsibility lie with the poor individual, with some other body, or was it the entire structure of society that was to blame? In these processes of social bargaining the category of the poor was soon divided into the undeserving and the deserving. 'Undeserving poor' meant that the individual was to blame. The invention of the concept of the 'deserving poor' shifted responsibility from the individual to some other body. Which body was the subject of social debate: was it the parish, the city, the employer, the state?[1] In the 1880s a new concept was invented in this bargaining process: the 'unemployed'. This new differentiation between the poor and the unemployed resulted from a growing recognition that the causes of poverty should be sought at a supra-individual level. Which specific level was, again, the theme of some fifty years of bargaining, before the decisive answer was proclaimed in the 1930s: the state. The response emerged under very different political labels: *front populaire*, national socialism, fascist corporatism, New Deal, Scandinavian red-green (worker-farmer) coalitions, etc.[2] However, in each case the change signified the same shift in the allocation of responsibility, from the individual to the supra-individual level, or, to adopt a more critical perspective, from a real to a fictional level.

The state responsibility that had been established in the 1930s was legitimatised and confirmed in economic theory during the 1950s and 1960s. The idea that emerged was that the economy, 'the market', was governable through politics. To a large extent this insight had gained importance as a result of the experiences in political planning and economic governance acquired during two world wars. Economic theory explained the connections between employment,

I am very grateful to Elizabeth Fordham for her many valuable observations and suggestions during the editing of this article, and to Peter Wagner for his important comments on an earlier version of the text.
[1] Castel 1995 and Topalov 1994.   [2] Mansfield, Salais, and Whiteside 1994; Stråth 2000a.

investment, and currency value, and argued that the nature of these connections was politically manageable. Political economy, mixed economy, *soziale Marktwirtschaft*, and economic planning became key concepts, while some thinkers talked about a long-term convergence between socialist and capitalist systems based on a belief in the indispensable role of political governance in the economy. This belief was shaken in the 1970s, when high inflation, mass unemployment and 'stagflation' returned, against the predictions of both economic theory and political economy, which had insisted that these conditions would never occur again.

However, belief in the state as a key instrument in the political economy paradigm had already been challenged before the crisis of the 1970s. Critiques of the 1960s, such as Althusser's,[3] had already maintained that the welfare state was conserving social injustice instead of providing equality. A more active political approach for more and better social equality was required. Within this framework, a gender-based emancipating language emerged. Moreover, the welfare state was held responsible for ruthless environmental exploitation. Ideas inspired by Marx about the state as an instrument of repression rapidly gained popularity.[4] It is these critiques and ideas that will provide the point of departure for my analysis.

This chapter will focus on the *transformation* of the image of the state in the wake of the challenges posed by the social movement of the 1960s. With the formulation 'the image of the state' I want to emphasise that, as David Runciman has argued in chapter 2, the state is a fiction, an abstraction that is given concrete form through reification and personification.[5] One element of 'the image of the state', or 'the state as a fiction', is that the state has been attributed purposes and intentions, or, in the form of the nation, an identity. During at least the two last centuries, the fiction of the state has gone hand in hand with a counter-fiction: the market.

In analysing the transformation of images of the state, my main concern is how critical language was transformed after the 1960s to emerge in the 1980s with an entirely new target. I consider this transformation to be a question of the appropriation of language and discursive struggle. Once a new problem is

---

[3] To take only the best-known example. See, for instance, Althusser 1969.   [4] Stråth 2002.

[5] The critique of the state as a fiction may also be found in the 1960s. Althusser defined the liberal state in terms of its *appareil idéologique*. By this he was certainly not denying the very real force of the state within capitalism, and Althusser was one of the most vocal opponents of the use of this *appareil* as an instrument of oppression and exploitation. However, the focus of Althusser's critique lay not so much on the material power of the state as on its intellectual domination. It was by controlling the domains of justice, culture, and education that the capitalist state maintained its hegemony, and it was within man's thought – and above all within the structures of language built up to express this thought – that the alienation of capitalist society was at once created and sustained. This critique found its most lyrical expression – though maybe not its most coherent – in Debord 1992.

critically identified, often in what has been labelled 'speech acts',[6] the whole framework of the debate changes and new power situations emerge; or, rather, the breakthrough of a new language reflects a new power situation. In my case I will demonstrate how the critics, who initiated the process, became themselves objects of counter-critique. Concepts like conservative and progressive, right and left became problematic and contested within the general transformation of the critical language from Marxism to neo-liberalism. In the Marxist view, progression was brought about though class struggle, whereas in the neo-liberal view the dynamic of class conflict gave way to the forces of market competition.

This study is inspired by a specific understanding of historical change. It is common practice for historians to divide time into periods and epochs, to discern discontinuities, when something new begins and an older order disappears. A realistic view of historical change, however, would not be one of abrupt shifts, where history is divided into well-demarcated phases, but more a continuous flow, where continuity connotes the verb continue – meaning to go on, to proceed – rather than a static state of things, and where continuity may also be taken to refer to the way in which key elements coexist with the addition of new elements. Therefore, revolutionary change, as it was understood during the French Revolution, is in this view of continuity less revolutionary than it pretends to be. *Plus ça change plus c'est la même chose.* This does not mean that nothing changes, but simply that the main problem lies in the investigation of precisely *what* changes and *what* remains the same. As Reinhart Koselleck has argued, continuity represents continuous change. Repetitive structures are not more or less static, as in the view of Braudel, but undergo permanent transformation.[7] In this sense long-lasting repetitive structures are unique in each particular situation and context, because their embedding is unique. The long-term structures, which make change possible, change themselves with the changes they have initiated.

One justification for this repudiation of caesurae is that each proposal and every decision in social bargaining and problem resolution is invariably challenged. There exists a perpetual cacophony of voices, never a single megaphone succeeded by another. Social bargaining is discursive contention, and attempts to appropriate key concepts and give them specific meaning. Such discursive contention transgresses the division of time into phases or periods. Rather than a sharp and frontal confrontation between two conflicting views, and sharp discontinuities in development, a pattern of coexisting and competing tendencies emerges. Their mutual challenge to one another entangles them in a bundle of continuities rather than separating them into distinct phases, where only

---

[6] Skinner 1999, esp. pp. 69–71 and 1996 ch. 4.
[7] Koselleck 2000. On Braudel's key concepts *la longue durée*, *l'histoire conjoncturelle*, and *l'histoire événementielle*, see Braudel 1969.

one tendency exists. There is a continuous tussle over social bargaining, and a continuous redefinition of interests. In retrospect we can see how the mutual strength of the competing tendencies has changed. The breakthrough of one specific problem solution means new challenges and a new point of departure for problem formulation and the discursive struggle. Social change is transformation as opposed to formation. This emphasis on transformation does not mean that the velocity of the change is equal. Discursive breakthroughs in specific and condensed situations are filled with their own Καιρός, the basic meaning of which was time and weather, but which in a transferred sense describes a condensed and fateful situation full of alternatives, one that provokes immediate action and discursive innovation, opens up new horizons and establishes new points of departure for the continued social contention.

The dynamics of the critique of 1968 varied from context to context. However, they all shared an individualist thrust. The cries for freedom and equality were cries for individual emancipation from state or parental authority. The 1968 movement belonged to youth. The hippie movement in the USA, the anti-war movement against the Vietnam War, the generational revolt against parental mendacity about the Nazi heritage in Germany, and the environmental protest all had their focus on the emancipation of the individual, although this was often concealed under the language of class-struggle. This focus on the individual was consistent with other simultaneous histories of modernity at that time such as clothing, culture, and education, according to which the individual, in the name of self-expression, took responsibility within the formation of new communities in contrast with the collectivity of the welfare state and the core family.

Individualist demands were inspired by a severe Marxist critique, which cast the state as an instrument of bourgeois repression. The critique occurred within the framework of the general disintegration of world-images. The progressive, functionalist, evolutionary image of Western modernisation, industrialisation, and democratisation, gradually occupying the whole world, was rapidly eroded by the dollar collapse, the oil-price shock, and the recurrence of mass unemployment during the first half of the 1970s. The critique, which emerged in the second half of the 1960s, was itself confirmed and strengthened by these developments. The combined effect was the emergence of new uncertainties in a world that, after 1945, had with astonishing speed gained confidence in its own governability. The welfare state provided security and assurance, and these feelings provoked demands for even greater equality and social justice, which, together with the pressures from the international economic order and the physical environment, paradoxically created a widespread sense of insecurity. A possible explanation for this paradox lies in the contradictions of 1968 – contradictions that are, indeed, inherent in Marxism itself. For if one of the great achievements of Marx was to recognise that in the modern world power lay on a *supra-individual* level (in fictions like the state, the market, the class or the people), his great failure was to underestimate the degree to which the locomotive for change still remained on an *individual* level. Until the language of power can be made to represent the experiences of the individual actor, then revolutions, like that of 1968, will serve merely to perpetuate the alienation they seek to resolve through invocation of the state, the market, or other such fictions.

These new individualist demands were interpreted and underpinned by economic theory. Until the crises of the early 1970s, economic theory had guaranteed that it possessed the necessary instruments to prevent another Great Depression. Reacting to the breakdown of their model, economists began to argue that overly strong trade unions and rigid wage politics had pushed wages too high and pressed governments to spend too much. Their prescription was wage flexibility – that is, that supply and demand in the labour markets should determine wages, which would in turn re-establish full employment – budget rigidity and tight monetary politics. The market replaced the state as the icon in economic theory. The neoclassical 'Keynesian' language of the 1950s and the 1960s shifted to neoclassical/neoliberal rhetoric.[8] At the beginning of the 1980s the fiction of the market replaced, in paradigmatic terms, the fiction of the state.

This general paradigmatic shift of the 1970s is illustrated in the transformation of the language of labour markets. The core of the radicalised language in the 1960s was a massive critique of the Western capitalist model of social organisation. (However, there was also a parallel and related, although less observed, critique of the Soviet model.) The new class language culminated in slogans like co-determination, *Mitbestimmung*, and *autogestion*, and under the development of new practices like sit-ins, work-ins, factory occupations, and so on. The massive critique formulated in the new language provoked a heavy challenge not only to organised capital, but also to organised labour, that is, to the trade unions. However, the interesting historical question is how to interpret the fact that shop-floor protests did not culminate in a Marxist appeal for a classless society, but in a new neo-liberal language emphasising values like nearness and flexibility, and a growing role for the individual worker not in class-based antagonisms but in friendly relations with the employer. The old *Arbeiter* became the *Mitarbeiter*, the worker became the co-worker. How can we understand the way in which the explosion of class language in 1968 was not followed by the triumph of the working-class but by its gradual dissolution as a historical category?

The ability to launch new concepts that carry conviction, and the ability to appropriate these key concepts, and positions of priority, and even to monopolise

---

[8] See Purdy 2001 for a critical discussion of the epithet of 'Keynesian' for the economics and economic politics in the 1950s and 1960s, which he prefers to describe in terms of a particular version of neoclassics in demarcation to the later neoliberal version of neoclassical theory.

the interpretation of them, is of critical importance to historical change. Of course, concepts do not in themselves cause change, but they do establish a particular horizon for potential action. They make change possible, on the one hand, and on the other, they set limits for possible change.

In the 1970s, not only militant class language, but with it the whole corporatist model, folded in upon itself. This was not a causative and necessary development, which could have been predicted *ex ante*, but one alternative development among others, discernible only in retrospect, and where the *ex post* analysis can only ascertain why the developments took the directions they actually did, given the existing social power relationships. In retrospect we can see that there was no breakthrough in shop-floor claims: class language never realised the classless society. Instead, radical class language was canalised and transformed in new directions. The target of the critique, 'capitalism' and its representatives, whether in private firms or in the state, was no longer an inflexible firm-standing target. The targets of the critique were in the process of developing new positions out of harm's way. The critical language therefore faced contentious interpretations and attempts to canalise the semantic and symbolic field around its key concepts into new directions. This may be seen, for example, in the way in which 'capitalism' responded to workers' claims for *Mitbestimmung* by granting rights to *Mitarbeiter* to form collegial relations with management.

From the end of the 1960s the language of critique was constructed around a bundle of key concepts such as co-determination, *Mitbestimmung* and *Selbstverwaltung*, *medbestämmande*, concepts that set the horizons for a more radical language. One question here is, what does the ambiguity between the particles *co-* and *auto-* in various languages reflect and express: how were these concepts appropriated and employed in order to occupy semantic fields, and how were they filled with political content in discursive struggles? This is a question for future research from a comparative perspective, which could possibly throw more light on the European differences in corporatist welfare capitalism already referred to above. However, it is clear that the languages with the prefix *co-*, *Mit* and *med* came from Social Democratic traditions reflecting ideas of shared responsibility and partnership, where more worker power would establish a new equilibrium. This language was particularly strong in Germany and Scandinavia. The languages with the prefix *auto* were generated from within the workers' shop floor movements and from Communist views, and they rejected the *co*-approach. This language emerged in countries like France and Italy that after the Second World War had strong Communist parties but relatively weak traditions of Social Democracy.

This tension between the *co*- and *auto*- approaches was dissolved in the post-1968 flexibility language within processes of protest integration. The two concepts were canalised in the same direction towards that of 'co-worker'. The key question here is the transformation of the language and industrial relations when claims by employees for *co-* and *auto*-determination gradually became an employer philosophy based on the co-worker concept. The breakthrough of the new radical *co-* or *auto*-determination language signified a fundamental change in the preconditions of industrial relations as they had been established in bargaining processes since the 1930s and even earlier. Nothing remained as it had been after this breakthrough. However, this does not mean that the future became what it had been imagined to become. This transformation of language and industrial relations, which took place under contention and attempts to appropriate positions of interpretative power, hardly represented a caesura, where everything prior to the events around 1970 disappeared and a new view emerged. There was a constant contest over the direction of the transformation, and over the content of the new language which had emerged – at the same time as the redefinition of the workers' interests and identities – from earlier concepts like social partnership. The language changed the historically established structures of industrial relations and work organisation. The focus moved from the central national level to the local company and shop-floor level. New rules for rights, standards, and negotiation – established in attempts to integrate the protests – had their focus on the shop-floor level. There the workers' militancy was at its strongest with their claims for power to the floor. The long-term effect of this shift of focus was that the vertical ties within the trade unions were strained. This transformation of industrial relations meant the redefinition of the employers' interests and the emergence of a new conceptual flora around concepts like co-worker, *Mitarbeiter*, *medarbetare*. One question which relates to this transformation, and also underpins the problem of the European variety of welfare corporatism, is why this emphasis on being one of the company family (*Mitarbeiter*, *medarbetare*) was so much stronger in Germany and Scandinavia than anywhere else. A concept like co-worker did emerge later on in English, as a translation from German and Scandinavian languages. However, the translation into French, *collaborateur*, did not have much mobilising power. The answer to this question could be formulated by considering the role of various political traditions and the organisation of industrial relations in the different countries.

The protests activated representatives of both organised capital and organised labour and the governments who intervened with new legislation and new regulation. The rewriting of the labour market laws at the beginning of the 1970s contained the same key concepts as did the critical discourse, such as co-determination and *Mitbestimmung*, but it was now much more a matter of shared employer–employee responsibility and determination than employee power. The prefix of *co-* (*med*, *Mit*) was given new, although still contested, meaning. The language remained but the content shifted during this integration of the protests. The old model of social partnership returned in new forms.

The bipartite bargaining model was re-established at the shop floor level in more de-centralised forms. Hierarchical ties of solidarity within the trade union movement developed over more than a century were severed during this de-centralising trend of response to the protests.[9]

Only gradually did the horizons and images of a new organisation of labour and of the economy as a whole emerge. Indeed, the direction of the transformation of the old order appeared in many respects only in retrospect. This can be seen, for instance, in the response to the totally unexpected recurrence of mass unemployment in the mid-1970s, where the first reactions were voiced through class language, but where, under the surface of this radical language, the development of new solidarity patterns were promoted. Management and labour, in competition for taxpayers' money with corresponding groups in rival companies, stood on the same barricades in struggles to rescue plants and jobs. Ties of solidarity between the trade unions, which had developed into national networks over many decades, were first stretched then severed in this shared struggle, and new ties of solidarity and identification with the company emerged. The overall impact, not only on trade unions and the labour market, but on the whole organisation of society, was tremendous when such national patterns of class solidarity began to mutate into company-related habits of identification.

Two other factors contributed to this transformation. In the short term these factors reinforced class language, but in the long run they presented an alternative image demarcated from and gradually eroding the class concept. First of all, the long-term erosion of 'class' language and corporatist structures was reinforced by an increasing tension between 'class' and 'gender' as categories of identity. In industrial society the gender dimension of the organisation of labour markets was from the very beginning male-dominated. The breadwinner metaphor provided the main argument for this bias. As we have already seen in chapters 8 and 10, there was a long tradition, since the emergence of liberal society, of struggle for women's rights. Although feminists made a significant contribution to the trade union movement, and although there was a long history of heated trade-union debates on the gender-work theme, the breadwinner interpretation predominated. The question of equality, for instance, was much more commonly reduced to a general low-wage problem than defined in terms of a specific gender problem. This changed in the 1970s with the more definite transformation of industrial society towards an information society. One aspect of this change was increased female labour market participation. From this point on, under severe tension in established union structures, union strategies and labour relations started to reflect gender-specific inequalities in new ways.

[9] Stråth 1996.

'Emancipation' became a key word in political debate, and its implication was that the gender dimension as a mobilising identity category had clear political aims of its own.

The other factor working in the same long-term direction was the environment debate. In the short run the work-place and working-life environment became targets for improvement, but in the long run the whole mass consumption–mass production model, which underpinned the growth economy, came under pressure. The prefix of consumption changed from mass to quality, and industrial production was in many respects seen as an obstacle to the claims of the green movement, which questioned the whole philosophy of growth while the working class in their show of strength wanted more growth and affluence. Much of the green critique was absorbed and transformed in the new nearness, flexibility, and small-is-beautiful language which emerged as the semantic entourage of the *Mitarbeiter* concept. This in turn was reflected in new management approaches, and was connected to the co-worker approach. Both the working-life environment and the production philosophy changed.

The concept of 'flexibility' played a key role in this dramatic transformation of the 1970s and 1980s. This concept was primarily coined as a term that applied to work organisation and the labour market, although there was a clear correlation with the debate on society in general in the demand for flexibility versus bureaucratic sclerosis and political inertia. The protests against robotisation, piecework stress, and conveyor-belt monotony were canalised into new wage-earner and co-worker rather than worker ideals. Instead of being a specialist on a line with a narrow competence, the employer looked increasingly for all-round and flexible 'generalists' with a competence to carry out various tasks by rotation in an emerging team-work organisation. The clear demarcation between blue- and white-collar employees was erased. The guarantee of job performance ('productivity') was increasingly looked for in psychological models of individual motivation and comfort, in opposition to the older and more coercive conveyor-belt and piecework models of Taylorism, which also had psychological connotations, but of a different kind. A simultaneous doctrinal shift in the economic and social sciences underpinned this transformation of worldviews. A new interpretative order emerged – based on older models of liberal thinking long superseded by the idea of political management of the labour markets and the economy – embedded in concepts like monetarism, budget equilibrium, and the reduction of government expenditure. This emerging neo-liberal rhetoric became attractive through frequent use of social Darwinian language, in which 'healing' meant 'slimming down', and in which State welfare arrangements were described as 'unsanitary', 'unhealthy', yes, 'suffocating'. Right in the middle of the prevailing mass unemployment a concept like 'labour hoarding' emerged with interpretative power. The market and flexibility were the main figures in this reshaping of the conceptual and symbolic topography.[10]

In a curious way 'flexibility' went hand in hand with its opposite, 'rigidity', in the new rhetoric. The prescription for the individual was flexibility and adjustment to the requirements of 'the market' while the simultaneous prescription for the state was rigidity and budget discipline. Not only 'the market' but also 'the state' took on personified proportions as actors who must follow prescribed regimes in order to be cured of their Beveridgian sickliness, and which respectively provided the necessary medicine for this healing.

The term flexibility emerged as an economic prescription against the unexpected blow of mass unemployment in the early 1970s. Taken by surprise, economists began to advocate wage flexibility, that is, that wages should adjust to the demand of the market. It was believed that lower wages (the necessary outcome of wage flexibility) would create more jobs. Wages higher than what the market could digest had created the situation of mass unemployment. The other side of this emerging economic language of flexibility was the argument that excessively strong trade unions and rigid wage policies had pushed wages too high. Counter-theories about labour market segmentation, and about long-term regimes of 'structural regulation' (*l'école de la régulation*) were not able to prevent what can be described as the main trend in the theoretical rhetoric from state to market orientation. The fact that mass unemployment, contrary to conventional economic wisdom, occurred within the framework of high inflation provided arguments that underpinned this doctrinal transformation. High inflation was caused by too much government spending, which, in turn, was caused by pressures from too strong trade unions. The theoretical prescription was to match the wage flexibility with budget rigidity and monetary discipline.[11]

One important element of this transformation was a social Darwinist division between the fit – the new kind of core labour, the *Mitarbeiter* – and the weak – the margin of unemployed or casual low-wage labour. Flexible, casual labourers and the unemployed each rise in numbers in situations where conditions exist which are, in this respect, reminiscent of the era prior to the introduction of labour legislation. The Darwinian element in flexibility language mediates continuity with the nineteenth century, when a Darwinian metaphor existed not only in the liberal doctrine of harmony through competition, but also emerged in a Marxist framework.

The decisive difference between Marxist and neo-liberal Darwinian languages is that the former was based on the collective idea of class identity, whereas today's flexibility language claims to have at its heart an idea of the free and unbound individual. This neo-liberal claim is in opposition not only to

---

[10] Stråth 2000a.   [11] Stråth 2000a.

Marxist theory but also to the images of classical liberalism.[12] Visions of work were the foundation of the chiliastic ideas of 'the New Man' in Soviet Russia. With socialism as a basis, the emergence of a new type of man was anticipated: a man who was solidaristic instead of egoistic, collective-minded instead of individually oriented. The icon of this New Man was a male and muscular manufacturing worker with a powerful faith in progress. Today's flexibility has its own liberal counterpart to this Soviet model New Man, a figure as strong but also as imaginary as the older one. The 'Flexible Man' is an all-rounder, highly adaptable to new challenges, creative and innovative. He is independent and emancipated from all restraining social bounds. From the self-realisation of the Flexible Man the emergence of a new and better society is postulated. The tension between adaptability and creativity is not, however, addressed. Thus a critical question arises as to how creative and innovative the remote-controlled Flexible Man really is. Does not his ability to roll with changes make him an achievement-oriented rather than a socially stable – or politically loyal – character?

As wage labour and the idea of full employment are being replaced, the whole socio-cultural pattern of community, identity, and solidarity, and core institutions like 'the state', the family, and the division of the population that is of working age into employers and employees, is affected. The conceptualisation of society had wage labour and employment as one of its most important points of departure during most of the twentieth century. Established institutions and patterns of community and solidarity in labour markets had a tremendous impact on the whole of society. The political controversy surrounding unemployment, working-hours, labour legislation, and wages since the 1970s can be seen as a symbolic struggle over deeper problems affecting the whole of society as old ties of solidarity and identity patterns and responsibilities break down.

The changing image of the state and the accompanying fundamental shift in the whole complex of social integration provoke the question of what communities enable solidarity to be created. Is the idea of solidarity exclusively a worker question as was class identity in industrial society? Is it more of an employee–employer question (for those who have a job) based on identification with a company? Or does this question also involve the relationship of the state and the unemployed? Old industrial communities based on the identities of wage labour and class do not provide much of a political foundation

---

[12] Adam Smith envisaged a role for governments. Indeed, Book V of the *Wealth of Nations*, on government revenue and expansion, outlines the basis of a liberal social programme. His views on education and training far from endorse minimum state intervention. Thatcher and others of the neo-liberal persuasion were absolutely wrong in this respect when they cheerfully cited Adam Smith in support of these policies. Smith was more pragmatic than utopian. It was thus not by chance that Marx referred to Smith as 'the Luther of political economy'. See Stråth 2000a, p. 75.

today, but the question of solidarity and social integration is more relevant than ever.

Around 1990, the topography of flexibility, the market, and 'nearness' language began to be supported by a new concept: globalisation. In the 1990s 'globalisation' developed the neo-liberal market language of the 1980s into a new master narrative replacing the old one of progress, growth, and welfare. In the semantic field that emerged, counter-concepts were mobilised, although not to express opposition, as is usually the case with counter-concepts, but on the contrary to establish unity: 'global' went hand in hand with 'local' in a contradictory but consistent way. The two were connected through the 'nearness' language, for in a curious way global connotes nearness. In a contradictory but nevertheless consistent fashion, expressions like the global village and 'globalisation' mediated this unification of the remote and the near. To this semantic field, the concept of market was added. Or, better put, the globalisation language connected to and supported the neo-liberal market language which had emerged in the 1980s. Globalisation as a concept plays a similar role to that which 'emancipation' and 'equality' played in the 1960s. It is a highly ideologically charged, indeed, overcharged universal concept that explains everything and nothing.[13]

The globalisation rhetoric has taken on mythical proportions, in Roland Barthes's view of myth as the transformation of the cultural products of history into something apparently natural.[14] At a certain moment whites have power over blacks, and a myth then emerges arguing that whites are of superior nature. Today the laws of the market are considered as laws of nature. The metaphorical language employed to describe society is a case in point. The clock that described the world in the eighteenth century, and the railway engine of predetermined progress that did the same in the nineteenth century has become during the last quarter of the twentieth century the network. What all these terms have in common is that they do not address the question of social power relationships. They all describe society as an automatically functioning category without conflicts.

From its very beginning in the 1990s, the discourse of globalisation has differed both between Europe and America, and within Europe. Within America it has been dominated by a debate within the social sciences between libertarians and communitarians. This debate, in fact, started some twenty years earlier, and could, from a long historical view, be seen as a continuation *under transformation* of the long debate between Kantians and Hegelians. It is true that the biased emphasis on the free individual and the idealised view of the small community is more an illustration of Turner's well-known frontier thesis about the importance of the life in the Wild West for American culture than something

---

[13] Offe 2002.   [14] Barthes 1967. See White 2000 for a discussion of Barthes in this respect.

which fits with European political philosophy and nation- and state-oriented cultures.[15] Nevertheless, these European cultures, inscribed in the Westphalian order of post-1648 Europe, an order based on the idea of sovereign states that do not intervene in each others' internal affairs, are being rapidly eroded by the globalisation rhetoric. Globalisation is an American economic order based on the ethic of creative destruction. American experts, economists, lawyers, and political scientists write constitutions for new governments in Africa and Central Asia. Economics as an academic discipline preaches a universal logic of axiomatic dimensions based on individualism, contract freedom, and of a state that is reduced to the role of guaranteeing private interests.

That this language is an intrusion in the context of Europe is obvious. The European transformation of values under the impact of globalisation has been demarcated by the welfare state idea and focuses more on the citizen concept, in a way bypassing and transgressing the debate between libertarians and communitarians. In its European context the Citizen is an historical rather than a universal category, as it tends to be in America, and it is historical in two main senses – as well, of course, as being based on ancient originals. It is historical in the sense formulated by Thomas H. Marshall in 1949, where the citizen is seen as the carrier of a sequence of rights which have emerged over time: from civil rights to democratic participation rights to social rights in the welfare states of the twentieth century.[16] This may be referred to as the 'English sense'. However, the citizen is also historical in a second sense, the 'French sense', in that the concept is widely connected to various histories and translations from its political breakthrough in the French Revolution. Marshall had the English development as his primary example. In both the 'English' and the 'French' formulations the term citizen connoted not only rights but also duties, in the form of civic virtues, although this emphasis on duties was more pronounced in the French case. The emergence of the bundle of duties and rights that constitutes citizenship gained their precise shape in processes of nation building and constitutional developments.[17] The fact that the French *citoyen* became the German *Staatsbürger* reflects a number of such processes.[18] The image of an unambiguous, universal, and stable category of the citizen breaks down when it is confronted with historical developments. In modern European societies, the status of citizenship emerged over long periods, and was less an equally and automatically distributed category than a hard-won status that only gradually spread to larger groups and segments of society.

There is a certain truth in the cliché that America was 'born liberal'. American political traditions, as well as her political languages, lack the same sense of historical relativism that they posses within European societies. To take just one

---

[15] Stråth 2001.   [16] Marshall 1963.
[17] Conrad and Kocka 2001, pp. 12–17.   [18] Koselleck 1989, pp 52–67.

example, and to put it rather simply, within American political discourse the citizen is defined as either holding all power (libertarians) or holding no power (communitarians). Within Europe, however, the citizen is conceived, not as dominant or dominated, but as holding different *degrees* of power. The precise degree depends on how civil society functions, and how images of civil society have emerged historically in relation to images of the state. Within Britain, for instance, citizen power is defined socially, or economically, in terms of birth, whereas in France, the citizen is an intellectual or political animal, who has risen to power through will.

Different definitions of the citizen reflect historically developed differences between Western European nation-states and the United States of America. In both cases, liberal legislation on freedom of trade and commerce was introduced during the decades around 1850 in order to fix the rules of the game for industrial and commercial capitalism, and in Western Europe as a way of adjusting the old society of estates to new challenges and requirements; rules for shareholding and limited responsibility, for banking, etc., emerged. At the end of the nineteenth century a much stronger collective social protest by organised labour emerged in Europe, but not in the USA. The containment of this protest promoted the introduction of rules of the game for labour as well. In Europe, ideas of legal social protection and labour standards were much stronger for this historical reason. This is not to say that there was no social responsibility in the USA, but that the framework was different from that of the European welfare states. In the 1980s both the American philanthropic model and the European welfare state models were cut off from their historical roots. In the new flexibility language, and in the adoration of the strong individual there was little place for social responsibility. In America the philanthropic tradition of Carnegie and Rockefeller was abandoned, while in the emerging European media world, with icons like Tapie, Murdoch, or Berlusconi, there was little place for long-term thinking or for the value of human dignity – whether based on private philanthropy or on public welfare capitalism. Of course, these developments do not mean that some form of organised social responsibility cannot be reconstructed. However, such a reconstruction will never be identical with the original since it will have to be undertaken from new points of departure.

The citizen of the French Revolution was the carrier of the nation-state. The category of the citizen in this revolutionary version presupposed a strong state, although a state of a new democratic kind. This state also reflected a strong opinion of the Other, the enemies of the Revolution. The parallels between the political conceptions of the French Revolution and those of the European Community today have been discussed elsewhere,[19] and are important to my

---

[19] See, for example, Siedentrop 2000. In contrast to Siedentrop's rather narrow definition of politics, this chapter intends to open up the parallel to include the whole of civil society. An interesting variation on this theme is given by Frank 2002.

present argument. The idea of a European citizenship was supported by the idea of a European identity. When, in 1973, a European identity was politically proclaimed at the European Community (EC) summit in Copenhagen, the concept was inscribed in the tradition of a connection between the citizen and a strong nation-state. The link to ideas of a strong Euro-state was obvious. This link was particularly emphasised towards the end of the 1970s when serious attempts were undertaken to establish a tripartite Euro-corporatist order. The idea of European identity as an instrument to re-establish Europe's place in the collapsing international order as it had been formulated in Bretton Woods was also obvious, that is, Europe's definition of its Others was pronounced. The identity idea was based on the principle of the unity of the Nine, on their responsibility towards the rest of the world, and on the dynamic nature of the European construction. The meaning of 'responsibility towards the rest of the world' was expressed in a hierarchical way. First, it meant responsibility towards the other nations of Europe with whom friendly relations and co-operation already existed. Secondly, in the framework of the oil-price shock, it meant responsibility towards the countries of the Mediterranean, Africa, and the Middle East. Thirdly, in the wake of the dollar collapse, it referred to relations with the USA, based on the restricted foundations of equality and the spirit of friendship. Next in the hierarchy was the narrow co-operation and constructive dialogue with Japan and Canada. Then came *détente* towards the Soviet Union and the countries of Eastern Europe. At the bottom of the list came China, Latin America and, finally, a reference was made to the importance of the struggle against underdevelopment in general.[20]

When these attempts to re-establish the place of Europe within the world order quickly failed, the concepts of European identity and citizenship moved to support the emerging neo-liberal market language. The European citizen came to support individualism, as opposed to the old-fashioned nation-state, and vague ideas of a European Community/Union rather than a United States of Europe. Ideas of European driving licences, a European flag, and a European anthem supported this transformation of the identity and citizen concepts at a European level.[21] The French model of citizenship as unity was replaced by a British model of citizenship as rights.

Within Marshall's perspective, the focus of the citizen concept was on rights guaranteed by the state, which can be seen as a kind of 'passive' citizenship. Claims and rights of protection are emphasised in this view. Marshall certainly also mentioned citizens' duties. However, they occupied a less prominent place than rights in his welfare-state language. A more 'active' side of the citizenship has in reaction been suggested, with an emphasis on social commitment, responsibility, participation, and self-organisation. The growing discursive role

[20] For this discussion, see Passerini 1998, pp. 4–5. Cf. Stråth 2000b.
[21] Shore 2000, Stråth 2000b.

of the concept of civil society – in demarcation from the welfare state – is an element of this emphasis on active citizenship. It is not necessary to state that this distinction between passive and active citizens has quite another meaning than the corresponding distinction in the French Revolution. The modern version of active citizenship connotes republican virtues rather than universal liberalism. In concordance with the theory of democracy drafted by Tocqueville, voluntary associations and the citizens' public commitment are seen as production sites of social capital and trust.[22] With this discursive development, the citizen concept becomes ambiguous in its connection with neo-liberal market language. It also becomes not only ambiguous but even contradictory in its emphasis not merely on individualism, but also on ethnicity. The connection to ethnicity signifies a disconnection from the universal welfare state ideal. Ethnically based citizenship means the exclusion of millions of poor immigrants and socially marginalised individuals. These are not contained in the citizen rhetoric that emerged at a European level in the 1980s. They were inscribed in the citizenship of the French Revolution only for a brief moment, as we shall see in chapter 9. However, they were inscribed as *une idée pensée plutôt qu'un fait réel*. The question for the future is whether the connection to the idea of a European civil society will change anything in this respect. Instead of citizenship, 'inhabitantship' might be a concept to express territorial solidarity. Such a concept could be used in new forms of post-ethnic and post-religious community construction, including all denizens in a specific territory, post-ethnic in the sense that ethnic origin or race does not matter, and post-religious in the sense that religion does not play a role in the definition of political community. Given the great number of Muslim immigrants in Europe, for instance, Islam must be considered a European religion today, which no less, or rather no more, than Catholicism or Protestantism should play a role in the definition of the polity. The image of a citizen concept, not only transgressing ethnic demarcations but also integrating the socially excluded, emerges.[23] The interesting question is whether the concept of civil society can play a mediating role in such a development.

Implicit in this question is the historical continuity of the critique of '1968' and its failure. The '1968' consciousness was marked by a kind of Enlightenment belief in the effects of social critique, according to which autonomous and reason-endowed human beings were able to organise a free society once certain obstacles had been removed. However, the views on society after successful liberation were in the '1968' movement as vague as in Karl Marx's prognostication of the future, and remote from the conditions prevailing in Western society. The tension between the two elements of any political project, critique,

---

[22] Kymlicka and Norman 1994; Hildemeier, Kocka, and Conrad 2000.
[23] Jacobson 1998; Soysal 1994.

and reconstruction, was solved by a complete neglect of the latter element. The individualism which certainly was emphasised in the '1968' discourse was of quite a different kind from the individualism that emerged in the 1980s. The latter emerged by default, as a consequence of the failure to construct a viable political form for the critique.[24]

A central question today is whether the 'anti-globalisation' language of critique, which is emerging on a massive scale in response to globalisation, has in this respect improved. Rather than taking the argument of globalisation as a natural unbound force for granted, a situation has emerged from which a new critique can be formulated and developed. This critique cannot be the same as the critique of '1968', of course, since the old narrative of modernisation and democratisation in the wake of welfare capitalism, which was the target of '1968', is no longer applicable. Moreover, if '1968' failed, it was because the language of class-conflict proved just as alienating as the state-system it was trying to overthrow. The individual demands that fuelled the revolts of the 1960s simply could not be contained within the language of Marxism; however, they would not have been effective at all without some form of collective agreement, as the *de facto* emergence of a new collaborationist language in the 1970s suggests. Therefore, the challenge today is to find a critique that *represents* individual demands in the sense of giving them social force whilst at the same time avoiding social reification. As a form of compromise between English and French traditions of citizenship, where the pragmatism of the one is animated by the idealism of the other, this would be the ideal European solution to the problems of world organisation today.

In formulating this new critique, it is important to keep the distinction between critique and terrorism clear. Critique is not terrorism, and terrorism should not be connected to a specific civilisation. It is important not to make Huntington's prophecy self-fulfilling.[25] Fighting terrorism should not be carried out as a clash between civilisations; terrorism should be isolated through international cooperation and communication between civilisations.

The new critique could take as one of its points of departure the construction of a new history, where events described by figures like '1789', '1848', '1917', the 1930s, '1968', and '1989', and empirical observations subsumed under concepts like 'the social issue', 'solidarity', 'responsibility' are connected and brought into today's context through new critical arguments. However, a new history must also expand beyond the Euro-centric view that such figures express, and address the question of resistance in history, to globalising forces, be it in the name of colonisation, imperialism, Americanisation, Soviet domination, or globalisation. This would mean the writing of a new social history for the twenty-first century. If the connection of these concepts to Marshall's passive

---

[24] Wagner 2002.   [25] Huntington 1996.

social citizenship based on rights guaranteed by the welfare state has become problematic, the question is what role the concept of civil society could play if engaged alongside a more active notion of citizenship.

To what extent a new critique in the name of 'the people of Seattle', Attac, and other new transnational movements will provide a new socio-political framework for such a historiographic project is an open question. So far the new transnational social movements have hardly found a convincing form. The critique is certainly there, but much less so the imaginary force that again could broaden the gap between experiences and expectations to pre-'1968' dimensions. And even less does the important connection of the imagined future society to the issue of political organisation and collective forms seem to exist.[26]

One problem is that the target of the critique has become more elusive. It is not so much, as it was in '1968', the nation-states as representatives and instruments of capitalism, but a much vaguer and more anonymous 'world capitalism' released from mediating connections to politics. Citizenship and subjectivity are no longer so state-centred. National governance has become one institutional sphere among several. Governance is increasingly a matter of international politics, supra-national institutions, international treaties and laws – and not always hard laws. Soft laws and mutual agreements and understandings of how to implement them make the developments even more complicated to conceptualise through the conventional terminology based on nation-states and their citizens. These processes of critique and response involve macro-regional bodies, transnational corporations, transnational citizen groups and media, interacting in complex, turbulent, and multi-centric ways. The concerns and the critique of environment, population, and resource distribution have a global dimension, which is the other side of the globalisation discourse. The public articulation, not least in UN global conferences, can at best be interpreted as the slow beginning of the emergence of a global public sphere with a growing pressure on political instances, although technological and political accomplishment and awareness have so far not resulted in a convincing collective capacity of action.[27]

A connected problem is the transformation of the image of the state. The fiction of the State is no longer the homogeneous rule-governed Weberian hard structure, but the soft market-oriented service state that adjusts to the shifting claims of its citizens without intervening in the prerogatives of the Market. New state activities emerge in this transformation and old ones disappear. The ideal of rule-governance is changing to discretionary practices, and the distinction between politics and administration is blurred in the new image of the state

---

[26] Stråth 2002.   [27] Nederveen Pieterse 2000, pp. 1–2.

and in the practices exerted by its representatives both as a response to and an underpinning of this shift of image.[28]

It is a commonly held view that globalisation has opened up the possibility for cosmopolitan citizenship. Cosmopolitan citizens are seen as citizens of an imagined world community that has replaced the national community. However, today it is capitalism, not citizenship, that is truly cosmopolitan. Capitalism has become disconnected from its traditional national and democratic containments. Globalisation means the disconnection of economy and politics from the public culture of citizenship, which was originally a state-led project that was integrated through a critique emanating from nationally demarcated civil societies. Citizenship appropriated an economic as well as a political space in which the rule of law provided personal autonomy. The economic and political faces of civil society, that is, the institutionalisation of both capitalism and democracy by public debate and by legal regulation, encapsulated the ambivalence of citizenship, as Gerard Delanty puts it. The formation of the modern nation-state prevented this tension between capitalism and democracy from collapsing. The problem today is that there is no effective constitutional state and no guarantee of democracy in the international arena comparable to the nation-state. There is no transnational welfare state. Social rights and labour legislation are still mainly negotiated and arbitrated within the national framework. This situation sets clear limits to the concept of cosmopolitan citizenship.[29] The very interesting future question is what the long-term potential of the European Union and the project of a European citizenship will mean in this respect.

A connected problem contained in the link between globalisation and the idea of a cosmopolitan citizenship is, as Gerard Delanty has emphasised, that the concept of the citizen in neo-liberal rhetoric replaces the citizen with the consumer. Margaret Thatcher's well-known statement that there is no such thing as society, only individuals, denies the social in favour of individual consumers. The idea of social citizenship has been extended into the world of consumption. The increased consumption of goods has created the need for new kinds of rights, which have little to do with equality. Citizenship in market discourse loses its equalising function and becomes a highly privatised matter requiring often only regulating bodies to secure its effectiveness.[30]

---

[28] This transformation of the state is analysed in a major research project by Bo Rothstein, Lena Sommerstad, and Lotta Westerhäll at the Gothenburg University and the *Institutet för Framtidsstudier*, Stockholm ('The Fall of the Strong State') and in an EU framework programme project coordinated by Bo Stråth and Anna Triandafyllidou at the European University Institute in Florence, 'Does Implementation Matter? Informal Administration Practices and Shifting Immigrant Strategies in Greece, Italy, UK and Germany' (IAPASIS) (www.iue.it/RSC/IAPASIS/welcome.html).

[29] Delanty 2000a, pp. 2–5.   [30] Delanty 2000a, p. 21.

Peter Wagner is another author who has critically reflected on the tendency towards individualisation in contemporary social life, where the citizen concept has been one important element in the argument. Without even taking into account the spread of rational-choice thinking in political science and sociology, Wagner argues that the neo-liberal emergence and assertion of the individual as a being without predetermined binding connections to and within collectivities has become the centre of sociological interest. Together with the parallel debate on globalisation, a sociological image of the contemporary world emerges according to which there are no social phenomena 'between' the singular human being, on the one end, and structures of global extension, on the other. The neo-liberalism in politics and economics that advocates both 'individualism' and 'globalisation' is one, but only one, possible proposal. Opposed to this solution, although connected to it, is the new nationalism and, in weaker terms, communitarianism, both of which criticise the thinness of liberal notions of political membership and communication, as well as individual market relations, and aim to provide stronger substantive underpinnings. Beyond this duality between globalisation and new nationalism, Wagner discerns a possible role for the European Union.[31]

Wagner's proposal can be compared to Delanty's idea of a civic cosmopolitanism, which goes beyond the European framework but which does not seek the transcendence of political community in an international organisation of states at a global level but in a pluralist world of political communities. In Delanty's view, the cosmopolitan moment occurs when context-bound cultures encounter each other and undergo transformation as a result. Only thus can the twin pitfalls of the false universalism of liberalism's universalistic morality and the communitarian retreat into the particular be avoided. This differentiated particularism requires a cosmopolitan critique of globalisation in so far as the latter is a discourse that succumbs either to the false universalism of an empty world culture or to the romanticism of the particular.[32]

This differentiated particularism is also the problem addressed by Lucien Jaume in chapter 9 of this volume, although he phrases it somewhat differently. Citizenship is not only challenged by the erosion of the nation-state but also by other developments where the universal dimension in the concept of citizenship is contested: labour rights move from the level of national regulation towards company-based agreements and soft European Union (EU) law, specific gender-based rights emerge, as do minority rights for territorial, religious, and sexual minorities, and civic and political rights for individuals deprived of national belonging. This explosion of *citoyennetés plurielles* confirms that the universal citizen of the French Revolution was only as strong as the state that could

[31] Wagner 2000, pp. 55–9.   [32] Delanty 2000a, pp. 144–5.

guarantee it. The question for the future is how to reconcile liberty and equality, plurality and unity.

In the 1990s there was growing recognition, by the International Monetary Fund and other similar institutions, that it is not necessarily the market that fills the gap when a state retreats. The vacuum can also be filled by organised crime or anarchy. The German experiences of the collapse of the German Democratic Republic have demonstrated that it is not the market but the building up of state capacities that provides the solution.

How may these experiences of the 1990s be translated into new concepts and expectations after the failure of neo-liberal rhetoric? The lack of horizons of expectation can be formulated in terms of a conceptual crisis, which is visible in international politics as well as in the system of representational government established by the French Revolution. In international politics the Westphalian order has obviously collapsed when individuals open war on states and when state consortia in turn declare war on individuals. The system of representation, on which the modern concept of democracy is built, is clearly eroded when the dichotomy of state and local government is exchanged for more diffuse concepts of governance that blur the distinction between state and society, and when public responsibilities migrate to private enterprises and private life becomes public. In these developments the tensions and the complexity in the concept of citizenship are exposed: between universal and particular, active and passive (as defined above), autonomous individuals and individuals in a collective framework.

From the present analysis it seems clear that the organisation of modern societies based on states and citizens concepts is facing a major challenge. Is it then justified to call this challenge *post-modern*? If we understand the foundation of modernity not only as a belief in the human capacity to control, manage, and govern, a belief in human autonomy, but also as scepticism and critique, based on self-reflection, and in constant tension with the belief in autonomy, then the very concept of post-modernity obscures the radicalism of modernity itself.[33] The post-modern impulse is modernity itself and the discourses of modernity began earlier than the conventional watershed of the Enlightenment, which was less a rupture than an early culmination of a process that had begun long before. Modernity contains the experience of scepticism and critique. Scepticism is normally attributed to post-modernity, but it is a much older attitude, and as a matter of fact one of the central dimensions of modernity, in particular with regard to knowledge and power, and to the very idea of the self. 'Postmodern' is, as Gerard Delanty has formulated it, the extension of scepticism into the realm of knowledge and the discursive contestation of power into the domain of the self, where the radicalism of the

---

[33] Delanty 2000b, pp. 1–3; Koselleck 1997.

modern project can be found to have reached its limits.[34] The alternatives to modern scepticism are rationalism, that is, the belief in the limitless nature of knowledge and the centrality of the cognising ego; or else relativism, the rejection of absolute certainty, the historicisation of subjectivity, and a turn to culture.[35] These alternatives are permanently present in the debate. The globalisation discourse is a rhetoric based on rationalism, and the point of departure of the idea of multiculturalism is relativism.

The conventional view of modernity, according to which religious legitimation was replaced by legitimacy based on science and Enlightenment, must be revised, since the epistemic experiences of modernity resulted rather in a deepening of uncertainty. Compensation for this uncertainty was looked for in the social construction of certainty and the emergence of new beliefs. New investments were made in human autonomy. One continuing expression of these social processes has been the quest for identity and community over the last decades. These ideologies are not dead and the grand narratives have not broken down, as the post-modern approach argues. The globalisation language fills every criterion of a grand narrative. However, 'post-modernity' could perhaps be understood as a feeling for the declining scope of action in the shrinking space between expectations, formulated through ideologies and grand narratives, and experiences. If the Holocaust marked the culmination of the modern quest for mastery and of the priority of the Self over the Other, postmodernity, according to Delanty, is a post-colonial and post-Holocaust discourse that forces us to see the Self through the eyes of the Other. In the reversal of the priority between Self and Other, subjectivity is reconstituted around a new responsibility for history and nature. Underlying such a shift is scepticism about the durability of any narration of the identity of the Self, since the question of non-identity must always be raised. In the context of value pluralism and multiculturalism and the collapse of the self-confidence of the Eurocentric worldview, the long-term prospect of any universal discourse of identity is questionable.[36]

The growing scepticism after the Holocaust is not, however, unequivocal. The Holocaust was not the last case of genocide and ethnic cleansing, as the developments in Europe, the Middle East, Africa, and Asia show us. The victims have become the victimisers in a new quest for mastery and priority of the Self over the Other. The globalisation discourse is a story of another kind of mastery through the market concept. The relevant question is the long-term outcome of the tension between scepticism and critique, on the one side, and the social production of new beliefs, on the other. This is not a question that can be answered by history and experience alone, for it is highly contingent on will and ability. The legitimacy crisis of the global order both underpinning and underpinned

---

[34] Delanty 2000b, pp. 1–3; Stråth and Witoszek 1999.
[35] Stråth and Witoszek 1999.   [36] Delanty 2000b, p. 3.

by the globalisation ideology is indicated in the growing critique during the last decades of the environmental situation and of the global distribution of jobs and incomes. This legitimacy crisis is inscribed in a long history of struggle between ideas of instrumental rationality, supporting political and economic power, and a cultural critique based on demands for democratic containment and control of this expansion. Scepticism, discursive struggle, and reflexivity are elements of a contingent social history which began much earlier than the Enlightenment. Neither '1968' nor '1989' was the end of this history. There is a profound challenge, but the challenge is not post-modern but inscribed in modernity.

BIBLIOGRAPHY

Althusser, L. (1969). *For Marx*, New York: Vintage.
Barthes, R. (1967). *Le système de la mode,* Paris: Seuil. Translated into English by M. Ward and R. Howard as *The Fashion System*, London: Sage 1983.
Braudel, F. (1969). *Ecrits sur l'histoire*, Paris: Flammarion.
Castel, R. (1995). *Les métamorphoses de la question sociale: une chronique du salariat*, Paris: Fayard.
Conrad, C. and Kocka, J. (2001). 'Einführung' in C. Conrad and J. Kocka (eds.), *Staatsbürgerschaft in Europa*, Hamburg: Körber-Stiftung.
Debord, G. (1992) [1967]. *La Société du spectacle*, Paris: Gallimard.
Delanty, G. (2000a). *Citizenship in a Global Age. Society, Culture, Politics*, Buckingham and Philadelphia: Open University Press.
    (2000b). *Modernity and Postmodernity. Knowledge, Power and the Self*, London: Sage.
    (2002). 'The Meanings of Europe in French National Discourse: A French Europe or an Europeanized France?' in M. Af Malmborg and B. Stråth, *The Meaning of Europe. Variety and Contention with and among Nations*, Oxford: Berg.
Ginsborg, P., Passerini, L., Stråth, B., and Wagner, P. (2002). '1968–2001 – Measuring the distance. Continuities and Discontinuities in Recent History' in *Thesis* 11, no. 68, February.
Hildemeier, M., Kocka, J., and Conrad, C. (eds.) (2000). *Europäische Zivilgesellschaft in Ost und West*, Frankfurt am Main: Campus.
Huntington, S. (1996). *The Clash of Civilizations and the Remaking of World Order*, New York: Simon and Schuster.
Jacobson, D. (1998). *Rights across Borders. Immigration and the Decline of Citizenship*, Baltimore: Johns Hopkins University Press.
Koselleck, R. (1989) [1967]. *Preußen zwischen Reform und Revolution. Allgemeines Landrecht, Verwaltung und soziale Bewegung von 1791 bis 1848*. Stuttgart: Deutsche Taschenbuchverlag/Klett-Cotta.
    (1997) [1973]. *Kritik und Krise. Eine Studie zur Pathogenese der bürgerlichen Welt*, Frankfurt am Main: Suhrkamp. Translated into English 1989 as *Critique and Crisis*, Cambridge: Cambridge University Press.
    (2000). *Zeitschichten. Studien zur Historik mit einem Beitrag von Hans-Georg Gadamer*, Frankfurt am Main: Suhrkamp.

(1994). 'Return of the Citizen: A Survey of Recent Work on Citizenship Theory' in *Ethics* 104, pp. 352–81.

Mansfield, M., Salais, Robert, and Whiteside, Noel (eds.) (1994). *Aux sources du chômage 1880–1914*, Paris: Belin.

Marshall, T. H. (1963) [1949]. 'Citizenship and Social Class' in *Sociology at the Cross-roads*, London: Heinemann.

Nederveen Pieterse, J. (2000). *Global Futures. Shaping Globalization*, London: Zed Books.

Offe. C. (2002). '1968 – Thirty Years after Four Hypotheses on the Historical Conse-quences of the Student Movement' in *Thesis* 11, no. 68, February.

Passerini, L. (1998). 'Dalle ironie dell'identità alle identità dell'ironia' in Luisa Passerini (ed.), *Identità culturale Europea. Idee, sentimenti, relazioni*, Florence: La Nuova Italia.

Purdy, D. (2001). 'Economic Theory and Policy from the Keynesian Revolution to the Third Way' in L. Magnusson and B. Stråth (eds.), *From the Werner Plan to the EMU: In Search of a Political Economy for Europe*, Brussels: PIE-Peter Lang.

Shore, C. (2000). *Building Europe. The Cultural Politics of European Integration*, London and New York: Routledge.

Siedentrop, L. (2000). *Democracy in Europe*, London: Allen Lane.

Skinner, Q. (1996). *Reason and Rhetoric in the Philosophy of Hobbes*, Cambridge: Cambridge University Press.

(1999). 'Rhetoric and Conceptual Change' in *Finnish Yearbook of Political Thought* no. 3, pp. 60–73.

Soysal, Y. N. (1994). *Limits of Citizenship. Migrants and Postnational Membership in Europe*, Chicago: Chicago University Press.

Stråth, B. (1996). *The Organisation of Labour Markets. Modernity, Culture and Gover-nance in Germany, Sweden, Britain and Japan*, London: Routledge.

(2000a). 'The Concept of Work in the Construction of Community' in Bo Stråth (ed.), *After Full Employment. European Discourses on Work and Flexibility*, Brussels: PIE–Peter Lang.

(2000b). 'Introduction: Europe as a Discourse' in Bo Stråth (ed.), *Europe and the Other and Europe as the Other*, Brussels: PIE–Peter Lang.

(2001). 'Community/Society, History of the Concept' in *Social Encyclopaedia for Social and Behavourial Sciences*, Oxford: Pergamon.

(2002). '1968: From Co-Determination to Co-Worker. The Power of Language' in *Thesis* 11, no. 68 February.

Stråth, B. and Witoszek, N. (1999). 'Introduction' in B. Stråth and N. Witoszek (eds.), *The postmodern Challenge: Perspectives East and West*, Amsterdam: Rodopi.

Topalov, C. (1994). *Naissances du cômeur 1890–1940*, Paris: Albin Michel.

Wagner, P. (2000). 'The Exit from Organised Modernity: "Flexibility" in Social Thought and in Historical Perspective' in B. Stråth (ed.), *After Full Employment. European Discourses on Work and Flexibility*, Brussels: PIE–Peter Lang.

(2002), 'The Project of Emancipation and the Possibility of Politics, or, What's Wrong with Post-1968 Individualism?' in *Thesis* 11 no. 68, February.

White, H. (2000). 'The Discourse of Europe and the Search for a European Identity' in Bo Stråth (ed.), *Europe and the Other and Europe as the Other*, Brussels: PIE–Peter Lang.

12 Citizenship and equality of the sexes: the French model in question

Michèle Riot Sarcey

I

Since the 1789 Revolution, Liberty and Equality have remained closely linked in France, as if an abstract reference to these concepts suffices to make them a social reality. Yet with each new regime, the tutelary reference to these principles has been accompanied by a differential implementation of social roles. Historically, successive adjustments of social hierarchy have made the real discourse and its signifier seem identical.

In its evolution, the State has not in itself been responsible for the various orders of rationality[1] practised by the various political systems that have operated since the French Revolution. In reality, the state is the concrete expression of the practice of power relationships. It thus seems more judicious to consider the question of domination through the mediation of 'government of men'. This allows us to decipher the historical process as a whole that largely exceeds the legislation.

The word *féminisme* was forged in France in the 1870s. At first it was used pejoratively, then it became emblematic of women fighting for universal rights. If we examine the various ways that 'feminists' themselves defined feminism, we see that the use of the word associated the two liberating principles of freedom and equality: '[Feminism] is a doctrine of individual happiness and general interest . . . of justice and harmony which proclaims natural equivalence and asks for social equality between the two components of humankind' (Nelly Roussel 1906 in Bard 1995, pp. 213–17). Yet, over the course of history, citizens' liberty has been acquired to the detriment of women's liberty, as if the history of political freedom and women's liberty advance in opposite directions, as if politics can only conceive of equality in terms of identity.

In order to understand the impossibility of reconciling citizenship and the equality of the sexes, we must expose, in all its forms, the powerful system of

---

[1] Originally *dispositif de rationalités*: there is no satisfactory English equivalent for *dispositif*; in this text, the words 'mechanism' and 'system' have been employed alternately to convey a widespread, human-made (though often unconscious) entity both influencing and influenced by thought and action (translator's note).

individual representation that has hindered women's progress toward liberty. Women could only extricate themselves from the specific category in which they were imprisoned through a process of individual desubjectification. Yet personal freedom became largely incompatible with collective emancipation, the group being the sole possible historical actor in the teleological sense of the term. This is why the idea of equality could only be envisaged in terms of the identity of the groups aspiring to achieve it.

II

Democratic countries – and France in particular – have mainly understood political representation in terms of social organisation based on gender division. Whereas women spread kindness and gentleness in the home, men, participants in the electoral process, are required to embody masculine values. This system has continually proved its legitimacy through its rigidity, its rebirth after each revolution, its resistance in the face of multiple protests, and its ability to adapt. Its very foundations have been so difficult to contest that even today women's access to political power has necessitated a new law: *la parité*.

In order to understand the commonly acknowledged 'Republican' reasons behind this violation of universal laws, we must adopt an historical approach that sets political reality in the context of the development of differentiated identities. In principle, the French Revolution liberated individuals, both men and women, from the exclusionary system of aristocratic privilege. The break from the *ancien régime* therefore appeared irreversible, opening onto a horizon of new possibilities. From that moment, the idea of liberty captured the collective imagination, building hopes of an emancipation far beyond the realities of the Restoration. The power of this idea has endured for the past two centuries.

While wider ambitions during the nineteenth century were buried under the debris of the Industrial Revolution, or were reduced to mere shadows in the triumphant bourgeoisie's velvet interiors, political representation was elaborated and deployed within the social sphere in a manner which created an opposition between equality and liberty. The egalitarian, 'universal' principles set aside by political representatives were slowly manipulated to describe the profoundly unequal social reality.

Often justified by the complementarity of the sexes, but far from being a 'natural' reality, the historical conflict between men's and women's rights is the legacy of a repeated but still misunderstood historical phenomenon. Conceived in terms of 'inferiorisation', the difference between the sexes essentially escapes the law, and is rarely a subject of debate within representative political structures. It is made invisible and therefore taken for granted.

As of 1789, 'sovereignty, one and indivisible' became the trump in the game of interpretations and exclusionary practices which, little by little, rendered the integration of different individuals impossible. Women's greatest visible difference from men, the ability to bear children, served as a pretext to keep them out of the public sphere. At the time of the Revolution, political representation was reserved for free men, who, in the Kantian sense of the term 'free', were independent of all tutelage. At the same time that the Revolutionaries were elaborating the principles of representative democracy, French society divided social roles according to an already long established system of social representation.

During the Revolution, despite the public activities of women who called themselves '*citoyennes*' – without actually possessing citizenship – the only public acknowledgement of women's place in society was made by the citizen Amar, who spoke on 9 Brumaire Year II (1793) in the name of the *Comité de sûreté générale*:

Citizens have these political rights: to discuss and advocate, through comparative deliberation, the accomplishment of resolutions relative to the interest of the State, and to resist oppression. Do women have the moral and physical force which the exercise of either of these rights demands? Universal opinion dismisses such an idea . . . Nature herself has destined women to fulfil the private functions that uphold the general order of society; this social order results from the difference that exists between men and women. Every sex is called to the kind of occupation proper to it; its action is circumscribed within a boundary it cannot cross, for Nature, which has imposed these limits on Man, commands imperiously and is subject to no law.

On the mere basis of rhetorical argument, women were thus excluded from the civic community. Placed outside the law, they were deprived of universal rights by this so-called 'universal opinion'. Official legislation excluding women from political rights was no longer necessary; in order to project an exclusionary representation of identity, one only needed to elaborate a system of rules based on a discursive technique of valorisations, injunctions, and prohibitions. Its effects sufficiently restrained women's identity to the point that their exclusion from the public sphere was transformed into a social norm.

In fact, the construction of the state of otherness, in the name of 'natural' reason, was that which allowed a citizen to be identified: a citizen modelled on the unicity of a political community that allowed the 'one and indivisible sovereignty' to come into being. Any person in some way 'different' became an 'other', and was classified elsewhere, either in a position of waiting to achieve freedom or outside the public domain. Individuals' diversity and social disparities were reduced to categories based on abstractions such as 'the common people', 'the proletariat', 'the foreigner', and 'woman'. The family remained the 'elementary structure' of society at the heart of this hierarchical social construction, the place of 'the' woman was predetermined, and her consensual subservience guaranteed the citizen's (father's or husband's) access to the status of representative, as if relationships of domination were the prerequisite for 'representative democracy'.

Under the *ancien régime*, domination, the political instrument of arbitrarily named authority, was at the foundation of 'voluntary servitude'; under the representative governments of the nineteenth and twentieth centuries, domination was used by the minority of free men who held the 'capacity to exercise power'. The invocation of Nature alone rendered the rules of cultural oppression acceptable.

In the nineteenth century, the relationship between two uses of the word 'representation' – one, the representation of citizens, the other, the idea of being represented by a collective identity – attests to an historical process that would be invisible if one were exclusively reading the law of the period. During representative democracy's early career, 'citizens' saw themselves as reflections of the categories that founded their social hierarchy. This is why the notion of representation is both globalising and constantly in flux: inscribed in discourse, it is equally a projection of the collective imagination, and an appropriation transformed at the whim of successive interpretations.

Representations create 'the real more than they depend on it', thus blurring 'conventional codes of referentiality'[2] to the point of concealing the issues at stake. This confusion disturbed Bernard Lepetit:

Although not explicitly, the nature of the relationship between representation and action is contained in the following definition: *representation* and *action* belong to separate spheres. On the one hand, there are norms, values, and categories that give meaning to the world, and on the other hand, there are behaviours and acts that instrumentalise them . . . Representation precedes action, motivates it, and gives it meaning.[3]

Yet all our difficulties are completely inscribed in this non-explicit tension; we must bring to light this form of the 'unthinkable' or the 'repressed' which, like Nicole Loraux, I will qualify as political. This task becomes all the more important since successive repetitions of the system of representations increase interpretative possibilities by producing meanings detached from the original statements. Slowly but surely, the past escapes us, leaving behind a discursive substitute that is supposed to be representative.

As the Century of the Philosophy of Progress, but also that of Revolutions, the nineteenth century invented representative democracy. By revisiting the question of representation from the viewpoint of its political mediations we can perhaps restore the relation between 'collective representations' in Durkheim's sense of the term, and the rules of political representation. In the maze of discursivities by which the symbolic power to persuade is married to institutional

---

[2] Kalifa 1999, p. 1352.   [3] Leptit 1995, p. 116.

power, we can discover a dependency between normative elaborations and regulatory systems, as Louis Marin and Michel Foucault have similarly demonstrated: for example, the practice of economic and social liberty presupposes an ordered and moral society. The nineteenth century developed formidably efficient techniques of coercion, if one measures their development by the majority's internalisation of 'moral' values: 'One cannot liberate individuals without disciplining them',[4] Michel Foucault affirms. In fact, the concept of representation relates the exercise of power to the social constructions resulting from this internalisation, and to the different 'modalities of self' affecting its production.

III

The legitimate representatives of the Revolutionary Assemblies pronounced exclusions, first provisionally and later definitively, by justifying distinctions established between passive and active citizens, between men and women, between 'free' men and others still under tutelage: household servants, foreigners, and soon afterwards the proletariat. The universality of the enlightened representative's status had not yet been acquired. However, little by little over the course of the nineteenth century, the sovereign common people lost their right to exercise power directly. By interpreting texts and professions of faith concerning liberty, the constitutional monarchies were the first to justify, explicitly, limiting the power of representation to the privileged. Contested at first as the permanent renewal of homogenous, identically free beings (*des mêmes*), legally ordered political representation was invested with rules whose founding principles would never be questioned by any regime. Thus the delegation of power became an historical given.

Profoundly attached to the preservation of individual liberties, Benjamin Constant had demonstrated the necessity of representation by distinguishing between Ancient and Modern liberty, since in ancient Greece the practices and experiences of liberty were quite different from those of modern societies: 'It is this [difference], my good men, which necessitates a representative system. A representative system is nothing but an organization of a few individuals to whom a nation entrusts that which she cannot or does not wish to do herself.'[5] In Constant's estimation, representation involved procuration, not delegation. However, during the Restoration, a period that designed a myth of the past based on the rejection of the present, representation was thought possible only through the exercise of power by a 'government' identified as representative. This idea was so severely detached from reality that it was presented as a 'metaphor'[6]

---

[4] Foucault, 1994, p. 92.   [5] Constant, 1980 [1819], p. 512.
[6] Royer-Collard, pronounced in the Chambre des députés, February 1817, *Séances et travaux de la Chambre des députés, Procès verbaux pour l'année 1817.*

during a discussion in the Chambre des députés, and the defence of the *Charte*, from which power emanated, assumed the metaphor unfit to do justice to the word. Rhetorical argument thus demonstrated the absolute incompatibility of government and representation, for the functional definition of representation could not correspond to concrete political practice.

During the constitutional monarchies, under the regime of suffrage based on property qualification, the metaphor of representation was tailored to a different conception of 'government' whose most pertinent theoretician was François Guizot. In the mind of this political figure and prolific historian, the principle of representation inherited from the Revolution was of little value: since the idea of 'representative government' had run the course of centuries and was accomplished in the 1830s, respecting the *unwritten* rule of representation only by the privileged would thereafter constitute the law. Invoking ideas such as 'truth', 'justice', 'the good', 'the true', and the 'law' amply legitimised the visibly paradoxical syntagma of representative government; furthermore, these ideas inspired a demand for security and power, values expressed for a long time by contemporary historians of Western civilisation: 'Representative government does not attribute the sovereignty of law to anyone . . . , those in power work within the law toward the formation and faithful practice of the rules which must preside over their action.'[7] The word 'representation' was imposed in order to signify proof of political practice; representation was no longer questioned because simply by subtly deploying this system its sovereignty was imposed. Through successively shifting applications, the abstract idea of popular sovereignty was eventually replaced by 'representative' sovereignty. The empire of the signifier[8] masked the practice of power by the government 'of the capable', and the preoccupations of Benjamin Constant, particularly his attachment to the control of appointed representatives, were consequently dismissed. 'When no boundaries are imposed upon representative authority, the representatives are no longer defenders of liberty, they are prospective tyrants, an assembly whose power is unlimited is more dangerous than the common people.'[9]

At the end of the nineteenth century, the debate concerning representative government was rekindled in the interests of universal suffrage, the mere idea of which, once again, created hope for the peaceful transformation of social relations. The Republicans seized upon the idea, having forgotten that the insurrection of 1848 was a symptom of political representation's dysfunctional nature. The Republican 'elites' desperately wanted to believe in the accuracy of the 'metaphor'. From Gambetta to Jules Ferry, everyone sought to articulate a *real* correspondence between the representatives and the individuals represented by them, even if the *République*, which considered such a correspondence to

---

[7] Guizot 1851, p. 93.   [8] Expression borrowed from Michel Foucault.   [9] Constant, p. 293.

be purely decorative, imposed itself as 'government'. Social disparities and in-equalities were only transitional stepping-stones, according to the Republican spirit's reconciliatory vision. Schools would close the gap between the rich and the poor, rendering Enlightenment and political power equally accessible to all men; in this way, class conflict would be avoided. As Clemenceau declared, 'I affirm that a democracy's entire political purpose is to emancipate the least enlightened group, as quickly as possible, with the aid of the group possessing the advantage of Enlightenment and education.'[10]

'Liberal illusion' and Republican 'utopia' were introduced into discursive representation in order to mediate between, on the one hand, the desire to be-lieve in the attainability of liberty and equality, and, on the other, the necessity of a hierarchically ordered society. Legitimised by the assertion that society was progressing toward egalitarianism, these constructions only worked by in-venting another form of 'representation' conveniently labelled 'collective'. In effect, the prerequisite for functional political representation requires the con-comitant formation of identity-based categories that constitute individual and collective representations. However, let us beware of homonyms: here, the same word, used in many different contexts, refers to a similar practice belonging to the power to persuade, but does not belong to the vocabulary of the period. Political representation is legible in the order of the law; its visibility is di-rectly accessible to the historian. All other representations are either 'collective representations' or 'individual representations', assumed to be contemporaries' mental and autonomous expressions. Exclusively considered as historical data – as are mentalities, for example – these social constructions may also be viewed as an analytical tool, allowing us to elucidate the perpetual movement between public display and internalisation, between accepted restrictions and deviating appropriations, and, essentially, to expose that which Foucault designates as 'relationships meaning'.

IV

Given this possibility of historical analysis, we must distinguish between in-dividual and collective representations. Modes of existence are differentiated according to models of referentiality and the desire to obtain public recognition. The restraining or mystifying aspects of representations may be denounced just as they may be internalised or consciously claimed.

What is important for our purpose is to consider the interdependence of political and 'mental' representations. In effect, this process juxtaposes the functions of representation: though socially similar, the individuals represented are no longer one with their representatives but, by claiming a representation that

---

[10] Clémenceau, in Barral 1968, p. 274.

others have constructed as their identity, they become passive but consensual accomplices in the reproduction of political and symbolic domination, which, linked together, constitute the agency of power. 'This form of power is exercised in daily life by classifying individuals into categories, making them dependent upon their category-based identity, and imposing upon them a law of truth that they must recognise and that others must recognise in them.'[11]

What is at stake as regards signification is precisely located at the confluence of the visible and the invisible, political representations and representations of the self, the internalisation of norm-values and the affirmation of one's own subjectivity. The social categories from which these values issue are formed around words of multiple usage: 'the common people', 'the proletariat', 'woman' – in the singular to emphasise the ideal she must embody – 'enlightened men' – in the plural to acknowledge their individual abilities – 'men of reason' as opposed to men who live by instinct, women subject to emotions, and many more such creations. Each construction, accompanied by epithets, was employed in minor or major mode: 'the common people, immature and immoral in their behaviour', 'the proletariat, prone to barbaric agitations', 'woman, socially determined by nature', 'man, endowed with the capacities of culture', and so on. Through the intermediary of this hierarchical classification, the individuals subject to representations were therefore able to consent 'freely' to being represented without necessarily being present, in both the social and symbolic senses, in 'representative' instances.

Thus charged with meaning, reductivist discursive mechanisms (*dispositifs énonciateurs*) proliferate. A few examples will sufficiently demonstrate the process by which an abstract idea is whittled down to a pure signifier whose efficacy imposes univocal meaning.

In the 1840s, the most significant and conflictual debate in France revolved around the expansion of suffrage. No one imagined the possibility of the 1848 insurrection; between the advocates of universal suffrage, seeking to give the common people political rights, and the liberals, attached to the hierarchical representation of society, the interpretative conflict revolved around the idea that one constructed of the common people: were they capable of becoming representatives or were their labouring functions the expression – the concrete representation – of their natural inferiority? Even some proletarians were involved in the debate. They rediscovered the original categories of the Revolution, borrowed a vocabulary of emancipation from the Enlightenment, and situated themselves in the framework of the proposed political system, although they reoriented its function by imposing another meaning upon it: thus Le Louédec defined the 'revolutionary' as one who 'wishes to change not only men, but the order of things . . . A Revolutionary wishes the country to be

---

[11] Foucault 1994, p. 227.

represented by the country and the government to be the clear, frank expression of the general will.'[12] It seemed useless to specify the general will, as the reference to Rousseau sufficiently 'represented' the common people by embodying them in a majority. Conversely, the authorities sought to orient 'collective representations' according to their own vision of the world: Lamartine, for example, preoccupied with integrating 'the most populous and poorest class',[13] wanted to erase the word 'proletariat' from the French vocabulary, by conceiving of the 'dangerous class' as a class of landowners in the making. This representation was intended to allow these subjects of the law, though still under social tutelage, to enter into politics: 'What name do *I* give the proletarians? I do not address them as they were addressed one day, here, in a moment of sinister agitation, I do not address them as the barbarians of our society, I address them as the children of the social family.'[14] Thus were slowly woven the group identities that the historian risks hastily assimilating into collective representations.

Women were very rarely thought of as candidates for citizenship or, *a fortiori*, for political representation; they were therefore viewed as privileged objects of normative representations. Yet some women sought to unveil the superficiality of such identity-based attributions. Among the women of her time in full possession of critical faculties, Flora Tristan was particularly attentive to mechanisms of subservience. 'I know of nothing more powerful than forced, inevitable logic that stems from a stated principle or from a hypothesis representing it. – Once the inferiority of woman is stated and proclaimed as a *principle*, you see what disastrous consequences result *for the universal well-being of women and men of all humanity*.'[15] During the Second Empire, contemporaries were compelled to forget the political meaning of representation: the substance of the word was diluted either by identity-based categories or social models. The idea was incarnated even in fashion, for a wife's clothing inevitably represented her husband's social position. André Léo, engaged in the Paris Commune, rejected the way this function of representation was imposed upon individuals, perpetually preventing them from adopting autonomous discourse.

Life resides, not in society, but in the single being, in the individual that feels, thinks and desires, whose impressions, especially in exchange with others', exalt or rectify him. These affairs only take place within himself, and cannot exist elsewhere. We have not yet fully understood the consequences of these insane concepts formed outside of the self, the unique residence of human life, nor have we recognized the inanity of an ideal accomplished anywhere other than the interior of the human being.[16]

[12] Letter to Cabet, 2 September 1847, Papiers Cabet, BHVP, MS 1052.
[13] Expression from the period, borrowed from the Saint-Simonians.
[14] Lamartine, pronounced in the Chambre des députés, session 15 avril 1845, *Séances et travaux*, année 1845.
[15] Tristan 1986 [1843], p. 191.   [16] Léo 1990 [1869], p. 116.

The historian's difficulty stems from this phenomenon: how to think about representations in this permanent play between the real and the imaginary, between the represented subject and the symbolisation of a presence, between the presented idea and the thing as it is signified, between production of truths and resistance of models? For this reason we have privileged the political act of representation in relation to the formation of mental representations, and hoped to distinguish between discursive invention as historical data and representation as social construction. In effect, analysing the formation of social norms and political rules through discursive mechanisms authorises the historian to examine ordinary historical assumptions by questioning the words that identify, such as 'woman', and the categories that unify, such as 'Republicans'. This process eliminates the possibility of envisaging 'collective representations' in any other way than in terms of relationships between normative constructions and their internalisation, and between the expression of needing social recognition and the desire to belong. This constant play between 'I' and 'we', between 'them' and 'me', is accessible to an historian attentive to multiple forms of expression: their confrontation informs the movement of history. The historical source in the form of text, image, or manuscript is not in itself a representation, it is a construction that allows different interpretations, events, practices, and represented objects to be understood as singular enunciations. Thus, representations must be examined in the historicity of the confrontation, as contained in the text, between what is said (*énoncé*) and how it is said (*énonciation*).

V

The system of representation must constantly avoid threats engendered by the horizon of the possible – a liberating perspective always at work – never definitively hidden away, for individuals seeking to release themselves from tutelage never cease to undertake the paths to emancipation. On the other hand, legislators also make a point of constructing obstacles to civil emancipation by establishing restrictive norms. By virtue of the Civil Code, masculine domination entered the law through the indirect route of regulation, and, in spite of diverse protests, this chapter of civil law has evolved remarkably slowly; women in France did not acquire equal rights until very late in the century (for example, parental equality was only recently obtained).

This is why the conservation of family hierarchy – the central pillar of the social structure – preoccupied every regime. Long excluded from egalitarian principles, both out of propriety and because it was the domain reserved for the expression of feeling, the family never entered the public debate, whatever the level of revolutionary commitment of the writers – the Utopians being the only exception to this rule. Successively, the liberal regimes, Republicans, Socialists, Communists, and other political parties, attempted to protect this privileged domain of consensual submission from any and all revolutionary tremors. From Proudhon to Jules Simon, from Jules Ferry to Jeannette Thorez-Vermeersch, the great figures of the workers' movement and the Republican Party largely replaced women's individuality with maternal identity. But the valuation of maternal qualities alone was not enough to impose a particular mode of existence upon women; it was necessary, over the course of history, to deny not only their inclusion in universality, but also their ability to reason. In this domain, Proudhon was an expert: 'The woman author does not exist, that would be a contradiction. Woman's role in letters is the same as in manufacturing; she is useful where genius is no longer necessary; she is like a spindle or a spool'. If these normative representations have endured throughout the last two centuries, it is because they disguise diverse forms of resistance, invalidating protests against the injustices that victimised women.

However, despite these oppressive measures, women over the course of the last two centuries have continually sought the path to universal rights. Yet, believing they would find allies in similarly disadvantaged men, they ran into other obstacles, particularly the difficulty of reconciling 'collective emancipation' and 'individual freedom'.

Having taken account of the different interpretations of the concept of liberty, confusion arose between 'individualism' and 'individuation', between the freedom of the individual and the liberation of the group to which he or she was supposed to belong, and for whose liberation he or she was fighting.

It is important to understand the different impasses that eventually consume the person wishing to circumvent multiple prejudices without confronting them since, in practice, breaking free does not always signify genuine emancipation.[17] In order to become a free individual, one must undertake to follow the path of freedom by oneself and for oneself, in the absence of all mediation: this process leads the individual to become a subject. Releasing oneself from all tutelage is therefore indispensable in order to access universal liberty. However, this struggle is particularly difficult, as Maria Deraismes phrases it, for women who are 'parked in maternity'. Rendered inferior by the Civil Code, placed under their fathers' and then their husbands' tutelage, women could not relinquish their domestic obligations without endangering the social order, since familial hierarchy was considered essential to the functioning of a perfectly ordered society. Furthermore, familial duty, understood as the acceptance of the father's superior (public) reason, extended to all social classes. Liberated from domestic tasks, even a non-property-owning citizen could consecrate the time necessary to the management of the commonwealth (*respublica*). Long a taboo, the family

---

[17] Here, breaking free (*affranchissement*) refers to liberating oneself from bondage, slavery, or any kind of arbitrary rule, whereas emancipation (*émancipation*) signifies becoming a free, self-determining subject in the Kantian sense of the term (translator's note).

was at the heart of feminine alienation because it represented the foundation of profoundly hierarchically organised modern society. In 1848, in a state of paranoia, the authorities feared losing this bastion of order; for this reason the Republicans inscribed, in the preamble to the constitution of the Second Republic: 'The Republic's principles are Liberty, Equality and Fraternity; its foundation is Family, Work, Property, and Public Order.'

The extremely slow progress in civil rights reform reveals the liberal, Republican institution's long resistance to all forms of evolution in the domain of familial relations – a revelation all the more pertinent in the light of works by Alexis de Tocqueville, in which equal civil rights are asserted as the necessary prerequisite for democracy. However, Tocqueville's conception of universality was limited to its masculine constituents.

In 1907, in France, women were legally able to have direct access to their salaries for the first time, and in 1938, married women's capacities as autonomous individuals in the public domain were finally recognised. However, the husband remained head of the family, he chose the couple's place of residence, and could prevent his wife from exercising a profession. This restriction was not repealed until 1965. Every step towards women's civil liberty underwent intense scrutiny, as if the inequality at the heart of the family structure became the precondition from which democracy was concretely put into action.

However, even in the face of the most widespread prejudice, women continued to denounce the injustices victimising them. As early as 1835, Madame Bernard wrote, 'Rendez, rendez la femme indépendante de l'homme!'[18] Yet this personal independence was found incompatible with the idea of collective emancipation cherished by the organised workers' movement. Also, from the beginning of the twentieth century, while feminists were acquiring a public standing, the majority of women chose the path of social integration by adopting a newly forming identity entailing specifically feminine activities. In France, women overwhelmingly privileged 'their social duty' to the detriment of 'their legitimate rights'. This choice seemed necessary to activist organisations, which needed to assemble a large number of women without disrupting contemporary norms. As is largely recognised, at the heart of French suffragist associations – in contrast to the English case – philanthropy and feminism were easily reconciled, for their practices were taken up by women who naturally situated themselves in a different sphere of social intervention than men did. This is what allowed the historian Christine Bard, author of *Filles de Marianne* to write: "to conceal the transgression of a social order, they sought to neutralize their transgression by conforming to gender rules, that is to say, to the social norms that defined femininity'.[19]

[18] Mme Bernard, letter to Globe, *Journal saint-simonien* 25 January 1932.
[19] See Bard 1995.

Notwithstanding, this kind of feminism, even in moderation, inherently respected every woman's individuality – an individuality that was quickly associated with individualism, however, by the spokespeople of the newly forming workers' movement. From their point of view, individual freedom became a hindrance to class struggle and an obstacle to the collective liberation of inferiorised groups. From then on, feminism and socialism appeared incompatible. In the minds of the socialists, women's liberty negated men's independence. As if the expression of political abilities relied on the unbalanced distribution of public space – organised under the democratic model – and private space – organised under the aristocratic model. Though previously overshadowed, this conflict marks the entire history of organised social movements: every foundational moment in the workers' movement was marked by measures taken towards the exclusion of women. In 1849, in the name of nascent socialism, Pierre Joseph Proudhon rose up against Jeanne Deroin, who dared to appear at the legislative elections. In the 1860s, the first Internationale declared itself by majority against women in the workforce. In 1913, the Couriau affair revealed the union's restrictiveness in the matters of tolerance and the organisation of women in the workforce. The typographers' union refused to admit Madame Couriau and expelled her husband because the couple refused to comply with the organisation's rules prohibiting women's access to different areas of the printing house. In 1916, Adolphe Merrheim, the secretary of the Confédération Générale du Travail (CGT')s metal workers federation, was able to affirm, without incurring even the militants' wrath, 'No matter what the result of the war may be, the employment of women constitutes a serious danger for the working class.' In 1936, some unions declared themselves in favour of firing married women whose husbands worked in the same factory. In other words, from the perspective of union leaders engaged in class conflict, the father of the family had to protect his wife: he guaranteed her the benefits of his income, allowing her to raise their children without 'burdening' her by renting out her services in competition with men's.

Women's emancipation considerably destabilised the head of the family's established position: the working-class father could no longer pose as 'man, armed with superior capacities'; men and women became equals. In its universal meaning, the social and political equality of women assumes an egalitarian practice in both the private and public domains. Yet society's equilibrium depended entirely on the asymmetry of familial relationships. One can understand, under these conditions, the Civil Code's very slow evolution. The abandonment of egalitarian principles, taken up again by the parties on the Left, resulted in the 'conservative' vision of the Communist Party, long hostile to contraception and abortion. Thus Thorez could denounce the 'bourgeois vices' in the 2 May 1956 issue of *L'Humanité:* 'It does not seem superfluous to us to recall that the path to women's liberation involves social reform and social revolution, not abortion clinics.'

Issuing from a hierarchical vision of modern societies and the prerogative of partisans for the exercise of power through social domination, the gendered division of sexual roles was not questioned by supporters of the leftist opposition. Quite the contrary, in practice it was a requirement for the liberation of the most disadvantaged groups. Previously announced by the Revolutionaries of 1793, the creation of a feminine territory based on the specificities of gender – the power to reproduce the species – was taken up once again, organised, and rationalised by the different political parties hoping to exercise power. Little by little, the majority of women espoused this form of self-representation. Given the efficacy of this process, it is easy to understand why the majority of women chose social integration by accepting representative norms.

It was and remains difficult to challenge commonly acknowledged ideas. Yet, if social recognition occurred through the internalisation of family values and therefore through a very specific conception of universal rights, confusion arose between the identity of genders and the principle of equality of the sexes.

VI

Finally, and parallel to the achievements of citizenship, women rose up against the untruths of liberationist discourse and the inexactitude of the value of words. In these fleeting moments of social disorder, hope was reborn, flourished in gaps of discontinuity, and contributed to the undoing of the legislative arsenal by invalidating the identity-based constructions upon which order rested. Numerous women protested against unequal rights by demanding, for example, in the 1830s, access to public education, in 1848, the right to universal suffrage, and in the 1870s, integration in the Republic. Their efforts were always vain, for after each revolution, 1830, 1848, and 1871, the fabric of domination was always forcibly rewoven. The recourse to new definitions, by 'rationalizing mechanisms that organise modes of action',[20] reconstituted defeated ideas; the system's survival depended upon it. These modalities of hierarchical stabilisation were reproduced or reinterpreted by the majority of both liberal and socialist candidates to political power. For example, as Christine Planté comments, Larnac, an emulator of Barbey d'Aurevilly, could, without shocking his contemporaries in 1929, express himself in these terms: 'The word *historienne* does not exist in our vocabulary. We have had women authors of memoirs, even women chroniclers, like Christine de Pisan . . . We have not had a woman historian comparable to Augustin Thierry or Michelet, for they are lacking in reason and mindpower.'[21] This line of reasoning legitimised the practice of political representation without women. Furthermore, having established proof

[20] Expression borrowed from Michel Foucault.   [21] Planté 1989, p. 243.

of women's inferiority, it was no longer necessary to create a law to ensure the authority of mens' government.

For a long time, and doubtless even today, many have confused, or wanted to confuse, identity and equality. Because of this, any visible difference, whether physical or cultural, has been a pretext for elaborating a hierarchical system founded on social disparities. For this reason, the most lucid feminists rose up, from the beginning, against this semantic confusion that served to conceal true inequality. In 1871, Julie Daubié, the first *bachelière*, denounced this fraudulent strategy:

> The society that hereby methodically claims to substitute itself for nature demonstrates an insanity incompatible with public harmony and order, for it is enough to be free from prejudice to understand that the most comprehensive liberty cannot be accomplished to the exclusion of women, and to know that equality, which is nothing but the respect of individual rights, cannot lead to identity for the very simple reason that we cannot remake nature, not even by opposing it, nor by compromising it, nor by stifling it.

This system allowed the decades-long separation of men's rights from women's: men, as we know, gained 'universal' suffrage in France in 1848, whereas women only acceded to the right to vote after the edict of April 1944. However, this right, in itself, has not opened the doors of public representation much more widely for women. Even the upheavals of the 1970s, in the course of which women achieved autonomy from their reproductive functions, still did not shatter the foundations of the gender role division, particularly in the domestic arena. Given the impossibility of envisaging the rules of government through other modalities besides political liberalism – whose standing rests on a permanent system of delegation – it is illusory to imagine access to the exercise of power by any means other than identification with the dominant model. The efficacy of this model must be measured against the effectiveness of its permanence.

In accordance with the new law that substitutes the word *parité* for equality, legislators justify differential otherness, and through this law they confirm the impossibility of women's access to universality. Certainly, *parité* allows women access to political representation, but only in the current state of hierarchical, unequal social relationships. This is why the 'French model' paradoxically risks condoning social inequalities in countries where disparities are even more pronounced. The only hope of exercising power against this system is to circumvent it, by unveiling the 'illusion' of power founded on the model of 'one and indivisible' representation, thus laying the groundwork for a diversified representation of individuals, in which all differences within a represented group are acknowledged. In this case, duality is insufficient. Associated with the family and with property, which depend upon the maintenance of mechanisms of domination for their perpetuation, representation is only viable at the heart of an exclusionary system. For this reason the true threat perceived by legislators did not manifest itself during the vote on *parité* – the near unanimity of which demonstrates its low risk factor – but at the 'painful' moment of the vote on *PACS* (*Pacte d'action civique de solidarité*), which was perceived as posing a tangible threat to the fundamental structures of the family.

We remain within the framework of unwritten laws of exclusion that characterise the current authorities' system of preference. Recently, these authorities have presented Louis Dumont as an expert in the matter. A partisan of hierarchy, this eminent anthropologist considers the inferiorities of others compensated by their superiorities at secondary levels. In this way, he authorises the dismissal of equality in the name of complementarity, all the while composing rather questionable statements: 'I uphold this: if the advocates of difference demand, in the name of difference, both equality and recognition, they are demanding the impossible. One is reminded of the slogan "separate but equal" which marked, in the United States, the transition from slavery to racism.'[22]

Liberty and gender equality of the sexes remain *after all* irreconcilable, according to the so-called democratic values in force in a Republican state that claims to be attached to the fundamental equal rights of all men *and* women.

BIBLIOGRAPHY

Bard, C. (1995). *Les Filles de Marianne, Histoire des féminismes, 1914–1940*, Paris: Fayard.
Barral, P. (1968). 'Discours de Georges Clémenceau Prononcé au Cirque Fernando le 25 mai 1884', in *Les Fondateurs de la Troisième République: Textes choisis et. présente's par Pierre Barral*. Paris: Armand Colin.
Clémenceau, G. (1968) [1884]. 'Discours du 25 mai 1884, Cirque Fernando', in P. Barral, *Les Fondateurs de la Troisième République*, Paris: Armand Colin.
Constant, B. (1980) [1819]. 'De la Liberté des Anciens comparée à celle des Modernes', oration given at the Athénée Royal de Paris in 1819, *De la liberté chez les Modernes*, presented by M. Gauchet, Paris: Hachette Pluriel, 1980.
De la liberté des femmes, lettres de dames au Globe (1992), [1831–2], ed. Michèle Riot-Sarcey, Paris: Editions Côté-Femmes.
Dumont, L. (1983). *Essais sur l'individualism, e, Une perspective anthropologique sur l'idéologie moderne,* Paris: Seuil.
Foucault, M. (1994). 'Entretien avec Michel Foucault', 'conversazione con Michel Foucault' with D. Trombadori, *Paris fin 1978, Il Contributo*, n.1, Jan.–March 1980, in M. Foucault, *Dits et Ecrits*, vol. IV, Paris: Gallimard, 1994.
Guizot, F. (1851). *Histoire des origines du gouvernement représentatif en Europe*, Paris: Didier.
Kalifa, D. (1999). 'Usages du faux, Faits divers et romans criminels au XIX siècle', *Annales, Histoire, Sciences sociales*, no. 6, Nov.–Dec.
Léo, A. (1990) [Paris 1869]. *La Femme et les mœurs, Monarchie ou liberté*, Paris: Tusson, Du Lérot.

---

[22] Dumont 1983, p. 260.

Lepetit, B. (1995). 'L'Histoire prend-elle les acteurs au sérieux?' *Espaces Temps*, nos. 59–61.

Planté, C. (1989). *La Petite Sœur de Balzac*, Paris: Seuil.

Séances et trabaux de la Chambre des députés, Procès verbaux pour l'année 1817 (1817), Paris: Bibliothèque national.

Tristan, F. (1986). [Paris 1843]. *L'Union Ouvrière*, ed. D. Armogathe, and J. Grandjonc, Paris: Editions des femmes.

13   States, citizens, and the environment

Andrew Dobson

I

First, some orientating remarks. There is no 'green theory of the state' in the sense that there is, for example, a Marxist theory of the state. The Marxist notion is derivable from key explanatory features of Marxism more generally, in such a way that the belief that a society's economic base ultimately determines its political and administrative superstructure leads to the conclusion that the state is never neutral, representing the general interest, but rather embodies the interests of the dominant social class. This view is a systematic one, and it would be hard to find a Marxist who did not – in broad compass – agree with it.

There is no equivalent green position, derivable, as it were, from first principles. There is, indeed, no definitive green view of social organisation at all – no particular set of social arrangements, that is, to which all greens will subscribe, in the belief that that set is either univocally derivable from broader green objectives and values, or especially likely to bring about those objectives and instantiate those values. So while there is a distinct tendency towards decentralisation in green thinking, and while this is derivable from green principles in the sense that many greens believe that sustainable living is best achieved by bringing points of production and consumption closer together, this very same objective – sustainable living – leads some greens (sometimes the same greens) to the conclusion that large social configurations, such as states, have a role to play.[1]

A widely endorsed – if still disputed – view of the relationship between social organisation and the values that greens would like to see instantiated in society is that outlined in Robert Goodin's *Green Political Theory*. Goodin argues for a distinction between what he calls a 'green theory of value' and a 'green theory

I am very grateful to my Keele University colleagues, Margaret Canovan and John Horton, and to Quentin Skinner, for having pointed out weaknesses in an earlier draft of this chapter, and for their astute suggestions for improvement.
[1] The exception to this rule is principled ecoanarchism of the sort described and defended by Alan Carter (1993 and 1999). Carter argues that all actual and conceivable states exhibit an 'environmentally hazardous dynamic' (1993: p. 45) driven by the need to develop environmentally damaging 'hard' technologies in competition with other states.

of agency', and suggests that the second should be in the service of the first. In deciding the question of agency greens should be guided, advises Goodin, by what works. This instrumental view of organisation and agency has come to dominate most discussions regarding sustainability and social organisation in general, and the state in particular.

This promiscuous approach to social organisation leads most green political theory in the direction of a 'yes, but . . .' position in regard to the state. John Barry, for example, offers two reasons why greens should support state-orientated solutions to problems of sustainability, but simultaneously makes it clear that non-state levels of activity are also necessary. The two reasons are, first, that the state provides a counterpoint to the argument that market-based and purely fiscal measures – such as environmental taxation – are sufficient for sustainability; and second, that the state is the only agent able to realise green-related objectives such as deepening social justice.

In the context of the first reason, a key notion is that of 'ecological modernisation'. This concept, says Barry, 'challenges the idea that improvements in environmental quality or the protection of nature are necessarily inimical to economic welfare, the fundamental position which dominated the early response to the "environmental crisis" '.[2] Ecological modernisation is a discursively powerful idea, linking, as it does, the central themes of ecological sustainability and modernity in a way that appears to make them realisable simultaneously.[3] Indeed some of its articulations suggest that they can *only* be realised simultaneously. For our purposes, the central point is that the state has a key role to play in this modernising project, through, for example, setting statutory standards that will encourage a 'race to the top' as far as commercial and other environmental behaviour is concerned.

The state has a role to play in this sense even (or, perhaps, in particular) in relation to so-called 'strong' forms of ecological modernisation, according to which the *scale* of an economy in relation to available natural resources (or 'natural capital') is critical. On this reading, a planet of finite size cannot sustain infinite economic growth, so an eye must be kept on the scale of an economy and its impact relative to available 'source and sink' resources. Advocates of 'strong' ecological modernisation will say that while the market is good at collating and responding to price information, it has no 'eyes' for the scale at which an economy is operating. Robyn Eckersley points, therefore, to the state as the locus of the kinds of audits necessary to determine 'carrying capacity', and to plan the appropriate scale of economic activity:

Whereas environmental economics is limited to ensuring an optimal *allocation* of resources (an efficiency issue), ecological economics *also* seeks an optimal ecological *scale* of resource use. The added requirement of scale is considered essential because

---

[2] Barry 1999, p. 114.   [3] See, for example, Jacobs 1999a.

Pareto optimality can be achieved irrespective of whether or not the scale of material-energy throughput in the economy is sustainable in relation to the ecosystems in which the economy operates.[4]

Even here, though, it is clear that states and their environmental policies cannot and do not exist in isolation from one another – statutory environmental regulations in one country will be affected by multilateral terms of trade with other countries. This is the kind of thought that leads John Barry to warn against exclusively state-centred approaches to the business of bringing about environmental sustainability: 'The institutionalization of green values within collective ecological management should be thought of in terms of "governance" as opposed to "government". That is, while the state has a role to play in creating and maintaining a sustainable and ethically informed metabolism with the environment, it is not the only or the pre-eminent institution in the process.'[5]

This warning points both 'upwards' and 'downwards' – upwards, that is, to international arrangements of various sorts, and downwards to regional and local spaces of action aimed at environmental sustainability. From an international relations perspective, sustainability has tended to be recast in the mould of 'security', in such a way that a new type of security – 'environmental security' – has been added to the lexicon.[6] The provision of security has, of course, traditionally been regarded as the most basic function of the state, so once sustainability comes to be viewed from a security perspective, it is almost inevitable that the state will loom large as the instrument for bringing it about. Much empirically informed research on sustainability issues, though, leads to the conclusion that a focus on the state as the engine and engineer of sustainability is misplaced. In a representative case drawn from the Himalaya, for example, Michael Thompson argues that we should resist the assumption that environmental insecurity results from, first, 'an *increasing population* combined with a static or, worse still, a declining resource base', and second, 'from the failings of a *weak state*'.[7] 'The idea', he writes, 'that what is needed is a state strong enough to install, and then pull on, the levers that will bring a whole mass of ignorant and fecund peasants back into line, can never be right. It can never lead to an increase in security but . . . it can all too easily result in the opposite.'[8] Thompson concludes that multi-level responses of people (not 'population') to environmental insecurities are appropriate, and that things can be made worse by 'strong state' action and by international programmes which undermine historically tested ways of dealing with those insecurities.[9]

---

[4] Eckersley 1995, p. 17; italics in the original.   [5] Barry 1999, p. 103.
[6] Dalby 2000; Evans *et al.* 2000; Lonergan 2000; Barnett 2001.
[7] Thompson 2000, p. 194; italics in the original.
[8] Thompson 2000, p. 194.   [9] See also Sergen and Malone 2000.

Even where there is no outright rejection of the state, then, in green thinking, there is considerable scepticism as to its efficacy in dealing with environmental problems. It is perhaps no surprise that the bulk of reflection on this incongruence has taken place in international relations theory. It has become *de rigeur* to point out that many environmental problems are international problems – global warming, ozone depletion, acid rain – and that they are *constitutively* international in the sense that they do not, cannot, and will never respect national boundaries in their effects. So as Karen Litfin writes: 'Observations about the incongruity between the political world, delineated by territorial boundaries, and the natural world, made up of interconnected ecosystems, have become something of a truism. The implication is that there is some fundamental incompatibility between sovereignty and ecology.'[10] The most common point of critical reference here is the 'Westphalian model' of states and their mutual relations (after the 1648 Treaty of Westphalia), summed up as 'territorial sovereignty, the formal equality of states, non-intervention in the domestic affairs of other recognized states and state consent as the basis of international legal obligation'.[11]

The claim is that this model is inadequate, both descriptively and normatively, for dealing with problems which are essentially international in character. But this claim surely needs clarifying, for it is not the existence of states that is the problem, but the degree to which state *sovereignty* is regarded as absolute. A belief in absolute sovereignty, if this is taken to mean the exercise of a state's Westphalian-type rights irrespective of the effect on other states, is indeed an obstacle to effective international management. This conception of sovereignty was articulated by US Attorney General Hudson Harmon in 1895 when he rejected Mexican claims that US use of the Rio Grande was having adverse environmental effects on Mexico. 'According to Harmon', writes Paul Wapner, 'the United States had the legal right to use waters within its territory as it saw fit, independent of external effects. The so-called Harmon Doctrine was based on the view that, "The fundamental principle of international law is the absolute sovereignty of every nation, as against all others, within its own territory." '[12]

But it is clear that neither the existence of states nor the notion of sovereignty are, in themselves, the key problems here, and the Harmon doctrine has indeed been modified since it was first articulated:

Subsequent cases and advancements in legal thought and practice, especially relating to air pollution and riparian rights theory, moderated Harmon's absolute notion of sovereignty and required that states use resources within their territories in ways that do not damage adjoining states or coriparians. This notion, which was codified in the doctrine *sic utere tuo ut alienum non laedas* [you must use your own so as not to injure

---

[10] Litfin 1998a, p. xi.   [11] Held *et al.* 1999, p. 37.   [12] Wapner 1998, p. 277.

others] and supported by the general principle of good neighbourliness stands at the heart of contemporary conceptions of sovereignty and environmental protection.[13]

Not only is it that states and sovereignty are not the problem in themselves, they are arguably essential to the task of arriving at the *sic utere* modification of the Harmon doctrine. The international environmental agreements signed over the past three decades have been formulated by nominally sovereign states, whose *bona fides* are guaranteed by the very fact that they *are* sovereign states. Neither the development of liability nor regulatory international environmental regimes (such as the Montreal Protocol on substances that deplete the ozone layer) would have been possible without states and their assumed sovereignty. Karen Litfin is therefore surely right to point out that 'the negotiation, implementation, and enforcement of environmental treaties are largely in the hands of states. A decline of sovereignty might even undermine the ability of the state to comply with international obligations and actually protect the environment.'[14]

This brief survey indicates, so far, that greens adopt a fundamentally instrumental view of the state. The objective for greens is the 'sustainable society', however we conceive such a thing, and the state is to be regarded as one among many instruments for arriving at it. It is a commonplace to point out that environmental problems are located both 'below' and 'above' the state, and that therefore the appropriate levels of environmental action will vary with the case. At the same time, enough of the Westphalian world survives to persuade greens to regard the sovereign state as pivotal in regard both to local and international sustainability initiatives. This pragmatic approach is illustrated by the fact that, ecoanarchism aside, there is no thoroughgoing green theory of the state which seeks to link a view of its institutions with green principles and objectives, either positively or negatively.

II

The foregoing has been about the state as a focus and lever of 'governance'. From this point of view, states can be made to appear essential features of any plan for a sustainable future, both locally and globally. But states are also articulations of 'political space'; they are both a version of what 'political space' might mean, and constructors of political space itself. This 'spatial' understanding of states is much more complex and potentially problematic for environmental questions than the governance perspective outlined so far in this chapter. Let me consider the implications of this for a key theme in this book: citizenship.

Most mainstream accounts of citizenship regard it as a matter of playing out reciprocal rights and responsibilities between the individual citizen and

---

[13] Wapner 1998, pp. 277–8.   [14] Litfin 1998b, p. 4.

the state. Given the Westphalian model of political geography it is plausible to claim that this is an exhaustive account of what citizenship consists in. Yet this 'Westphalian moment' is not only questionable in its own terms (has the sovereignty, integrity, and equality on which it is based ever been more than formal?), but it is clearly a historically quite specific moment, sandwiched between situations which are more complex and confused than putative post-1648 arrangements would have us believe. It is no coincidence that the term 'new medievalism' has been applied to the contemporary states' system.

The existence in medieval times of an array of authority structures from the local to the transnational and supranational, coexisting with an evolving system of territorially defined political units, has similarities to the contemporary period. This is not to argue that nothing has fundamentally changed. Rather, it is to suggest that a 'new medievalism' may be a useful metaphor for thinking about the present era.[15]

What does this mean for citizenship? If one adheres strictly to the state-centred view, and if one accepts that most states' positions as sites of authority and legitimacy are being eroded in a globalising world, then one might conclude that citizenship, both as theory and practice, must be in decline. Yet even a cursory glance at the political discourse of the Western world, at least, over the past decade, reveals citizenship's stubborn presence in the hearts and minds of both political elites and 'citizens' themselves. How is this to be explained? In part it has to do with the effects of widening disparities in wealth and opportunity across the globe. The contemporary world is marked by unprecedented movements of 'economic refugees', and the direction of movement is always towards countries perceived to possess greater wealth and opportunity. In citizenship-speak, these economic migrants are seeking membership of communities that offer better citizenship entitlements than their countries of origin. This, then, is one very good reason for the current interest in citizenship, organised almost entirely around the question of qualifications for membership of the citizen body, and focused on a discourse that sees citizenship as fundamentally a matter of rights-claiming.

There is, though, a subordinate tradition – subordinate viewed from a contemporary perspective – that views citizenship as about the exercising of responsibilities as well as the claiming of rights. It is this tradition, recast in an international and even an intergenerational context, that environmentalists find most interesting and productive. Environmentalists focus on the *practice* of citizenship rather than the state as the unique political space in which this practice is carried out. Environmental political theory has recently been full of attempts – more or less systematic, more or less complete, more or less convincing – to articulate an 'environmental' or 'ecological' citizenship as one of the means of

---

[15] Held *et al.* 1999, p. 85.

bringing about a sustainable society.[16] This is in part a reaction to the dominant focus on macroeconomic and macropolitical approaches, such as the ecological modernisation agenda referred to above. It is also because there is a clear sense in which no amount of *dirigiste* initiatives will work unless citizens play their part. As Will Kymlicka and Wayne Norman have pointed out: 'the health and stability of a modern democracy depends, not only on the justice of its "basic structure" but also on the qualities and attitudes of its citizens'.[17] They cite environmental policy as one area where this remoralisation is most absent and most required, pointing to 'the failure of environmental policies that rely on voluntary citizen cooperation'.[18]

The key question, though, is whether a conception of environmental citizenship can be coherently articulated at all. One reason why it perhaps cannot is that the state exerts such a powerful grip on our political imagination as the primordial articulation of political space that the only citizenship that makes sense is state-centred citizenship. At first blush, while environmental citizenship is in part about the relationship between the citizen and the state – in the guise, for example, of citizens demanding that their 'environmental rights' be redeemed – it also seems to be about much more. As I pointed out above, environmental problems 'overflow' attempts to keep them within the state, and so the putative responsibilities that go with environmental citizenship point well beyond the standard citizen–state relationship. The question I want to ask here is whether, conceptually, citizenship can sustain this kind of relocation?

To a large degree, of course, the answer depends on what we think citizenship is. If it is, by definition, about the political relationship between citizens and the state, then all attempts at political relocation beyond (or beneath) the state will fail. Yet the development of the concept[19] suggests that we can talk of it in respect of social configurations other than the state: the city, for example, and, today, supra-national organisations such as the European Union. This suggests that linking citizenship with the state, uniquely, is a mistake. If it makes sense to talk about citizenship of the European Union, this is because the European Union possesses the structural characteristics required by citizenship-talk: individuals exercising rights and discharging responsibilities within a political community. Thus far, then, it seems possible for the concept to 'track' the international character of environmental problems or, to put it differently, to think of environmental citizenship as one kind of response to those problems.

Yet the 'spatial imaginary' suggested by even transnational political communities such as the European Union (EU) is still a *bounded* political imaginary. From this point of view it is only possible to speak of citizenship *within* those

---

[16] van Steenbergen 1994; Smith 1998; Barry 1999; Dobson 2000.
[17] Kymlicka and Norman 1994, p. 352.   [18] Kymlicka and Norman 1994, p. 352.
[19] Reisenberg 1992.

boundaries. This makes particular sense, of course, if we focus on citizenship as rights-claiming. It is only appropriate for me to talk of my European citizenship right to vote and stand in member-state municipal elections *in connection with the European Union*, since that right – and any claims I might make in respect of it – can only be redeemed in the territory where the EU's writ runs. But as I pointed out above, citizenship is clearly about obligations as well as about rights, and while these obligations can also be thought of in respect of the citizen's relationship with the state (e.g. the obligation to pay taxes where levied), political obligations are surely not exhausted by this relationship. The question is whether these other obligations can be thought of as obligations of citizenship. This is important from an environmental point of view, because while the obligations of the putative environmental citizen are in part to do with the nation-state, their nature, and to whom they are owed, take us beyond and between states. Citizenship is a powerful political idea, thought important enough by a number of states – most recently the British one – to warrant a statutory presence in secondary or high-school curricula. Citizenship matters, therefore, and this is why it is important to determine whether the 'environmental project' of sustainability can be articulated in the citizenship idiom.

III

We have established that it is a mistake to confine citizenship to the state, and we have broached the question of whether citizenship needs to be territorially confined at all. One way of reading Michael Walzer, almost certainly against his own grain, suggests not: '[A] citizen is, most simply, a member of a political community, entitled to whatever prerogatives and encumbered with whatever responsibilities are attached to membership.'[20] The word 'community', of course, suggests a physical space, but we are well enough acquainted with other sorts of community – an 'epistemic community', for example – to see that it need not be. Perhaps the most thoroughgoing contemporary attempt to take citizenship beyond the state goes by the name of 'cosmopolitan citizenship', a notion that trades on the possibility of political communities being defined in other than territorial terms. One of its most articulate exponents, Andrew Linklater, is well aware of the conceptual problems associated with it:

Appealing to cosmopolitan citizenship may inspire fellow nationals to honour obligations to peoples elsewhere, but this distorts the notion of citizenship in their [i.e. opponents'] view. From their standpoint, to be a citizen is to have concrete rights against, and duties to, a specific sovereign state rather than voluntary and inexact duties to the rest of humanity . . . Traditional approaches argue that appeals to cosmopolitan citizenship amount to little more than an exercise in moral exhortation while the nation-state is the

---

[20] Walzer 1989, p. 211.

dominant form of political community. Their contention is that the idea of world citizenship may have considerable moral force, but, on any strict definition of citizenship, the term is self-evidently and unalterably oxymoronic.[21]

In other words, 'critics of world citizenship protest that its exhortatory and rhetorical purposes are entirely divorced from the Aristotelian idea of active involvement in the democratic public sphere'.[22] Not so, says Linklater. For him, 'involvement in the democratic public sphere' can take many forms, and one of them is political argumentation. In Linklater's view, the 'central aim' of cosmopolitan citizenship is the liberal one of ensuring that 'dialogue and consent' replace force as the means by which disputes are settled in the international arena.[23] He goes on to claim that, 'it requires political action to build communication communities in which outsiders, and especially the most vulnerable among them, have the power to "refuse and negotiate offers" and to contest unjust social structures'.[24] Linklater calls this a 'dialogic' approach to citizenship, according to which the central idea of involvement in the public sphere is not abandoned, but rather recast in the non-territorial context of an incipient discursive democracy. This seems genuinely non-territorial, in the same sense that an epistemic community, or a community of the diaspora, is non-territorial.

Environmental citizenship is an example of cosmopolitan citizenship in this dialogic sense. The public sphere in this context is the dialogic sphere in which debates regarding environmental values and objectives take place. From an environmental point of view, this sphere is intergenerational as well as international. In this regard, environmental citizenship is rooted in Hannah Arendt's view that, 'If the world is to contain a public space, it cannot be erected for one generation and planned for the living only; it must transcend the lifespan of mortal men. It is what we have in common not only with those who live with us, but also with those who were here before and with those who will come after us.'[25] The discursive focus for the debate is the idea of 'sustainable development' – an idea endorsed by virtually everyone, but whose meaning is continually, even perhaps 'essentially', contested.[26] In this context, the environmental citizen 'does' citizenship by articulating, defending, and practising particular answers to general sustainability questions such as, what is to be sustained?, for whose benefit?, and for how long? This is citizenship because it conforms to a broadly accepted notion of what citizenship consists in, at least in part: active involvement in the public sphere.

By deploying the dialogical idea, then, Linklater hopes to have headed off one kind of territorial-based criticism of cosmopolitan citizenship. But there is another. It is clear from the long quotation above that Linklater is sensitive to

---

[21] Linklater 1998, pp. 23–4.   [22] Linklater 1998, p. 27.   [23] Linklater 1998, p. 25.
[24] Linklater 1998, p. 25.   [25] Arendt 1989, p. 55.   [26] Jacobs 1999b.

the charge that not only the *context* of citizenship, but its *duties*, too, are quite precise – that 'to be a citizen is to have concrete rights against, and duties to, a specific sovereign state rather than voluntary and inexact duties to the rest of humanity'. As Linklater goes on: 'the argument is that, if it is to have any real meaning, cosmopolitan citizenship must involve rather more than moral commitments not to exploit the weaknesses of others – more than the ethical resolution to treat all other human beings with care and compassion'.[27] To resist this criticism, the discursive, or dialogical, moment in cosmopolitan citizenship is once again enlisted. Linklater's contention is that the commitment to dialogue and discussion is somehow more 'political' than more 'voluntary and inexact' commitments. So he says that while 'world citizenship may embody commitments to treat the vulnerable with compassion . . . it must also embrace the principle of engaging others as equals within wider communities of discourse'.[28]

Quite why 'engaging others as equals within wider communities of discourse' is 'political', unlike 'the ethical resolution to treat all other human beings with care and compassion', though, is not clear to me. They both share the key citizenship idea of active involvement in the public sphere, so the only difference can be that the activity of 'discourse' is somehow more political than the activity of care and compassion. But this is open to the feminist objection that we should pause before consigning apparently 'private' practices and virtues to the category of the non-political. From this point of view, the determination to regard care and compassion as non-political virtues is ideological rather than analytical. It may be that Linklater is giving too much ground to his critics by seeking to 'shore up' the world citizen's commitment to treat the vulnerable with care and compassion with the somehow more political – and therefore more citizenly – principle of dialogical equality.

IV

The only way to sort out these difficulties is by developing a comprehensive analytics of obligation so as to see what it is that distinguishes the duties we might have towards 'humanity in general' and the duties we have as citizens. We would then be in a position to say whether cosmopolitan and environmental citizenships are citizenships at all. Although beyond the scope of this chapter, a full analytics of citizenship obligations would have to take into account at least three dimensions of obligation: their source (why are we obliged?), their nature (obligation to do what?), and their object (to whom or to what are obligations owed?). Usually it is assumed that the *nature* of citizenship obligations distinguishes them from other types of obligation, but my contention is that we

---

[27] Linklater 1998, p. 28.   [28] Linklater 1998, p. 34.

should focus on the *source* of obligation instead. I shall return to the significance of this shortly.

Traditional liberal, state-centred, citizenship offers quite specific kinds of answers to these questions: citizens owe obligations to the state for reasons of what we might call reciprocity, and the obligations they owe are those that the state determines (pay taxes, seek work if unemployed, do military service, and so on). Those who believe that citizenship can *only* be state citizenship will regard cosmopolitan citizenship as failing the citizenship test on at least two of these dimensions. Most obviously, cosmopolitan citizenship's obligations are not owed to the state. Furthermore, they are of the wrong type: a 'commitment to unforced dialogue' is simply not a citizenship-type obligation. Only in respect of the source of obligation – reciprocity – is there any similarity between state-centred and cosmopolitan citizenship. In the state-centred case, reciprocity consists in the state honouring the rights of citizens in return for citizens fulfilling their obligations to the state. For cosmopolitanism, reciprocity resides in the commitment to free and unforced dialogue.

On the face of it, Linklater's response to his state-centred critics of cosmopolitan citizenship is organised around the second of these dimensions. He claims that commitment to dialogue is indeed a citizenship-type obligation and, as we have seen, he makes this claim by contrasting dialogue with what he regards as broader and therefore non-citizenly virtues. But what is it about such virtues as care and compassion that makes them non-citizenly? Linklater appears to think it is because care and compassion are owed too broadly (their 'non-specificity'). But this cannot work for him since the point, precisely, of cosmopolitan citizenship is to urge us towards the idea that the obligations of citizenship extend beyond the nation-state. Is it, then, that these are private virtues that fall foul of the requirement that citizenship virtues be public virtues? This view, though, is vulnerable to the feminist point canvassed above, that equating 'the private' with the 'non-political' is a mistake, as well as to the more prosaic point that so-called private virtues can of course be exercised in public.

We appear, then, to be left with the *source* of obligation as that which will distinguish citizenship obligations from other types. Is there something about the source of citizenly obligation that is specific to citizenship, and that marks it off from other more general ethical obligations? The common source of obligation for both state-centred and cosmopolitan citizenship is reciprocity. Perhaps this is the answer to the question of what makes some obligations 'citizenly'. As I pointed out above, the nature of the reciprocity in the two cases may be rather crudely different. In the state-centred context it is a reciprocity of something approaching mutual advantage (even if motivated by an ethical view of the state), whereas for cosmopolitanism reciprocity is contained in the dialogical commitment to truth. But reciprocity is nevertheless common to them both. There is indeed something to be said for reciprocity as a distinguishing foundational mark of citizenship obligation. It will certainly allow us to rule out some relations of obligation as being of a citizenship type, thereby undercutting the tendency to criticise cosmopolitan citizenship for being too all-embracing. The Good Samaritan, for example, was not acting as a citizen but, as Jesus says, as a 'neighbour' when he bound the wounds of the man attacked by thieves on the way to Jericho.[29] It is worth adding that, if we focus on reciprocity as the key distinguishing characteristic of citizenship obligation, then we must allow a wider range of virtues to be regarded as virtues of citizenship. Care and compassion cannot be ruled out *as such*, for example, so long as they can be shown to have been generated by demonstrable relations of reciprocity.

Let me sum up the story so far. I began this discussion by suggesting that the spatial imaginary supplied by the state as a bounded community has corralled our conception of citizenship. It has been pointed out *ad nauseam* that many environmental problems cannot be confined to the bounded territories of states, and that therefore measures to deal with them will inevitably have an international dimension. If we cleave to the idea that citizenship is definitionally associated with states, then we must conclude that environmental action in the international arena cannot be conceived in terms of citizenship. The political disadvantage of this is clear: politically, citizenship is a valuable exhortatory resource. For example, it is broadly recognised that global warming is caused by wealthy countries, and that these same countries are best placed to adapt to its impacts because of the capital and technological resources at their disposal. Conversely, the countries least best placed to deal with global warming are those which have had relatively little to do with causing it in the first place. Citizenship might be regarded as a powerful rhetorical tool to engage the political imaginations of 'first world' populations with a view to encouraging them to reflect on their responsibilities to those affected by inappropriate habits and practices. This tool will only be available, though, if citizenship can be released from the shackles of association with the state. I have suggested that the idea of cosmopolitan citizenship is useful in this context, and that it is defensible *as* a citizenship. This defence is not based, though, on the standard attempt to show that cosmopolitan citizenship's virtues are distinct from broader 'human' virtues, but on the relations of reciprocity that call for the exercise of virtues (whatever they may be).

V

From the point of view of a putative *environmental* citizenship, however, this small victory – if such it is – may have been won at a high price. As I have said,

---

[29] Luke 10:36. I assume that neighbourly acts are not carried out in the expectation or on the understanding that favours will be returned.

environmental citizenship is as internationalist as cosmopolitan citizenship; this much they have in common. But environmental problems have a temporal as well as a territorial dimension. The half-life of Uranium-235, used as a fuel in nuclear reactors, is 7.1 × 10 (to the power of 9) years, which, given the problems associated with storing waste safely, offers this generation the possibility of inflicting damage on generations yet to be born or even imagined. Assuming we have a duty at least to consider the effects present practices might have on future generations, can this duty be regarded as a duty of citizenship?

On a strict interpretation of the reciprocity principle, it cannot. Although very interesting arguments to the contrary have been put,[30] I shall adopt the standard view that relations between generations follow time's arrow, and that future generations cannot therefore influence the life chances of the present generation. The idea of intergenerational citizenship seems to fall, therefore, at the reciprocity hurdle. Let me have a go at scrambling over it, neverthe-less. In the first place, the reciprocity principle is much better understood in the context in which I have been using it as an *interdependence* principle. 'Reciprocity' carries with it an implication of parity or equality of relation-ship that is clearly inappropriate in the environmental cases I canvassed above, such as global warming. Further, when we ask ourselves what it is *about* in-terdependence that calls forth the virtues of citizenship, we see that it is our capacity to affect those with whom we are in relationship, rather than interde-pendence itself, that counts. More accurately still, it is the recognition that our antecedent actions have already had damaging effects on others that gives rise to obligation.

Attempting to articulate a cosmopolitan view of international morality, Judith Lichtenberg distinguishes between 'historical' and 'moral' arguments. The moral view has it that 'A owes something positive to B . . . not in virtue of any causal role he has had in B's situation or any prior relationship or agree-ment, but just because, for example, he is able to benefit B or alleviate his plight.'[31] In contrast, the historical view suggests that, 'what A owes to B he owes in virtue of some antecedent action, undertaking, agreement, relationship, or the like'.[32] The moral view is exactly that adopted by the Good Samaritan, or by the purveyor of charity, and I have suggested that we should not view this kind of obligation as one of citizenship. Lichtenberg's 'historical' option is a version of the 'interdependence' thesis to which I referred above. It is far-reaching in its implications for a globalised world, in which 'relationships' are forged across the planet at an ever-increasing rate,[33] creating 'historical' obligations whose existence it would have been quite proper to deny until now. Lichtenberg describes this phenomenon in her own way as follows: 'My claim

---

[30] E.g. O'Neill 1993.   [31] Lichtenberg 1981, p. 80.
[32] Lichtenberg 1981, p. 80.   [33] Held *et al.* 1999.

is that history has involved the gradual (or perhaps not so gradual) transformation of the earth from a collection of many relatively open worlds to one closed one.'[34]

Perceptively, from an environmental point of view, Lichtenberg goes on to comment that, 'Some of the relationships in virtue of which the earth now constitutes one world are so pervasive and far-reaching that they are difficult to pinpoint or to measure. There are also actions that may have harmful consequences without any direct involvement between agents and those affected. For these reasons it is easy to ignore them as sources of obligation.'[35] It is increasingly pointed out, for example, that many so-called 'natural' disasters may in fact have anthropogenic origins. Climate scientists are fairly confident that, although the disaggregated impacts of global warming are very hard to predict, we are likely to experience an increased incidence of extreme weather events – so called 'strange weather'. When floods devastate large areas of developing countries, we congratulate ourselves on the generous quantities of aid we offer to alleviate the suffering. From the 'closed earth' point of view, though, the campaigning issue is not so much about how generous aid should be, but whether 'aid' is the appropriate category at all. If global warming is principally caused by wealthy countries, and if global warming is at least a part cause of strange weather, then monies should be transferred as a matter of compensatory justice rather than as aid or charity.

Note that what prompts the idea of obligation in this instance is not reciprocity but a version of the interdependence thesis – the recognition that our actions affect the life chances of distant strangers. But to call these obligations 'historical' in Lichtenberg's sense is to misunderstand their nature in a globalised world. Recall that for Lichtenberg the historical view has it that 'what A owes to B he owes in virtue of some antecedent action, undertaking, agreement, relationship, or the like'. In a globalising world the notion of 'antecedence' wears thin, as both space *and* time tend towards collapse. Thus, in post-modern parlance, inhabitants of globalising nations are *always already* acting on others, as when, for example, our use of fossil fuels causes the release of gases that contribute to global warming. It is this recognition that calls forth the virtues and practices of citizenship. Note once again that the distinction between the Good Samaritan and the Good Citizen is preserved. The obligations associated with the former are those that it would be simply desirable to fulfil, in some broadly virtuous, benevolent, and supererogatory sense; those of the latter are obligations that it would be wrong not to fulfil.

While this is a citizenship with international and intergenerational dimensions, it is not itself universalisable. This is a citizenship for those, precisely, with the capacity to 'always already' act on others. In a crucial insight, the

[34] Lichtenberg 1981, p. 86.   [35] Lichtenberg 1981, p. 87.

Indian environmentalist Vandana Shiva points out not only that the fruits of global free trade are shared unequally around the planet, but that the very possibility of *being global* is disproportionately distributed. She writes that, 'The construction of the global environment narrows the South's options while increasing the North's. Through its global reach, the North exists in the South, but the South exists only within itself, since it has no global reach. Thus the South can *only* exist locally, while only the North exists globally.'[36]

The North has the capacity to impose its own local view on the global environment – a capacity that is denied the South. Towards the end of 2001, practically unnoticed amid the sound and fury of the international attack on Afghanistan, 171 countries met in Marrakesh, Morocco, to finalise the operations rulebook for the Kyoto agreement on limiting global warming emissions. Thirty-eight industrialised countries signed the Marrakesh agreement – but thirty-nine had set out on the long road that began in Kyoto. One of the original participants, the United States, dropped out along the way. When George W. Bush's administration pulled out of the talks, critics dubbed the administration 'isolationist'. But it was never that. It was, rather, unilateralist – and unilateralism is, as Vandana Shiva points out, an option only available to the rich and powerful. It may be no coincidence that the power most capable of unilateral action – of existing globally as well as locally – chose the environment (perhaps the most global topic there is) as the arena in which to exert its own very specific and local version of 'the good life'.

This is not reciprocity, then, nor is it even interdependence, in any broadly accepted sense of the term. Shiva comments that,

There are no reflexive relationships. The G-7 can demand a forest convention that imposes international obligations on the Third World to plant trees. But the Third World cannot demand that the industrialized countries reduce the use of fossil fuels and energy. The "global" has been so structured, that the North (as the globalized local) has all rights and no responsibility, and the South has no rights, but all responsibility.[37]

The obligations of environmental citizenship sketched here are therefore obligations for 'industrialised' countries and their inhabitants, in recognition of the responsibilities produced by the political and social economy of globalisation – responsibilities that are all too often unilaterally eschewed.

These insights suggest that the most appropriate 'spatial imaginary' for environmental citizenship is the 'ecological footprint'.[38] This idea has been developed to illustrate the varying impacts of individuals' and communities' social practices on the environment. It is assumed that the earth has a limited productive and waste-absorbing capacity, and a notional and equal 'land allowance' – or footprint – is allocated to each person on the planet, given these limits. The

---

[36] Shiva 1998, p. 233.   [37] Shiva 1998, p. 234.   [38] Wackernagel 1995.

footprint size is arrived at by dividing the total land, and its productive capacity, available by the number of people on the planet, and the figure usually arrived at is somewhere between 1.5 and 1.7 hectares. Inevitably, some people have a bigger impact – a bigger footprint – than others (median consumers in 'advanced industrial countries' are generally reckoned to occupy about five hectares of ecological space), and this is taken to be unjust, in the sense of a departure from a nominal equality of ecological space. This approach to determining environmental impact is of course open to all the standard objections to 'limits to growth' and other Malthusian-type analyses of the relationship between human beings and their natural environment. It will be argued that such an approach underestimates the resources available, the capacity for doing more with less through technological advances, the possibility of substituting one resource for another with the same function, and that it ignores the historical evidence suggesting that resource availability is more elastic than 'finitude' analyses would have us believe. Its implicitly egalitarian view of distributive justice is also open to the objection that departures from the norm of equal shares are often justifiable.

I cannot fully review these criticisms here, and nor, I think, do I need to for present purposes. The relevance of the ecological footprint notion to environmental citizenship is broadly unaffected by the criticisms to which I have just alluded, unless we believe in a totally cornucopian world in which infinite substitutability of resources is possible. Its relevance is that it contains the key spatial and obligation-generating relationships that give rise to the exercise of specifically citizenly virtues. The *nature* of the obligation is to reduce the occupation of ecological space, where appropriate, and the *source* of this obligation lies in remedying the potential and actual injustice of appropriating an unjust share of such space. This, then, is an explicitly ecological version of Lichtenberg's 'historical' argument for obligation, transposed to the 'always already' context of ecological impact in which some countries, and some people within some countries, systematically affect the life chances of others in this and in future generations. It also explains and reflects the asymmetrical and non-reciprocal nature of environmental citizenship obligations. Obligations are owed by those in ecological space debt, and these obligations are the corollary of a putative environmental right to an equal share of ecological space for everyone.

In sum, every political project implicitly or explicitly contains an account of political space, and the quest for environmental sustainability is no exception. The state has its uses in this context, but the sub- and supra-national arenas of political action are also crucial for environmentalists. The recent history of citizenship, and its now-dominant articulation as the claiming of rights within the nation-state, suggests that citizenship can neither be talked of nor used in the contexts favoured by environmentalists. But I have argued that there are environmental resources (so to speak) in the burgeoning idea of cosmopolitan citizenship, and that these resources are best deployed by identifying what is peculiarly citizenly – as opposed to broadly humanitarian – about the source of obligations in an asymmetrically globalising world. Finally, environmentalism offers the earthy footprint – in addition to the state, the supra-state, or cosmopolitan citizenship's dialogic community – as the spatial imaginary within which citizenship and its obligations are best conceived.

BIBLIOGRAPHY

Arendt, Hannah (1989). *The Human Condition*, Chicago: Chicago University Press.
Barnett, Jon (2001). *The Meaning of Environmental Security*, London: Zed Books.
Barry, John (1999). *Rethinking Green Politics*, London: Sage.
Carter, Alan (1993). 'Towards a Green Political Theory' in Andrew Dobson and Paul Lucardie (eds), *The Politics of Nature: Explorations in Green Political Theory*, London: Routledge.
  (1999). *A Radical Green Political Theory*, London: Routledge.
Dalby, Simon (2000). 'Geopolitics and Ecology: Rethinking the Contexts of Environmental Security' in Miriam Lowi and Brian Shaw (eds.), *Environment and Security: Discourses and Practices*, London and New York: Macmillan Press and St Martin's Press.
Dobson, Andrew (2000). 'Ecological Citizenship: A Disruptive Influence?' in Christopher Pierson and Simon Tormey (eds.), *Politics at the Edge: PSA Yearbook 1999*, London: Macmillan.
Eckersley, Robyn (1995). 'Markets, the State and the Environment: An Overview' in Robyn Eckersley (ed.), *Markets, the State and the Environment*, Houndmills: Macmillan Education Australia.
Evans, Mary Margaret, Mentz, John, Chandler, Robert, and Eubanks, Stephanie (2000). 'The Changing Dentition of National Security' in Miriam Lowi and Brian Shaw (eds.), *Environment and Security: Discourses and Practices*, London and New York: Macmillan Press and St Martin's Press.
Goodin, Robert (1992). *Green Political Theory*, Cambridge: Polity Press.
Held, David, McGrew, Anthony, Goldblatt, David, and Perraton, Jonathan (1999). *Global Transformations: Politics, Economics and Culture*, Cambridge: Polity Press.
Jacobs, Michael (1999a). *Environmental Modernisation: The New Labour Agenda*, London: Fabian Society.
  (1999b). 'Sustainable Development as a Contested Concept' in Andrew Dobson (ed.), *Fairness and Futurity: Essays on Environmental Sustainability and Social Justice*, Oxford: Oxford University Press.
Kymlicka, Will and Norman, Wayne (1994). 'Return of the Citizen', *Ethics* 104 (January), pp. 352–81.
Lichtenberg, Judith (1981). 'National Boundaries and Moral Boundaries: A Cosmopolitan View' in Peter Brown and Henry Shue (eds.), *Boundaries: National Autonomy and its Limits*, New Jersey: Rowman and Littlefield.
Linklater, Andrew (1998). 'Cosmopolitan Citizenship', *Citizenship Studies*, 2/1: pp. 23–41.

Litfin, Karen (1998a). 'Preface' in *The Greening of Sovereignty in World Politics*, Cambridge, Mass. and London: MIT Press.

Lonergan, Steve (2000). 'Human Security, Environmental Security and Sustainable Development' in Miriam Lowi, and Brian Shaw (eds.), *Environment and Security: Discourses and Practices*, London and New York: Macmillan Press and St Martin's Press.

O'Neill, John (1993). *Ecology, Policy and Politics: Human Well-being and the Natural World*, London: Routledge.

Reisenberg, Peter (1992). *Citizenship in the Western Tradition: Plato to Rousseau*, Chapel Hill and London: University of North Carolina Press.

Sergen, Galina and Malone, Elizabeth (2000). 'Perceptions of Risk and Security: The Aral Sea Basin' in Miriam Lowi and Brian Shaw (eds.), *Environment and Security: Discourses and Practices*, London and New York: Macmillan Press and St Martin's Press.

Shiva, Vandana (1998). 'The Greening of Global Reach' in *The Geopolitics Reader*, ed. Gearóid O Thuatail, Simon Dalby and Routledge, Paul, Routledge: London.

Smith, Mark (1998). *Ecologism: Towards Ecological Citizenship*, Milton Keynes: Open University Press.

Thompson, Michael (2000). 'Not Seeing the People for the Population: A Cautionary Tale from the Himalaya' in Miriam Lowi and Brian Shaw (eds.), *Environment and Security: Discourses and Practices*, Macmillan Press and St Martin's Press: London and New York.

van Steenbergen, Bart (1994). 'Towards a Global Ecological Citizen' in Bart van Steenbergen (ed.), *The Condition of Citizenship*, London: Sage.

Wackernagel, Mathis (1995). *Our Ecological Footprint: Reducing Human Impact on the Earth*, Gabriola Island, B(ritish) C(olumbia): New Society Publishers.

Walzer, M. (1989). 'Citizenship' in T. Ball, J. Farr, and R. Hanson (eds.), *Political Innovation and Conceptual Change*, Cambridge: Cambridge University Press.

Wapner, Paul (1998). 'Reorienting State Sovereignty: Rights and Responsibilities in the Environmental Age', *The Greening of Sovereignty in World Politics*, Cambridge, Mass. and London, England: MIT Press.

Index

Africa, colonial rule of 150
Al-Biruni 148, 162
Almain, Jacques 101
Alsted, Johann 86, 88
Althusius, Johannes 4, 73, 83–84, 86–88,
  91–92
  Civilis Conversationis 87
  objections to 88–89
Althusser, Louis 168
Amar, André 193
American Declaration of Independence 17–18
  objections to 18
American Indians, Spanish dealings with 100,
  102
Anderson, Perry 82–83
Andreae, Johann Valentin 88
Anjou, Duke of 84
anthropology
  anti-feminist readings of 206
  Enlightenment readings of 124–125
Anti-Terrorism Act (2001) 25
Aquinas, Thomas 52, 100–101, 103, 105–107
  De regno 106
arbitrariness (of power) 12
Arendt, Hannah 216
Aristotle 30, 51–53, 131, 216
  medieval influence 60, 83, 88–90, 92
  post-medieval influence 102, 105–106,
  109
  Nicomachaean Ethics 106
  Politics 57, 88, 106, 109
armed forces
  citizens as 41–42, 45–46
  responsibility for 1
Arnisaeus, Henning 4, 83–84, 89–90
  De Republica 89, 108
Assemblée Nationale see French Revolution:
  legislative proceedings
associations
  in development of nationalism 153
  in early civic theory 86–88
  objections to 135–136

women's 122, 202
  see also trades unions
asylum, applications for 1
Auden, W. H. 35

B— B—, Madame 121, 125
Bacon, Francis 92, 108
'barbarian' society 117–118, 123
  versus modernity 125
Barbey d'Aurevilly, Jules 204
Bard, Christiane, *Filles de Marianne* 202
Baron, Hans 92
Barry, John 209–210
Barthes, Roland 178
Bartolus of Sassoferrato 60–61, 85, 87
Basle 69
Batavia 109
Bayle, Pierre 92
Bentham, Jeremy 18–20
Berlin, Isaiah 23–24
Berlusconi, Silvio 180
Bernard, Madame 202
Beveridge, William 176
Bharatiya Janata (BJP) *see* Jana Sangh
black races, debates on political/natural
  equality 124
Blanot, Jean de 56–57
Blockmans, Wim 65, 73
Bodin, Jean 4, 71, 73
  impact on political theory 83–84, 89, 92
  Les Six livres de la République 83
  modern commentaries 91
  objections to 85–87, 89
Bolingbroke, Henry St John, 1st Viscount 17
Bosanquet, Bernard 21, 23, 34
Bracton, Henry de 12
Braudel, Fernand 169
Braunschweig-Wolfenbüttel, dukes of 89
Bretton Woods summit 181
Brunner, Otto 65
Buchan, James 31
Burckhardt, Jakob 79–82, 92–93

bureaucracy, role in government 156–157, 161
Burke, Edmund 141, 151
Bury St Edmunds, liberty of 54
Bush, George W. 222
Butler, Judith 128

cahiers de doléances 121, 124
Calvin, Jean 86
canon law 51–52, 56–57
capitalism, critiques of 171–172
Carnegie, Andrew 180
Carré de Malberg, Raymond 142
Carter, Alan 208
caste system
    functioning/terminology 148–149
    interaction with political systems 148–151,
        157, 159–160
    role in Indian society 6, 147, 149, 159
categorisation (of social groupings) 198, 200
celebrity, nature of 35
change, nature of process 169–172
Charles I
    conflict with Parliament 14
    trial/execution 14–15
Charron, Pierre 108
China 2
Church
    freedoms of 11, 52, 66
    medieval hierarchy 54
Cicero, Marcus Tullius 87, 107
    De inventione 99
    De officiis 108
cities, medieval
    in Germany 65–66, 69, 72–73
    in Italy 66
    legal system 66–71, 73–74
    power struggles in 71–73
    as precursors of modern State 4, 42, 53–55,
        58–61, 65, 68, 71
    role in wider community 68–69
    role of Council 69–70, 72
    socio-political system 66, 68, 71
citizenship
    'active' (vs. 'passive') 105–108, 134–135,
        138, 181–184, 195
    aspects/definitions 39–44, 48, 107,
        131–132, 137, 212–215
    'cosmopolitan' 215–220
    'environmental' 213–216, 219–224
    European 181–182, 185, 214–215
    functions/limitations 133–137, 139
    international 7–8, 46–48, 142, 185–187, 214
        (see also 'cosmopolitan' above)
    lack of see statelessness
    and migration 47–48, 213

and national identity 2, 43, 46, 140
new developments 45–48, 213
obligations 217–224
as philosophical concept 3, 44–45
rights of see liberty; rights
territorial confines 215–216
(rival) traditions of 97–99, 179–181, 183,
    213
of women 118–123, 193, 199
see also French Revolution; state
city-states
    in Ancient world 42, 44–45, 117
    post-medieval theories of 98, 102–111
    see also cities, medieval
Civil War (English)
    basis of conflict 13–15, 109
    impact on civic theory 92–93, 104, 109
class
    economic theories based on 171, 174
    erosion as significant factor 171–172,
        174
Clemenceau, Georges 197
co(-operation)
    as basis of economic theory 171–172, 175
    vs. auto- approach
coercion, as function of state 28–29, 40, 64,
    83, 195
Coke, Sir Edward 12
Cold War 23
Coleman, James 45
colonialism 6, 100, 145
    diverse approaches to 150
    ethics of 102, 115, 153–154
    impact on post-colonial societies 146–147,
        152, 154–155, 161
common good, sovereignty of 106–107
Communism/Communist party
    impact on economic concepts 172
    policy on women's issues 203
Condorcet, Marie-Jean de Caritat, Marquis de
    6, 120, 123, 125, 131, 135–140
Conring, Herman 83–84, 88–90
'consociation', theories of 4, 83, 86–87, 91–92
Constance, Peace of 58
Constant, Benjamin 195–196
constituents, citizens as 42, 47
Constitution(s)
    British (lack of) 25
    French, (post-)Revolutionary 132–133,
        136–139, 142
    Indian 155, 158
    medieval notions of 52–53, 70
    role in state 29
consumers, citizens as 185
contract, role in rights theory 104–105

cordon sanitaire, in philosophy of liberty 21, 23–24
corporations (multi-national)
  assumption of states' functions 1–2, 25, 47
  power within state 45
  regulation 2
corruption 157
Couriau, M/Mme 203
Cowell, John 12
Cremona, Bishop of 53–54
Cresheld, Richard 14
Crowe, Cameron 32

Darwinism (social) 175–176
Daubié, Julie 205
De La Court, Johan/Pieter 86, 91
Déclaration(s) des droits des hommes et des citoyens 121, 132, 135–137, 139, 141
Dekker, Rudolf 122
Delanty, Gerard 185–188
Delfau, G., Deputy 136
democracy
  electorate's adjustment to 157–159
  and gender issues 7
  impact on civic/social life 39–40, 146, 158–161
  and party politics 44
  post-colonial 6, 146, 154–155, 157–159
  role in modern world 146
  success/failure 146, 161–162
Deraismes, Maria 201
Deroin, Jeanne 203
Descartes, René 92
'development', as function of state 155, 157
Dreitzel, Horst 88
Droysen, Johann Gustav 79
Dumont, Louis 206
Durand, Guillaume 56–57
Durkheim, Emile 44, 47, 194

East India Company 150–151
eating/drinking, role in civil state 87
Eckersley, Robyn 209–210
'ecological modernisation' 209–210, 214
ecology *see* environmental issues
economy/ics
  global 47
  impact on politics 43
  management of 167
  role in state formation/development 147
  theories of 171–177
  see also money; taxation
education
  in citizenship 215
  civic value of 137–138, 140, 142, 197

Eighty Years War 83
Emden 73, 88
employment, as focus of social theory 177–178
  see also unemployment
Enlightenment (C18) 5, 64
  development of civic theory 116, 123–125, 127
  influences on 92–93
  role in development of modern world 115–116, 128–129, 182, 187–188
environmental issues 7, 170
  and citizenship 213–215 (*see also* citizenship: 'environmental')
  diversity of viewpoints 208
  'footprint' analogy 222–223
  impact on economy 175
  and international politics 210–211, 214, 219–220
  temporal dimension 220–221
  theories of state 208–212
  value *vs.* agency, theories of 208–209
equality, principle of 44
  of gender 119, 121–123, 126, 191–192, 205–206
  in medieval cities 68
  obstacles to 45, 200, 205–206
  vs. identity 205–206
Ertman, Thomas 41
Europe
  comparisons with USA 180
  impact of globalisation 179
  unity/identity 180–181
  see also European Union; *names of countries/historical periods*
European Convention on Human Rights 25
European Union/Community 25, 46, 142, 214–215
  economic operation 46
  formation 181
  future 185–186
  international relations 181
  political system 46

family, central role in social theory 193–194, 200–201, 203
  as obstruction to women's rights 201–202, 205
feminism 127–129, 174, 205, 217–218
  origins of term 191
  vs. socialism 202–203
Ferguson, Adam, *Essay on the History of Civil Society* 115–119, 123
Ferry, Jules 196, 201
feudalism

and medieval law 56–58
    modern perceptions of 59, 64, 67
'fiction', state as 28–29, 35, 37, 54, 168, 171,
    184
Filmer, Sir Robert, *Patriarcha* 17
Flaubert, Gustave, *Madame Bovary* 35
flexibility
    role in industrial economics 175–177
    of wages 176
Florence 72, 79–80, 92
Foucault, Michel 40, 194–195, 197
France
    civic history 6, 191–192, 194–197, 202
    Constitutional Monarchies 195–196
    democratic ethos 7
    legislation 202–203
    medieval law 56
    modern politics 172
    political history 97, 104, 142
    Republics (Second/Third) 135, 142,
        196–197
    1848 Revolution 196, 198–199, 202
    Second Empire 199
    see also French Revolution
franchise *see* suffrage
Fraser, Nancy 127–128
Frederick I 'Barbarossa', Emperor 58
Frederick the Great, Emperor 81
freedom *see* liberty
Freiburg 69
French Revolution 5, 28, 64, 67, 162,
    169
    electoral system 134–135
    fundamental principles 132–133, 135–136,
        139, 141, 191–192
    ideals of citizenship 5–6, 44, 131–132,
        136–142, 179–182
    internal divisions 131–132, 135–141
    legacy for modern world 141–142,
        180–181, 187, 191–192
    legislative proceedings 121–124, 131–133,
        138, 195–196 (*see also* Constitution(s))
    military aspects 41
    and women's issues 119–122, 124, 135,
        193, 204
Freud, Sigmund 20
future, environmental obligations towards
    220–221

Gambetta, Léon 196
Gandhi, Indira 156, 158
Gandhi, Mahatma 145, 155
gender, issues of *see* citizenship; democracy;
    rights; suffrage; women
genocide 188

Germany
    development of political theory 83–84,
        86–91
    historiographical trends 80–81, 92
    medieval cities 65–66, 69, 72
    modern politics/economics 170, 172–173,
        187
    political history 83
    Weimar Republic 31, 81
    Wilhelmine era 80
Gerson, Jean de 101
Giddens, Anthony 40
global warming 219–221
globalisation
    critiques of 183–186, 188–189
    early examples/foreshadowings 115–116,
        123
    environmental effects 221
    impact on citizenship 46–48, 142, 184–187,
        213
    impact on state powers/functions 3, 37,
        46–47, 115, 213
    inequality of input/effects 221–223
    terminology 178
    theories/models of 178–179
Goffman, Erving 44
Goodin, Robert, *Green Political Theory*
    208–209
Gordon, Thomas *see* Trenchard, John
Gouges, Olympe de, *Déclaration des droits de
    la femme et de la citoyenne* 120
government
    identification of state with 28, 31
Gratian 51
    Concordance of Discordant Canons 51
Greek society/culture 41–42, 97–98
    (modern) Western referencing of 121, 123,
        125
Green, T. H. 21, 23
Grotius, Hugo 4, 83–84, 87, 91, 105
    comparisons with other philosophers 91,
        104–105, 110
    modern commentaries 91–92
    De Iure Praedae 84–86
    *Treatise of the Antiquity of the Batavian now
        Hollandish Republic* 86, 109
Guicciardini, Francesco 80
Guizot, François 145, 196

Habermas, Jürgen 126–127
Habsburg Empire 100
Hardtwig, Wolfgang 79–80
Harmon, Hudson, General/Harmon doctrine
    211–212
Hastings, Warren 151

Hedley, Sir Thomas 14
Hegel, Friedrich 21, 30, 79, 81–82, 178
Helmstedt, University of 89
Henry of Sousa (Hostiensis) 52
Herborn, University of 88
Hindu society/politics *see* caste system; Jana
    Sangh
Hintze, Otto 82
Hirschman, Albert, *The Passions and the
    Interests* 41
Hobbes, Thomas 19, 29, 32, 105, 110,
    131
  comparisons with other philosophers 91,
    104–105, 110
  influence on European thought 91
  later supporters 18–19, 24
  modern commentaries 91
  objections to 16–17
  Leviathan 3, 11, 15–16, 29–30, 32, 36,
    90–91, 140
  On the Citizen 108
Hobhouse, L. T. 23
Hohfeld, Wesley, *Fundamental Legal
    Conceptions* 97–98, 100
Holland *see* Netherlands
Holocaust 188
human rights
  impact on definitions of citizenship 47–48
  as international principle 47
  present-day debate on 126–129
  vs. civic rights 124
humanism
  'civic' 106–109
  northern (Dutch/German) 83–84, 88
  Renaissance/Italian 80, 99
Humboldt, Alexander von 63
Hume, David 18, 30
Huntington, Samuel 183

'identity politics' 116
IMF (International Monetary Fund) 1, 187
India 2, 6
  administration 152, 156
  British assumption of control 150–152
  colonial society/politics 6, 147, 150–152,
    154–155
  evolution of modern state 155–157, 161
  as example to other nations 146, 162
  formation of independent State 6, 145,
    154–155
  global significance 146
  internal politics 147–148, 151–161 (*see also*
    nationalism)
  languages 158
  modernisation, processes of 147, 152–153,
    155

political system (post-independence) 146,
    155, 157–158, 161–162
  population 146, 161
  social structures 149 (*see also* caste
    system)
  traditional (pre-colonial) society/practices
    148–150, 152–153
  transformations, social/political 150, 152,
    158–159, 162
individualism
  philosophy of 170–171, 183
  role in social developments 7
  vs. citizenship 43
  vs. collectivisation 185–186, 202–203
industrial relations *see* trades unions
Industrial Revolution 192
insurrection, popular 136–137
Internationale 203
interventionism 23
Islam
  among EU immigrants 182
  in pre-colonial India 148–150
Italy
  medieval political system 53–55, 58–59, 66,
    72
  modern politics 172

Jacobins, Society of 135
James II 16–17
Jana Sangh/BJP (Hindu nationalist parties)
    160
Japan 2
Jellinek, George 42
Jerry Maguire (1997 film) 32
John, King 53
Justinian, *Institutes* 52

Kant, Immanuel 21, 178, 193, 201
Keynes, J. M. 171
Knichen, Andreas, *De iure territorii* 64
Koselleck, Reinhart 169
Kymlicka, Will 214
Kyoto summit 222

Labour Party (UK) 23
Laclos, Pierre Choderlos de 123–124
  Des femmes et de leur éducation 124
Lagarde, Georges, *Birth of the Lay Spirit* 52
Lamartine, Alphonse de 199
language, role in rights discourse 128
Larnac, Jean 204
law(s)
  medieval 3–4, 12–13, 51–52, 54–58, 70 (*see
    also* cities)
  purpose of 52
  relationship with civic rights 100

relationship with State 33–34, 37
see also canon law; Roman law
Le Chapelier, Isaac 135
Le Louédec (1848 revolutionary) 198–199
Leibniz, Gottfried Wilhelm 79
Lembke, Sven 68–70
Léo, André 199
Lepelletier, Michel 140
Lepetit, Bernard 194
liberalism
    and nationalist politics 153–154
    philosophy of 21–24, 33, 153
    as system of government 39–40, 44
    see also neo-liberalism
libertarianism, philosophy of 23–24
liberty (civic)
    Ancient vs. Modern 195
    compatibility with feminism 191–192, 206
    compatibility with monarchy 15–16, 18
    demands for 14–15, 17
    differing theories/interpretations 24, 201
    evolving ideas of 2–3, 11–12, 18–19, 22–23
    medieval notions of 3–4, 51–54, 60–61,
        66–67, 72
    twentieth-century ideas of 23–24
    Victorian ideas of 19–23
    see also French Revolution: fundamental
        principles
Libri Feodorum 64
Lichtenberg, Judith 220–221, 223
Linklater, Andrew 215–218
Lipsius, Justus 108
    Monita et Exempla Politica 90
    Six Books of Politics 90
Litfin, Karen 211–212
Littleton, Sir Thomas 12–13
Locke, John 20, 30, 137
    Two Treatises of Government 16–17, 19,
        110–111
Lombard League 58
Loraux, Nicole 194
Lorenz, Ottokar 81
Louis XVI of France 132–133, 136, 137, 142
Luther, Martin 86
Lynd, John 18

M. de la M—, Madame de 121
Macchiavelli, Niccolo 80–81
    Discorsi 61, 107
magistrate, (theoretical) role of 85–88
Magna Carta 53, 55, 58
Maitland, F. W. 57
Malthus, Thomas 223
Marie Antoinette 120
Marin, Louis 194–195
market(s)

central role in contemporary thought 178
critiques of 171
interrelation with state 171, 184, 187
Marnix of St Aldegonde 84
Marrakesh agreement 222
Marshall, Thomas H. 42, 44, 47, 179, 181,
    183–184
Marsilius of Padua, Defensor Pacis 57
Marx, Karl 43, 158, 170–171, 177,
    182
Marxist theory 7, 20, 82–83, 156, 158, 168,
    170–172, 183
    of State 208
    vs. neoliberalism 169, 171, 176–177
'mask', state viewed as 36
medieval period 51–61
    governmental practice 54, 64–65
    'liberties', grants of 3–4, 53–54, 58–60,
        66–67
    modern commentaries on 56–58, 63–65,
        67–71, 73
    urban life/social systems 4
    see also cities; law; liberty
Meinecke, Friedrich 4, 79–82, 90–92
    Die Idee der Staatsräson 81–82
Merrheim, Adolphe 203
Michelet, Jules 204
migrations 47
    implications for definitions of citizenship
        47–48
Mill, John Stuart 19–20, 153–154
minorities, concern for rights of 138, 186
Mitarbeiter/Mitbestimmung see
    co(-operation)
monarchomachs 86–88
monarchy
    abolition 14–15
    challenges to (military/political) 11 (see
        also Civil War; French Revolution)
    and medieval liberties 60–61 (see also
        Frederick I)
    objections to (moral/philosophical) 16–17,
        72–73, 107 (see also republicanism)
    as representative(s) of State 11, 29–30, 36
    restrictions on 57, 133
    rights/duties of 14, 56
    support for 15–16, 106
money, as concept
    compared with state 30–31, 33–35, 37
    contrasted with state 34
    function/purpose 33
    Hobbesian analysis 36
    value, fluctuations in 31
Montaigne, Michel de 108
Montesquieu, Charles-Louis de Secondat,
    Baron de 30, 64, 135

Montreal Protocol 212
More, Sir Thomas 30
Mughal empire 151
Murdoch, Rupert 180

Nassau (German County) 88
national debt 34
national interest
    contrasted with civic society/rights
        117–118
nationalism 2, 43
    Indian 145, 147, 153–155, 158, 160
    new 186
natural resources, management of 209–210
'natural state' (of man) 84–85, 98, 194
    law(s) 100–101, 110
    rights 100–103, 119–120, 123–124,
        126–129, 134, 137
    vs. civic identity 99, 104–106, 110
    see also savage
Necker, Jacques 133
Nehru, Jawarhalal 155–158
neo-liberalism 169, 171, 175–177, 182,
    186–187
Netherlands
    development of political theory 83–86,
        91
    medieval cities in 66, 72, 86
    political history 83, 92–93, 104, 109
'new medievalism' 213
1960s society/ideology 7, 168, 170–171,
    182–183
    after-effects/backlash 172, 183
'non-coincidence, zone of' (in rights theory)
    98, 110
non-governmental organisations
    global 1
Norman, Wayne 214
Nozick, Robert 23
nuclear waste 220
Nuremberg 66

Ockham, William of 54, 101
Oestreich, Gerhard 90
ordo civitatis, theories of 4, 90
Overton, Richard 11

Painter, Sydney 56
Palacios, Miguel de 108–109
Paley, William, Principles of Moral and
    Political Philosophy 18
Palm-Aelders, Etta 121–122
paper, manufacture of 69–71
Paris Commune 199
Parker, Henry, Observations 14

Parliament (UK), relationship with monarchy
    57
parties, political 44
    ideological objections to 135
    in India 160–161
    in medieval cities 71–72
Patel, Vithalbhai 155
'P.B.v.W.' 120
'people, the'
    identification of state with 28, 31–32
    individual's subordination to 139–140
    sovereignty of 42–43, 86–88, 126, 133
Philip II of Spain 84
Piccart, Michel 109
Pisan, Christine de 204
Planté, Christine 204
Plato, Timaeus 20
Poliakov, Leon 124
Politica Christiana 86
politics
    citizens' involvement in 43–44, 46
    Indian developments 147–148, 158–159
    medieval (city-based) 71–73
    modern trends in 44
    theories of see under names of theorists and
        countries
    see also parties
postmodernism 36–37, 187–188, 221
'postsocialism' 127–128
poverty
    in Indian society 157, 160
    responsibility for 167
Price, Richard, Two Tracts on Civil Liberty
    17–18
Priestley, Joseph 17
Primus, Richard 98
Prohibition (USA legislation) 23
Proudhon, Pierre Joseph 201, 203
Ptolemy of Lucca 106
Pufendorf, Samuel 91
race
    linked to citizenship 182
    theories of 178
    in UK society 25
Ranke, Leopold von 79–82, 92
    Politische Gespräch 79
Rebérioux, Madeleine 121
reciprocity, role in civic theory 218–221
recognition, politics of 127–129
Reinhard, Wolfgang 63–64
religion(s)
    and civic rights 98–99, 103–105
    conflicts between 100
    and EU citizenship 182
    Revolutionary theology 140

role in Indian society/politics 147–148, 160, 162
wars of 104
see also Church
Renaissance
civic philosophy 99
cultural/political trends 80, 82–83
representation, doctrine(s) of 88, 133–134, 142, 194–197, 200
individual vs. collective 197–200
practical application 134–135
problems of 157–158, 187
republic(anism)
rise in medieval cities 66, 71–73, 88
theories of 4, 15, 28, 85–87, 110
'resistance theory' 104
Reynolds, Susan 64
Rhetorica Ecclesiastica (medieval law manual) 51
rights, civic 2–3, 5, 42
as definition of citizenship 179, 181
definitions/terminology 98–100
denial of 97
history of debate on 5, 11–24, 97–111, 202, 212
individual vs. group 159–160
in medieval world 53, 72, 100
problems of 111
significant developments in 100, 104, 109–110, 116
theoretical systems of 5, 104–105, 110–111, 116–119
vs. nature/religion 103–105
see also franchise; human rights; liberty; women
Robespierre, Maximilien 140
Rockefeller, John D. 180
Rokkan, Stein, The Formation of National States in Western Europe 82
Roman law/society 13, 42, 57
civic rights under 97–99
influence on English/UK law 13, 15, 17–18, 21
influence on humanist ideals 107
medieval study/adoption of 51–52, 56, 58, 60, 66, 70
Rorty, Richard 44
Rousseau, Jean-Jacques 122, 199
Du contrat social 131
Roussel, Nelly 191
Russia/Soviet Union 2, 177
Ryan, Magnus 66, 70

Sade, Donatien Alphonse, Marquis de 123
Saint-Just, Louis-Antoine de 139, 141

Salamanca, School/University of 102–103, 106
Samaritan, parable of 219–221
Sapiro, Virginia 119
savage(s)
(perceived) qualities of 117, 123
vs. 'barbarians' 117–118
Scaliger, Joseph Justus 84
Scandinavia
modern politics/economics 172–173
Schelling, Friedrich 79
Schilling, Heinz 72–73
Schlosser, Friedrich Christoph 80
Schubert, Ernst 65
Scotland, civic philosophy in 123, 125–126, 154
Second World War 23
separatism (male/female) 122, 204
Shiva, Vandana 221–222
Sidney, Algernon, Discourses of Government 17
Siedentrop, Larry 180
Sieyès, Emmanuel, Abbé 133–135
Qu'est-ce que c'est que le Tiers État? 133–134
Simon, Jules 201
slavery
as antithesis of citizenship 60, 97, 99
debate on 5, 121, 123–124
in Roman law 13
subject's lot compared to 14–15, 17–18, 52
woman's lot compared to 119–121, 123–126, 128
Smith, Adam, The Wealth of Nations 177
social bargaining, processes of 169–170
social responsibility, ideals of 180
society, as construct 177–178
soldiers see armed forces
solidarity, role in social theory 177–178
Soto, Domingo de 101–103, 105
sovereignty
colonial assumption of 150–152
compatibility with environmental concerns 211–212
definitions/theories of 83–84, 86, 89, 92, 149
as focus of conflict 83–84 (see also Civil War)
Revolutionary assumption of 132–133, 192–193
see also monarchy; 'people'; state: powers
Spain
legal/theological thinking 100–101
political history 97, 100
Späthumanismus see humanism

Spinoza, Baruch 79, 91–92
Srinivas, M. N. 159
state(s)
    assertion of rights/prerogatives 1
    budgetary restrictions 176
    definitions 39, 63–64
    demise (predicted) 1, 37
    domination of political ideology 7, 11,
        145–146, 214
    enduring qualities 2
    environmental theories of 208–212
    (excessive) demands on 156, 161
    as force for evil 80
    functions/responsibilities 1–2, 7, 29, 33–35,
        155–156, 161, 167
    historical development 3–4, 6, 55–56,
        58–60, 63–65, 67, 71–72, 90–93, 108
    image(s) of (1960–1990) 168–169,
        184–185
    within larger entities 45–46 (see also
        globalisation)
    medieval notions of 51, 55
    objections/challenges to 6–7, 24, 145, 208,
        210–211
    as philosophical concept 3, 28–29, 31–37
    power(s) 29, 32, 35, 37, 46, 92, 168
    relations between 116–117, 187
    relationship with citizenry 2–4, 7–8, 11–25,
        39–44, 89–90, 97, 215–218 (see also
        citizenship; liberty; rights)
    role in colonisation 145
    role in post-colonial societies 145–148,
        155–157
    spatial identity 212, 214–215, 219
    theoretical analyses 79–83, 85–86,
        92–93
    transformations of 185, 187
statelessness 2, 186
Stolleis, Michael 82
Stuart kings 11, 17
    see also individual names
subjects, citizens as 39–40, 43
    see also slavery
suffrage, universal
    French debates on 196, 198
    in India 155, 157
    see also democracy
suffrage, women's
    appeals/demands for 120–122, 137, 199,
        201
    denial of 135, 142
    granting of 203, 205
    ideological objections to 192–193,
        200–201
    obstacles to 201–202

(lack of) role in female citizenship 121–123,
    202
sustainability, role in environmental thinking
    209–210, 212, 216
suttee, practice of 152

Tacitism 90
Tagore, Rabindranath 145
Talleyrand(-Périgord), Charles Maurice de 119
Tapie, Bernard 180
taxation
    as basis of electoral system 134
    implications for citizenship 40–42, 46,
        215
Taylor, Charles 126–127, 175
technological developments
    impact on society 71
territory, role in formation of States 59–60,
    64–65
Thatcher, Margaret 177, 185
Thierry, Augustin 204
    Essai sur l'histoire du Tiers État 67
Thirty Years War 83
Thompson, Michael 210
Thorez-Vermeersch, Jeanette 201, 203
Tilly, Charles 64–65, 73, 83
Timpler, Clemens 86–87
Tocqueville, Alexis de 43, 141, 146, 158, 162,
    182, 202
Todorov, Tzvetan 124
trades unions 25, 174
    attitudes to female employment 203
    critiques of 171
    impact on economy 171
    relations with management 173–174
Treitschke, Heinrich von 82
Trenchard, John (and Thomas Gordon), Cato's
    Letters 17
Tristan, Flora 199
Turner, Frederick Jackson 178–179
tyranny
    counters to 118
    masculine 120–121, 123

United Kingdom
    contemporary society 24–25
    ideals of citizenship 179–181
    system of government 25
Ullmann, Walter 56–57
unemployment 167, 171–174, 176, 177
United Nations 1
United States of America 2, 23, 142, 162, 211
    civic theory 179–180
    comparisons with European societies 180,
        206

and globalisation 178, 222
  see also American Declaration of
    Independence
utilitarianism 18–21, 28, 151

Vázquez, Fernando 85, 87, 102–104
Vettori, Francesco 80
Victorian period
  philosophy 19–23
Vietnam war 170
virtue(s), role in civic theory 87, 106–107,
  131–132, 218–219, 221
Vitoria, Francisco de 85, 101–102
voting rights *see* franchise

wages, role in economic success/failure
  176
Wagner, Peter 185–186
Walpole, Sir Robert 17
Walzer, Michael 215
Wapner, Paul 211
war 34, 41
  'barbarian' attitudes to 117–118
  modern methods 45
  right to declare 85
  see also armed forces; *names of specific
    conflicts*
Wars of Resistance (C16) 5
Weber, Max 4, 29, 42–43, 68, 82, 147, 184

welfare, state provision of 23, 41, 167, 170,
  180
  critiques of 168, 170
  and immigration 47
Westphalia, Treaty of 211, 213
Wolff, Robert Paul 23
Wollstonecraft, Mary, *Vindication of the
  Rights of Woman* 119
women
  in armed forces 45
  'barbarian' attitudes to 117–118
  employment 174–175, 203
  (presumed) informal influence 120, 125
  (male) views of nature 125–126, 192–194,
    201, 204–205
  political representation *see* suffrage
  political stance 202
  rights, debate on/denial of 5, 7, 115–116,
    119, 192, 204–205
  rights, demands for 202, 204
  rights, granting of 202
  social position 118–119, 122–123, 125–126,
    199, 201–202
  as subject of political analogy 108–109
  see also citizenship; equality; French
    Revolution; slavery; suffrage
World Bank 1

Young, Iris 127–128